Sustainable Recovery

Keith Kay

ISBN-13: 978-1502478795
ISBN-10: 150247879X

Library of Congress Control Number: 2014919456
CreateSpace Independent Publishing Platform, North Charleston, SC

Self-Help / Substance Abuse & Addictions / General

Contents

PART III: Old Worlds, New World

PART IV: Sustainable Recovery

Preface

"Our deepest fear is not that we are inadequate. Our deepest fear is that we are powerful beyond measure. It is our light, not our darkness, that most frightens us. We ask ourselves, Who am I to be brilliant, gorgeous, talented, fabulous? Actually, who are you not to be? You are a child of God. Your playing small does not serve the world. There's nothing enlightened about shrinking so that other people won't feel insecure around you. We are all meant to shine, as children do. We were born to make manifest the glory of God that is within us. It's not just in some of us; it's in everyone. And as we let our own light shine, we unconsciously give other people permission to do the same. As we're liberated from our own fear, our presence automatically liberates others."

~ Marianne Williamson

My name is Keith. The business-card version of me is that I am a 50-something registered nurse and recovering alcoholic. I live in an average community and look like the average guy next door.

On scratching a little deeper, it comes to light that I started life as a musician, stumbled into the field of healthcare through no particular wisdom or insight, and later in life I became interested in alternative and complementary healing.

The thing about me that is not obvious is that I changed into a different person. I became the man I am today, who is literally a different human being than the man who suffered from the addictive disease of alcoholism years ago. In that context, this change is exemplified by the idea that, though formerly a man who could not go a day without a drink, I do not presently think about drinking in any situation or circumstance. I never want to drink. I no longer have the mind, personality, behaviors, and indeed, I probably no longer have the physical body of the active alcoholic I once was.

This transformation from previous version to upgraded Keith began inadvertently, and then became the heart of a deliberate and focused effort. Once I became aware of this phenomenon, I began to think more and more about this tremendous gift. In light of the fact that my experience was not the experience of the majority of recovering alcoholics, gaining a deeper understanding of what was happening became increasingly more important to me. Over time, I began to develop insight into my personal recovery and also what distinguished it from more common outcomes. Experiences, teachers, and lessons came into my life.

I was a true alcoholic and evidenced all the characteristics. A heavy daily drinker, I hid most of my consumption while stumbling through life from problem to problem, miraculously avoiding catastrophe. Almost daily, I operated a vehicle while intoxicated. By the end of my drinking days, my musical ambitions were in ruins; my livelihood was at the breaking point; my relationships were empty shells; I had no coping skills, and I could not envision my life continuing as it had been for another decade.

Yet today, I am that different man with a high-end recovery. At first, I accomplished this the same way millions have before me, by working the basic Alcoholics Anonymous twelve-step program of recovery. That took me to a point where I found myself asking, "So, what now?"

Almost daily, I hear others asking, "What now?" or something along those lines. Of itself, that's not a problem, but as I survey the recovery landscape I see something related to that question which disturbs me. With tremendous frequency, I hear and witness people in recovery struggling and failing, or, at best, achieving a poor outcome. That "thing" that people are asking about fails to materialize.

In my early recovery, I found that thing intuitively. Over time, exposure to many influences served to indirectly answer the "what now" question. Finally, in recent years, I've set about deliberately reverse-engineering my outcome. It was a byproduct of the numerous hats I wear. I am a man in recovery, a nurse in the traditional Western model, and a student of alternative healing. This combination created the perfect storm of experiences, which in turn created me. The bigger picture that did materialize, my version of the "thing," is the effect of science meeting spirituality meeting the traditional form of recovery: the steps, but on steroids. It is the best of the old, along with something new and wonderful, in short, a sustainable recovery.

Ever notice how when you buy a certain make and model of car, you suddenly become aware of how many astute people purchased the same car as you? You see them everywhere. It's really not that there are any more of that car model out there; you're just noticing it more. A couple years ago, I started to notice dozens of teachers, scientists, and spiritual leaders who have a variation on the "thing." Brilliant men and women, impeccably credentialed, and often with their own amazing stories, have written books, produced videos, set up programs, courses and workshops—all in the interest of facilitating personal transformation. Today, probably more than ever, people are interested in helping and changing themselves. With some amazing success, people are using these techniques to heal, change, succeed, and become enlightened. When I paid attention, I suddenly noticed how many different programs, approaches, and techniques, in essence "things," are out there.

Many of the "things" have a lot in common. Most are a variation on science meets spirituality, and many endorse meditation.

To the best of my knowledge, these new techniques have not been adapted directly for alcoholics and addicts. That is something else they have in common. None of these approaches to transformation addresses the specific issues, concerns, and needs of the millions of people suffering from diseases of addiction. It's time someone did. I don't see anyone else doing it, so I'm stepping up. This book needs to be written.

This book existed for years before becoming words on pages. I was in the process of becoming a walking version of it. There were numerous false starts before the start of the actual writing, but once I was truly ready and began working, the universe supported me in some significant and extraordinary ways. Having failed to write "on the side" while working as a nurse fulltime, I became a fulltime writer who did nursing on the side. I made a courageous (though some would say foolish) decision to quit a job that did not serve me, and pursue my dream of writing this book. Nursing side jobs materialized. After I established a writing routine, my nursing "on the side" swelled to 40 or more hours per week, and I eventually returned to a permanent position. I kept writing.

As I completed work on the manuscript, I began to explore publishing options. After a brief and futile exploration of literary agencies, I looked at various self-publishing alternatives. I selected one that initially seemed to be the best for me; however, this proved to be a learning experience. The self-publishing division of a prominent and seemingly genre-related publishing house turned out to be an extremely poor fit. Apparently my little book had some things that bothered people in the Content department. Maybe they were just unduly alarmed, or possibly I'm pushing the envelope; whatever the case, I chalked it up to a lesson learned.

The lesson was about compromise. Basically I couldn't... When stuck between the rock of the publisher's rigid criteria and the hard place of my true telling of an industrial-strength human experience, there was little I was willing to concede. I'd already used prudent judgment and contacted important people in my book and received their permission to tell their stories. Aside from changing a few first names, I wasn't budging. I adamantly refused to change, soften, omit, or otherwise adulterate my story.

Finally, in keeping with the Alcoholics Anonymous traditions of placing principles before personalities and personal anonymity at the level of media, I've used a pen name. If AA didn't exist, neither would this book. Neither would I for that matter. Those traditions are based largely on concerns from a bygone era; however, I come to praise AA, not rewrite it. I sincerely believe if Bill Wilson were alive today, he would be incredibly forward in his thinking, and the anonymity issue would no longer be written in stone. While some have tried to convince me otherwise, I've been resolute in my decision not to attach my real name to this, for the present anyway. The whole point of this work is just that, the work. It's not about me, nor is it about money. It's not about personal gain. As I said earlier, it's about a "thing."

So, my answer to that "What now?" question is my "thing." I call it Sustainable Recovery. It is the title of the book, and also my way of being. Allow me to explain...

Acknowledgments

I received inspiration for this work from a multitude of sources. Gratitude is a powerful thing. While the constraints of space prevent me from expressing my thanks in adequate detail, it's more about the failure of mere words to convey the true magnitude of my appreciation.

William Wilson and Robert Smith, the founders of Alcoholics Anonymous, gave the world something truly amazing. In finding the serenity to accept their disease and the courage to change their own lives, their accomplishment has made possible the life I live today. As they manifested something divinely inspired, their wisdom in creating a program of recovery that has saved millions of lives is the object of tremendous reverence for me. It is with a sense of awe and humility that I would stand on their shoulders, as have so many others they have inspired.

This work does not represent an effort to reinvent the wheel. While Henry Ford brought the automobile to the masses, today's cars are as different as they could possibly be while remaining the same form of transportation. Just as the Model T formed the basis for what we drive today, Alcoholics Anonymous and the Twelve Steps will remain the basis of recovery. Since that basis is the foundation of my recovery, I'm well aware that I've written a book that is steeped in the language, symbolism and general ways of that foundation. While I refer to it as the old model, I'm aware of its strong presence here. For those unfamiliar with *Alcoholics Anonymous* (frequently referred to as The Big Book) and *Twelve Steps and Twelve Traditions,* I suggest having them handy as you encounter the numerous references contained herein.

My AA sponsor of about 20 years cannot be acknowledged by name; that's how he would want it. His sharing of his experience and wisdom, in addition to his mere presence in my life, have made my journey what it is. To him, I say that I owe you so much. I love you. Thank you.

I have had the honor and privilege of working and serving with many brilliant men and women in medicine and nursing, and also in the greater body of healthcare. Through their knowledge, mentoring, and the shining examples of their excellence, I have learned a thousand lessons.

While specifically adapted for recovery from the disease of addiction, many ideas in this work did not originate with me. I've sampled from a wealth of knowledge and wisdom imparted by the world's greatest teachers and scientists. One in particular has been placed in my path; the model of personal transformation in this work is my adaptation of his teachings. Thank you, Dr. Joe Dispenza, for explaining complicated things in a simple way and for demystifying the mystical. You are my beacon, and you've helped me immeasurably. Thank you also to Paula Meyer, and everyone at Encephalon. Can't wait to see you again!

Joni Wilson, my personal editor, came into my life just when I needed her. With the perfect mix of objectivity and enthusiasm, Joni's guidance and support have been invaluable. Thank you so much!

Thanks to the most gifted Nicole Pero Laponius for her inspired cover artwork.

Thanks to the talented Patrick Brigham for his crafty design work.

Finally, acknowledgment and thanks go to the *Coast to Coast AM* radio program with George Noory. For open-mindedness, the spirit of inquiry, and the courage to ask the hard questions, I'm indebted to you for exposure to so many new ideas through the years, all of which helped make this possible. Perhaps I can share my ideas with your audience someday. Thank you for doing what you do.

Introduction

"You will not grow if you sit in a beautiful flower garden, but you will grow if you are sick, if you are in pain, if you experience losses, and if you do not put your head in the sand, but take the pain as a gift to you with a very, very specific purpose."

~Elisabeth Kübler-Ross

My goal in writing this book is to facilitate and enhance the promises of Alcoholics Anonymous for others. To put it simply, I stumbled into a recovery that is amazing. It works so well that I am now, for all intents and purposes, a different person than the man who could not go a day without a drink. The guy whose whole perception of the world revolved around the open bottle of vodka under the seat of his car has been replaced with a man who will stay sober under any and all circumstances. I've thought long and hard about that "thing" I stumbled into. I've worked very hard to gain a measure of understanding.

In the chapters that follow, I'm going to describe my experience of alcoholism and my experience of recovery. My personal version of the disease of addiction, while not intensely dramatic, is testimony to the enslavement the alcoholic, or any addicted person, experiences. The bottle was my master. I will describe what happened as I first became open to, and then ultimately embraced, the basic ideas of recovery as the foundation for what came next.

What came next was so amazing that I couldn't have imagined it happening. I experienced things I didn't believe were possible. I found out that both the world and reality were different than I thought they were. I began to learn about infinite possibility.

In *Sustainable Recovery*, I describe what happened, what I learned, and how I changed as a result. I will show you how I took some amazing knowledge and information and applied it to my old-fashioned recovery in Alcoholics Anonymous with unexpectedly wonderful results. I will explain how the things I was already doing became even more meaningful. And finally I will explain how I became a different man than the one who drank daily.

This book follows a standard self-help book structure, slightly modified. Instead of three sections, there are four; the first section is essentially divided in half. Part I discusses my childhood until my last drink. Part II, after a brief editorial of the situation in a chapter titled "The Nurse's Opinion," picks up the narrative from my first day of sobriety through my recovery. These first parts are very personal and honest, and I don't spare humbling details of my human failings in the interest of capturing the essence of my alcoholism. Parts I and II contain separate sections of present-day insight into the dysfunction of those past events and circumstances, in preparation for more information to follow. Except for the insight sections, Parts I and II together form a longer, more detailed version of the personal stories in Alcoholics Anonymous, relating how it was, what happened, and how it is today.

Part III begins to establish a way of looking at our recoveries and lives from three different perspectives, or three worlds. While most of us identify with the first two, the worlds of everyday life and our belief systems, the information and perspectives in the third world will require our open minds. Accepting the fact that our consciousness influences our reality, and that there is no separation between consciousness and reality is key. To assist with this, I offer some interesting examples and evidence; please consider the case I make for this new way of looking at life. After building this model of the three worlds in which we exist, I relate it to how we care for our bodies, our spirits, and how we recover in the twelve-step way. Sharing information from the perspectives of a man in traditional recovery, a mainstream nurse, as well as an alternative healer, I give the background of my own transformation.

Finally, and having set the stage, Part IV is about creation. After suggestions for the foundation of conventional recovery are outlined, discussion moves to establishing a new vision for that recovery, and ultimately how to move toward the realization of that vision—the recovery and life of our dreams. It builds on that idea about consciousness and how to strengthen and use our consciousness' connection to a greater reality. The valuable tool of meditation is used, and I share background on the practice, in addition to some specific direction in using an approach to meditation that has worked for many.

There is a saying around Alcoholics Anonymous. "It's not for people who need it. It's for people who want it." Not strictly for those who want it, *Sustainable Recovery* is for those who want more.

Instead of experiencing the fulfillment of the Alcoholics Anonymous promises, I see people, even after decades of recovery, continuing to drag the ball and chain of alcoholism through their lives. I see people living in fear of drinking. I hear people complain of being unhinged by going three days without an AA meeting. I see people reluctant to engage in the full potential and possibility of their lives and reality. I see people who are still the same people who drank; at best, they have a disease of addiction that has only been anesthetized. They live in a self-constructed prison, with that sleeping disease as their cellmate, terrified that it's going to wake up at any moment and have its way with them. They are the same people they were previously; the only difference is they have a habit of not drinking instead of drinking.

These people have somehow come to believe that, because they will always technically be recovering alcoholics, they will always think, feel, and be a certain way. I hear people say it all the time. "I'm an alcoholic and I'll never change."

I'm asking for a chance to show you that profound change is possible. I'm suggesting that you dare to believe that it is possible to become an upgraded version of yourself! I'm asking for a chance to show you that we are connected to one another and everything else at a basic level. Give me a chance to show you that there is more to reality than what we see, hear, feel, taste, and smell. Open your mind to the possibility that you can intentionally change into someone who stays sober under any and all circumstances. Let me tell you how you can have a recovery that is sustainable.

It's not enough for me to simply enjoy this gift. There isn't enough gratitude on the planet to express my feelings about the tremendous healing I've experienced. As the founders of Alcoholics Anonymous discovered many years ago, no one recovers alone.

Having reached a point where I want, actually need, to give back, my purpose in life is to gain better understanding of the way I've come to be, and to inspire others as I've been inspired. I found a way to experience my promises, which I simply think of as the life and recovery of my dreams. If I can do this, so can you.

I know there are some very challenging ideas in this book. There are wild and crazy notions that might feel uncomfortable. When that happens, know that something wonderful is starting to happen to you. Great things are always preceded by chaos. Things worth doing are seldom easy. I beg you to persevere, secure in the knowledge that you have nothing to lose but your old thoughts about recovery and an amazing way of being to be gained. On the other side of these challenging ideas lies a freedom you might not have even known was possible. This is so worth it. More than a book title, sustainable recovery is a way to live.

My vision is that these ideas might someday take on a life of their own. As more people begin to accept new ideas, more people will embrace new possibilities. My hope is that others will intention-ally transform into different people, into upgraded versions of them-selves as I have done. My hope is that this will become common-place, that the way people recover will modify, and, ultimately, that anyone suffering from the disease of addiction will have every means available to achieve profound change. My vision is a day when anyone with motivation can achieve a way of being in which they no longer obsess over alcohol (or drugs), or their consumption, or situations involving alcohol, and have absolutely no desire to drink. I want to see people with a harmonious balance in the ele-ments of recovery. And finally, I want people to have a sense of se-curity that accompanies a firm conviction that they will never drink again, as long as they continue to do what supports this way of be-ing.

I want to see people go from saying, "What now?" to saying what I can say today:

"I'm never drinking again."

Part I

Before

"A person often meets his destiny on the road he took to avoid it."
~ Jean de La Fontaine

CHAPTER 1

The Sixties, Seventies

I was born in interesting times, the sixties.

To be accurate, I was born in October, 1959. Though born in the fifties by just three months or so, I'm a child of the sixties.

There is a popular television show that dramatizes the sixties. The depiction of the excesses of that decade seems bizarre by the standards of the times in which I now write this. Particularly striking is the gratuitous drunkenness, but there is much more that is excessive by today's norms. Blatant sexism, racism, ageism, and radicalism were rampant. And if there was an "ism" for being more or less innocent by virtue of ignorance, that would also apply. The smoking of cigarettes everywhere seems especially strange. By illustration of all the above, this drama suggests ample commentary on our contemporary culture.

Yes, the sixties were interesting times.

My birth certificate says I was born at 12:42 PM at Richardson House, part of the Peter Bent Brigham Hospital, now Brigham and Women's. I was born to parents whose union exemplified the spirit of freedom that the sixties ushered in. Their cultures and backgrounds were as different as two people of the same race could be. I'm American mutt on my mom's side, first-generation Nazi refugee German Jew on my father's side; it's a mystery where my amazing sense of rhythm came from.

I'm the oldest of three and have two sisters. My first sister (18 months my junior) and I comprised the standard sixties model—an average of 2.3 children per household. My second sister was born eight years later, as the decade and my parents' marriage wound down. Her addition to the family might not have been in keeping with that model, because my parents' marriage was already quite rocky.

I was told that I began walking at 10 months and liked to push furniture around. From my earliest recollection, there were large toys—blocks and the like—for me to focus my attention on instead of the furniture. Even early on, I seemed to demonstrate a tendency to rearrange things to my liking.

Like the main characters of the popular TV show, my parents were living the American dream as it materialized for them. They built their dream house on a nice parcel of wooded land in a beautiful town, best known as the home of a famous World War II Army general, and also known for equestrian pursuits. My parents were interested in neither of those and settled there instead for the quiet setting and good schools.

My father went daily to the engineering company of which he was cofounder, while my mother stayed home, her graduate degree in early childhood education likely packed in a box in the attic. This sounds like a typical fairy-tale existence of the times, except, like the main characters of the TV drama, I don't think my parents were actually in love.

My parents were two people who chose to be together despite their marriage going against the grain. In the late fifties, it was unusual for people of their respective backgrounds and religions to marry. They were well-educated young adults residing in the greater Boston area, and both were reasonably enlightened, progressive people for their time. Introduced at a "college mixer," the German-born engineer and the early childhood educator were not the most likely of couples, and I imagine the wedding was interesting, if not contentious. According to my mother's youngest brother, their mother was openly contemptuous of her son-in-law.

There were many things my parents did well, especially in my early years. My sister and I benefited from enriching experiences, travel, and culture. As a family, we took vacations to resorts in the summer, skiing in the winter. There was often music in the house, something that would become quite important to me down the line. We visited museums. We had pets, a dog and cats, which evolved into a full-blown menagerie throughout the years with fish, hamsters, birds, rabbits, etc. There were art supplies in the house—paper, paint, crayons, pastels, and even modeling clay. We were taken to the circus, theatre, Disney movies, and my fifth birthday was spent in the audience of one of those children's television shows, Bozo the Clown. Our parents spent time with us, giving us the attention that young, forming minds thrived on.

The dark cloud forming over this enchanted picture of family bliss was my parents' marital discord. I remember one night, when I was probably four, hearing lots of yelling and screaming from downstairs. My parents were fighting, something I had never witnessed. I have no recollection of them interacting as a loving couple for that matter, no demonstrations of affection or intimacy. My memories of my father are of him coming down the walkway to the door, as I waited to greet him when he came home from work, and of him sitting at his place at the dinner table. I remember my mother doing domestic chores—cooking, ironing—and sitting opposite my father at the table.

One day when I was still quite young, I awoke from my nap and a disturbing dream. Maybe it was the arguing I overheard that planted the seed. Shaken and upset, I told my mother that I had dreamt that my father was going away. That was the moment she chose to tell her five-year-old son that his parents were separating. Maybe she felt it was the most honest thing to do in the moment, but I think it's likely that her master's degree in early childhood education had been sitting in the attic a little too long. Dad moved out.

In the mid-sixties, divorce was still rare. This is not the sort of thing a kid wants to be first on the street with. For my parents, this was in the nature of a trial separation, but it was absolutely the real thing to me.

I remember that life with a father who I only saw on weekends had just about become routine after a year or so. Whether it was normal is beside the point; to a five- or six-year-old kid, routine was important. It was sometime during the summer of 1966 that my father accepted a job in Germany, his country of origin. He was there for most of the summer. The big news, however, was that we were all going to live there. It was a happy day for me that my parents were getting back together!

I started the first two weeks of first grade in the states, and then my mother, sister, and I left to join my father, who had been there for months already. Off to Germany we went! How excited I was, taking off from Logan airport at 10 PM to arrive at 5 AM, Boston time, 10 AM, German time.

After driving for what seemed like forever to my jet-lagged, six-year-old awareness, we arrived at our new German home. It was a beautiful, and I mean exquisitely beautiful, house nestled on a hillside in a picturesque German village. Furthermore, while this house was certainly deluxe by American standards, it was downright palatial in the context of the houses and farmhouses in the vicinity. I can only assume we were viewed as the crazy Americans on the hill.

Completing this scene was our family dog, a St. Bernard that joined us as soon as he cleared quarantine, along with the "sensible" Land Rover my father felt compelled to buy. Looking back, I'm not inclined to think this was all about image, though none of my German friends had dogs, and their families generally didn't have more than one car. In the big picture, however, and from a business standpoint, I think my father's image required the presence of a wife and 2.3 children.

The plan was for me to attend German public first grade. The theory was that I would pick up the language as the German kiddies were learning it, but little thought was given to the socialization aspect. I felt isolated, thousands of miles from home, and unable to communicate with anyone around me. I was rather shy actually and didn't make friends as easily as some children do.

One experience that stands out, because it was traumatizing and serves to define the feelings of isolation I had around the whole Germany experience, was a day shortly after starting school. There was an early dismissal, unbeknownst to me or my parents, and when school let out in the late morning, I found myself alone in the small town. I had followed some neighbor children out of the school and become separated from them. Because my mother was the usual ride home in the carpool, they might have walked the several kilometers home.

Not being able to communicate with them, I wasn't sure what to do when they struck off, and found myself at the tender age of six, alone and scared in the middle of the town where no one understood what I was saying. Some women who saw me crying knew of a local woman who spoke English, and somehow they located her. She talked to me, calmed me down, and was able to reach my mother by pay phone. What an angel! She became an occasional babysitter for the duration of our time there.

On the plus side, there were some positive experiences, as a family and for me individually. We took lots of trips, locally, regionally and across borders. We were close to Munich and the Austrian border, and we went to beautiful Salzburg a number of times. In the late winter, we traveled to Belgium and Holland by car. We also went to Switzerland. I stayed in some nice hotels, ate in some fancy restaurants, and saw some incredible scenery. Old European architecture—castles and cathedrals—and the incredibly beautiful Alps were unforgettable.

I remember really bonding with my mother at this point in my life. Perhaps there was the element of us both feeling a little of the "stranger in a strange land" isolation, but this experience forged our relationship. Later in life, I learned that this is a normal thing, young children bonding with the parent of the opposite gender. Looking back on this through the lens of my adult awareness, I believe my mother was smart, sensitive, and knew what it took to be a good parent.

~~~~~~~~~~~~~~~~~~~~~~~~~~~~

My earliest recollection of drinking alcohol was probably around age four. It was a morning drink, to boot. My parents had hosted that mainstay of sixties social culture, the cocktail party. I remember them being busy with preparations on Saturday for the coming evening. It was neither summer nor winter; the weather was moderate when I played outside that day. My sister and I were fed, bathed, and pajamaed, then put to bed, what seemed to me, early.

I remember watching from the top of the stairs, which afforded a panoramic view of the high-ceilinged living room. There were about two dozen adults, standing around in small conversation groups. They all seemed to have a drink in one hand and a lit cigarette in the other... I took this scene in almost voyeuristically. I don't remember being noticed while I stared down at this live-action role modeling in progress. This scene is indelibly imprinted in my memory.

The next day I was the first one up, as I often was on Sunday morning. I went downstairs to the family room to watch my usual Sunday morning cartoons ("Popeye" and "Boomtown" were the Sunday AM staples). The house was a bit of a mess, a litter of well-used ashtrays and discarded drink glasses, many in various states of fullness. What I remember most were numerous half-finished and melted ice-watery bourbons, Scotches, martinis, and Manhattans. I clearly recall experiencing the taste of watered-down Scotch. The fact that it was forbidden completely canceled out what should have been a normal child's reaction to the taste and flavor of the adult beverage. The normal response would have been "YUCK!" Maybe I thought it, but I drank that watery Scotch, feeling that warm feeling in my stomach that was to become so, so customary later in life.

Whether my curiosity about adult beverages intensified after the experience with the leftover drinks or it was already there, I developed a true preoccupation with alcohol from an early age. I hounded my father for sips of his beer. One day after I pestered him, his European sensibilities must have gotten the best of him. He got a small version of the glass he had, put some beer in it, and gave it to me. This is, unfortunately, a defining early childhood memory of my father. It was not the type of bonding experience that any good came from. The fact that I remember it so clearly decades later—the circumstances, the taste, the smell, and that I wanted more—negates any cuteness. I had clearly demonstrated an unusual, if not abnormal, preoccupation with alcohol and its consumption.

~~~~~~~~~~~~~~~~~~~~~~~~~~

Our time in Germany ended as it began, only in reverse. My mother, sister, and I returned to the United States about nine months after we left, in the summer of 1967. My father remained in Germany, to complete business affairs it was explained. Originally forecast as only a matter of weeks, it turned into nearly six months before he returned.

Although three of us flew home from Germany, my mother was transporting a fourth little stowaway. My younger sister had been conceived in April or May and would be born in January 1968. We returned to the house we had left, which had been rented in the interim. Within a short time, life returned to normal, or at least to the way it had been.

In September, I started second grade. Something felt familiar... Because I missed American first grade, that disconcerting feeling of having no idea what was going on was there. While I spoke the language at least, I felt just as lost as I had back in German first grade the year before. Reading was the issue. With some extra help, I would catch up completely during the course of the next two years. The practice of the time was to group children of corresponding ability—there were three reading groups. By sometime in third grade the following year, I had gone from struggling in the lowest group to not struggling in the highest group.

Maybe it was these major life events during a window of formative time, my impressionable age, but the universe seemed to be sending me experiences that made me feel different from the other kids. As I mentioned, socialization was never my forte, and the feelings translated to uniqueness at best, inferiority at worst.

One little fringe benefit showed up during gym class. At the time, probably a component of the president's fitness program or some such mandate, part of the routine consisted of metrics—the recording of measurements for some standard athletic events. When I was overseas, the German kids all played soccer, which wouldn't catch on in the states for another decade or so. In the course of the backyard soccer games, I guess I had done a lot of running around. When the gym teacher back in the states had us doing the 40-yard dash, I could run faster than all the other kids could. The same thing happened with the standing broad jump; I jumped farther than the other kids in the class. It was good to have some minor positives on my side, because I would be feeling a lot different from the other kids soon enough.

My father returned before the Christmas holidays. About a month later, my youngest sister was born. It was only a short time after that, I think just a couple months, before my parents separated again. This time, they would divorce, something that was still uncommon in those days. Later in life, I would form insight about the things that were going on behind the scenes. At the time of course, it felt like it was all about little eight-year-old me.

Behind the scenes, my mother felt an intense social stigma. Divorce equaled failure in the eyes of society. The women's liberation movement hadn't quite gained its miniskirt-clad legs yet, and certainly hadn't filtered into the suburban cultural consciousness. A divorced woman in the 'burbs was an object of whispered derision. I remember my mother bemoaning lost friends. Though she held a graduate degree, she had never worked outside the home since starting her family. Although these things seem like contemporary adversities that many face today, I'm sure she felt as if she was in uncharted territory back in 1969 when the divorce was finalized. That timeframe holds my first recollection of my mother's drinking.

Also behind the scenes, I believe my father's remaining in Germany after we departed was not entirely about business. Based on the way events unfolded over the next few years, I believe my father met his next wife in that timeframe. Shortly after the divorce became final, we were introduced to a young (very young) German woman while visiting one of the family friends who dad had apparently retained custody of in the divorce. New to this country "by coincidence," she would first become an infrequent recurring acquaintance who evolved into a fixture and finally became my stepmother about six years later.

It was at this time that I caught the music bug. I blame it on Ringo. Somehow, it was always about the drums too. When I was young, I had a cool little Native American tom-tom type drum. A playmate accidentally broke the drumhead, and I was beside myself with disappointment. At age nine, I was given a toy snare drum for Christmas. There was no stopping me after that.

I was a huge Beatles fan. The reason I blame Ringo is because he always looked like he was having so much fun back there, wailing away on his old Ludwig drums. I had some of their records, had seen them on TV a bit—Ed Sullivan and the like—and was simply enamored of them the way the rest of the world was. Though unable to articulate the idea at the tender age of 10, I was quite impressed by their sociological impact. That intangible energy intrinsic in their music really spoke to me. Now I know that they instinctively utilized rather complex musical and compositional techniques; they were naturals, and I still love them and their music.

In fourth grade, I began taking lessons through the school. The band director did this as a class. We had to get practice pads and 2B drumsticks (specified size). I wanted a drum set of course, and this desire did not fall on deaf ears. My mother sensibly suggested that I needed to apply myself to that first year of lessons, after which time a drum set might be discussed. So I did.

As the hoopla from my parents' divorce had settled, at least somewhat, we had established a new routine. My father would come pick us up every Sunday afternoon at 12:30, then return us home in the evening. I still struggled with being the only kid whose parents were divorced that I was aware of.

This timeframe was also my earliest recollection of another childhood struggle. From age nine until my early teens, I was a chubby kid. Not obese per se, but heavy, maybe about 15 or 20 percent above my ideal weight. I became extremely self-conscious about this, but really never connected it to my affinity for the potato-chip drawer. I think this was in response to stressful events, such as the divorce. There was probably an emotional component. I love eating to this day, and know I have the potential for letting myself go. I'll always be someone who has to watch my weight and take care of myself with physical activity and exercise.

I had maintained a strong level of interest in the drum lessons throughout the year of fourth grade. Rather unexpectedly, my mother had made some inquiries into finding me a small, used drum set. On the band director/drum teacher's recommendation, she had gotten in touch with a local musical instrument dealer. We went to look at a little three-piece, orange-sparkle drum set, and it became my first kit, as the Brits like to call them.

The drum set appeared a few weeks before the end of school. My poor mother and sisters! I don't think she ever took into consideration how loud drums are. There was no effect of a novelty that wore off. I practiced for hours each day that summer. I had a little Radi-oShack stereo, and I would put on records and play along with them. The Beatles, the Rolling Stones, and Jimi Hendrix became my imaginary band mates. I was also in summer-school band, my first organized school ensemble experience, which I hoped would help me as I went into the regular school-year band.

During the summers, my family belonged to a "Beach Club." This was a family-based social club located in a nearby coastal town. Naturally there was a beach, along with saltwater swimming pool, large clubhouse with lockers, snack bar and regular bar, and tennis courts. We had begun this annual tradition sometime in the early sixties before my parents separated, and my mother made it a priority to continue. It gave my sister and me some structure and activity during school summer vacations. It also gave my mother her only real adult social outlet. She hadn't yet reentered the workforce, and she was quite verbal about feeling ostracized as a rare divorcee. I spent a lot of time in the pool. Mom spent a lot of time in the bar.

I had a separate cadre of summer friends. One significant and lasting relationship was with an older kid from the Beach Club. Alex was the leader of the little group of kids I hung around with at the club. He was smart, athletic, and... musical. He was a cool guy that a chubby, slightly younger kid would look up to and wish to emulate. Alex will have more mention later.

~~~~~~~~~~~~~~~~~~~~~~~~~~

At this point in my life, around age nine or ten, I became more aware of my mother's drinking. There had been some isolated incidents, even a hospitalization in the preceding years. On a couple of occasions, she drank too much and got sick. The first time this happened, I remember feeling shocked, scared, and helpless. I called a neighbor, who came over and cleaned up the vomit, nursed my mother a bit, and went home. I don't remember where my sisters were through that episode, probably because I was a little traumatized.

On another occasion, my sisters and I stayed with a family friend while my mother was "in the hospital." No one would really discuss the matter, but this was undoubtedly drinking related. While no physical ailment was ever mentioned, the timeframe fits the drunken episodes for which neighbors were called. Also, the general events surrounding the end of the hospitalization seemed to reinforce that the event had been about mental rather than physical health.

I became conscious of my mother's drinking on several levels. First, I developed a keen sense of what her level of intoxication was. By paying attention to her mannerisms, activities, and behaviors, especially her voice, I developed my own mental capacity for sobriety testing.

Second, another element of mom's drinking I remember distinctly was her attempt to hide her drinking. Opening a cupboard for a dish or cup, I'd frequently discover a tumbler with gin or Scotch in it. However, she never made any attempt to hide the supply. The bottles lived under the sink with the other hazardous chemicals.

Third, her driving was starting to become hazardous. The times then were much different as far as operating a vehicle under the influence was concerned. There was a Friday night when Mom took us out for pizza, only to make it as far as a stone wall a half mile from home. One of the neighbors drove by and found us there, moments after the car accident. My mother was out of it... and the kindhearted neighbor piled us into his car and drove us back to his house. Mom sobered up, the tow truck was called, and I don't believe the police were ever involved. It wasn't until the eighties that the heightened awareness of drunk driving became more prevalent.

My ability to assess and predict my mother's level of intoxication evolved into a kind of defense mechanism, or coping skill. It seemed that there was a proportionate relationship between her level of drunkenness and my need for some sort of parental assistance. Whenever I was depending on her for parental contribution to my general endeavors, for example, a ride somewhere—be it a school event, drum lessons, or to a friend's/social thing—she would be more intoxicated. This had two results. Having observed that the more important something was, the more drunken she seemed, I began to minimize the importance of things. The other result was that I took up hitchhiking.

I can only imagine how she felt. She was smart enough to appreciate fully the complexities and subtleties of her situation both personally and socially. She was intelligent and educated, possessed of all the tools to be the model of an independent woman. Perhaps that might have happened in a different environment, but probably not in the small-town, suburban community atmosphere where we lived. She was quite vocal about feeling abandoned by her social circle following the divorce. While this might have been the case as a result of a general stigma, her becoming an inebriate surely clinched the deal. I suspect she felt isolated, lonely, and trapped.

~~~~~~~~~~~~~~~~~~~~~~~~~~~~~~

Meanwhile, my father carried on the business of being a divorced guy in the swinging seventies. He had a small apartment in a town near us for several years, and then moved to Cambridge, Massachusetts, to another small apartment.

During one of our Sunday afternoon Dad visits, my sister and I were introduced to the young German woman. When we mentioned this to our mother, she became quite unhinged. Apparently, this young woman was somehow known to our mother and in an especially negative way. Our mother, likely in some degree of intoxication on our arrival home, screamed and ranted. She was absolutely hysterical, and my sister and I were both quite disturbed by this. My mother's reaction to the mention of the young woman gave us a negative association with her. My father somehow got us all past this, and we started to see more of his friend as time passed. The young woman had immigrated to the United States within a year or so of our returning from Germany. More specifically, she came stateside about the time my parents separated.

While my father remained ambiguous as to his relationship with the new woman, we saw progressively more of her on our weekend visits. She had her own place in Cambridge, just a few miles from my father's. Jumping out of narrative sequence now for a moment, my father remarried in 1975. It was years later, as I pondered events and timelines that I realized my father and much younger wife had likely met while we were living in Germany, or at least before my father left. Aside from the fact that he was married then, doing the math was also rather disturbing. In the late sixties, my father was in his mid to late 30s; she was 20 years his junior, most likely making her a teenager when they met.

I spent the majority of my time, Monday through Sunday morning, in the company of a parent, my mother, who was coping with lots of negative emotions. This was a constant undercurrent in our household. My insecurity festered, as it was continually reinforced that I could not rely on my mother. It wasn't until much later in life that I came to understand that children normally have absolute faith in their parents.

Every Sunday at 12:30 in the afternoon, Dad would get us for our weekly visit. Every Sunday there would be something to feel strange about. The awkward dynamic of the presence of the young woman, who was neither stepmother nor elder sister, often made the visits bizarre. Then, arrival back home always held mystery, more often than not resulting in some form of hysterics from Mom.

As the sixties became the seventies, the onset of puberty with all its hormonal weirdness still ahead of me, no real family support behind me, and dysfunction all around me, I felt lonely and isolated. These experiences and feelings were starting to define and shape my way of being.

CHAPTER 2

The Fermentation Process

I was not a natural athlete. We didn't watch sports in the house as such, no baseball games or NFL Sundays. Sometimes, I would watch Wide World of Sports, a Saturday afternoon television staple in the sixties and the seventies, but more as entertainment than out of interest in the athleticism. I remember seeing skiing and boxing. We did ski as a family, something that went away along with my parents' marriage. My father had never been one to throw the football around with me, or put on a glove and toss a baseball. He was unable to offer the requisite instruction in throwing, catching, and hitting. This left me at somewhat of a disadvantage socially.

One spring, probably around age 10, I contracted baseball fever. I suspect I caught it from the other boys who had fathers to teach them how the game was played. So on a Saturday morning in April, Mom took me to Little League tryouts. While I optimistically anticipated some sort of miraculous event that day, I was quite disappointed to perform as one might expect of a boy who'd had that steady relationship with the potato-chip drawer and no one to show him baseball basics.

My three seasons in Little League were all spent playing right field in the "farm" league. The leagues were ranked farm, minor, and major in order of proficiency. My failure to progress discouraged me, and I gave up.

Athletically speaking, the bright spot for me was swimming. The Beach Club we belonged to had a summer-league, swim team, and I did reasonably well at this activity. No doubt owing to my tendency to revert to some primal aquatic state during the summers and inspiration from the 1972 Summer Olympics, I practiced and developed proficiency at the various strokes. Breaststroke was my best event, backstroke my worst. It seemed like there were days when I would scarcely get out of the pool. I just swam and swam. In combination with a little motherly encouragement and peer pressure, my comfort in the water translated to some modest success in the age-based swim races. I had a little collection of ribbons, largely blue first-place ones.

My personal hero on the swim team was Alex, mentioned earlier. He was an exceptional athlete and all-round gifted kid—smart and good-looking. He was even musically inclined! He became my idol. He was a good kid to boot, tolerating a younger hanger-on. He had just been raised right and had a marvelous family who was nice to me later on. I'm not quite sure how it happened, the age difference between my 10ish and his 13 or 14 being rather significant, but we became friends outside the Beach Club.

As our friendship moved beyond mere swimming buddies, and the season moved beyond summer, it quickly became apparent that if I was going to hang with Alex, I would need to take up hockey. He being rather charismatic, I quickly caught hockey fever. It didn't hurt that the Boston Bruins were doing quite well at that point in time, or that places to skate were plentiful. I began to skate at every opportunity and hounded my parents for padding and equipment. Alex's previous years of hockey playing and natural athleticism allowed him to excel. This constantly reminded me that I was an average athlete, and it was frustrating.

To sum up about athletics, whatever attraction it held for me was much more about acceptance than love of sports, competition, or athleticism. While it was fun, exhilarating, and physically beneficial, underneath it was a simple desire to fit in.

Left to my own devices, I was basically introverted during this period of my life. I would reflect and think about the things of life, such as sports and being social, etc. It was all I knew, so I didn't realize that I was rather isolated and lonely a lot of the time. Feeling insecure and dealing with those insecurities is part of growing up, to be sure, but I seemed to be doing a lot of that on my own. Time spent with my father was minimal, one day a week, and I don't remember him ever really checking in about how I was emotionally.

I was intelligent enough, but my academic performance was only average. My parents were always of the opinion that I should be doing better. The only real concern about my emotional status stemmed from concern about my grades in school. There wasn't a lot of psychology going on in those days, but it's safe to say I was a little sad about life. My parents' divorce was a huge stressor, compounded by the drama, financial concerns, and the fact that I was the only kid with divorced parents in the early seventies.

My mother continued to drink, and a byproduct of this was her sharing too much information. I'm sure that she was just lonely and worried, not having enough adults to talk to. I remember her unloading her worries and fears about the mortgage and the taxes and the heating bill. This was definitely too much information for the oldest male child, approaching puberty, with a tendency to take things on. In this environment, I grew up fast. I was the man of the house and felt the weight of that in my head and heart.

Many years later, I would be sitting in a college psychology class listening to the teacher lecture on the family dynamics of divorce. The effects on children, he outlined, are more pronounced as they reach the age where they think of things outside themselves, abstracting. He went on—this will be compounded in a male child who is the oldest... Yikes, I was triply screwed. Good thing I thought that was just how life was at the time, didn't question it. As I mentioned, there just wasn't much psychology and counseling going on in those days, and I was mostly just left to deal with it on my own.

My little neuroses were within normal limits, I suppose. Still, because I didn't know that at the time, it was a period characterized by discomfort and anxiety.

I was an alcoholic waiting to happen.

The summer between sixth and seventh grade was like the ending of what little childhood I had left. I was 12. Physically, I was visibly maturing. All the swimming that summer (thank you, Mark Spitz) had leaned me a little bit, and I was getting taller. Socially, I had enjoyed acceptance as just one of the pack in the little beach circle of friends. I paid close attention to the older kids; they were interested in things that seemed grown-up. I was to start a new school in the fall, and I felt as if I had an opportunity to somewhat reinvent myself. And what better way to do this than in the image of my interesting, older acquaintances?

Sex and partying first came to my awareness, as I listened to the conversations of the older kids. I had little to contribute. Mutual interest developed between a young (though well-developed) girl and me. She was the first woman I ever kissed in a naïvely romantic way, and we fooled around a little. Then she got interested in… guess who? Alex! This did not result in any significant hurt feelings or jealousy for a couple of reasons. He wasn't really interested in her, and I don't think I had really formed an attachment with her. It was more about curiosity, experience, and doing forbidden things.

Labor Day came and with it the end of the summer. In a spur-of-the-moment way, Alex and I planned an impromptu sleep-out. After we said goodbye to all our summer friends for the season, he came over and we pitched his tent way out of sight in the woods in back of my house. I don't remember exactly how it came up, but I remember being right onboard with the idea of drinking that night. Alex somehow obtained and brought, secreted in his sleeping bag, two bottles of Boone's Farm wine (distasteful sound effect).

This was my first drinking experience. Well, to be more accurate, it was my first-ever *planned* drinking experience for the expressed purpose of getting drunk.

~~~~~~~~~~~~~~~~~~~~~~~~~~~~~~

Alcohol was not unfamiliar to me. As outlined earlier, there was the morning drink tasting of my early childhood. In the course of growing up, I had normal exposure to alcohol. However, what I had, in retrospect, was a more normal exposure for a kid growing up in Europe. My father had a much more "continental" perspective about alcohol and categorical drinking ages. During those Sunday visits, if he was having a beer, I would have a beer. We frequently had a glass, or even two, of wine with dinner. My father's point of view, no doubt, was the European one. It's probably healthier to avoid making alcoholic beverages into forbidden fruit restricted by age limitations, which really don't mean someone is mature enough to handle it anyway.

I liked being treated as an adult. A sense of precocious sophistication accompanied the experience of drinking around my father. That is to say, I felt grown-up beyond my years. Those positive associations set the stage. Having positive experiences and conditioning to drinking, in a more European or enlightened way did not transfer to any kind of ability to handle drinking in a different setting. In exactly the way that familiarity breeds contempt, I completely failed to recognize alcohol's power.

I certainly don't blame my father for creating the monster I became. I do think that the mixed message of the enlightened perspective on alcohol against the contemporary environment with its peer-based and adolescent social pressure played a huge role. Naïvely, I took alcohol for granted.

~~~~~~~~~~~~~~~~~~~~~~~~~~~

Predictably, the sleep-out did not end well. After drinking most of a bottle of the horrible strawberry wine, I quickly bypassed euphoria and went rapidly past silliness and just got stupid. Then came the inevitable spinning sensation and the vomiting. I don't think my older friend was too pleased with me, but fortunately, I had gone charging out of the tent (mostly) before puking my guts out.

I spent the following day sick on the couch. I don't think my mother ever suspected a thing. Alex went home, and it was a while before we spoke again, as I was now branded as a "puke artist" for some time to come. I started seventh grade the next day, and while I still felt the queasy effects of drinking, I couldn't wait to do it again.

My desire to reinvent myself was realized to a great extent. My experiences during the summer had improved my confidence. My body was maturing slightly ahead of the curve, with a little fuzz on my upper lip and where my sideburns would one day be; there was hair in my armpits and farther south. I was not the tallest, but still tall.

I made fast friends with a new kid in town. He was actually seated next to me in our new homeroom on the first day of school, and we quickly found we had something in common. His family had just returned stateside from living overseas for a year while his father worked for an American firm. He was a really good-looking guy and obviously athletic. I sensed that from the social politics standpoint, this would be a good acquaintance, but we genuinely had a lot in common and became true friends. His name was Mike.

While I began to establish an identity in my middle school years (referred to as junior high school at the time), it was largely based on being different. I can't quite say I dared to be different, because I did not really set out to be. Nor was I always happy about it at the time.

I "went out" for the junior high school football team. It was more out of some strange urge for conformity and did not end well. After I proved to myself (and anyone who was paying attention) that I had what it takes to make the team, I quit in a way that kind of said f%#k you. The impetus for this stemmed from a dumb remark I made. The junior high school football team was composed of kids from both seventh and eighth grades. Typically, the seventh graders get a little hazing and general abuse from the "veteran" eighth graders. I didn't like my helmet, and one day after the first three weeks of awful boot campy practices, as the first game was approaching, I remarked, "so, when do we get our game helmets?"

While it's probably just in the nature of kids that age to be ridiculously cruel at times, the barrage of grief I took because of that stupid remark was absolutely over the top. During the next few days, it only got worse, not better. I had withstood weeks of calisthenics, tackling drills, and wind sprints, but I was basically unwilling to suffer fools, and I quit the day before the first game. What does that say? First, that I was never in it for the football, but rather some false sense of pride or prestige, which I clearly wasn't getting at that point. And second, that I had the ability to go rogue, even if not consciously understanding what I was doing.

For the next few weeks, at least once a week or so, I had a habit of riding my shiny 10-speed bicycle by the football field, just about the time the team was doing push-ups. With my new spare time, I started hanging around more with Mike in the afternoon, which included the girls he attracted. As I always say, there are two ways to do everything.

In the course of that seventh-grade year, Mike and I and a kid named Bill, who I had already been friends with, became quite inseparable. I suppose we were regarded as edgy, but basically good kids. We could be a little disruptive, but avoided any serious trouble. I don't think it is a coincidence that we were placed in three different homerooms the next year.

I mention those two childhood friends for the reason that it was later pointed out that I was viewed by some as the leader. I never felt that way and was generally insecure about such things. The next year, in eighth grade, it was also said to me (or about me), and this was in front of the entire social studies class during a discussion of social things, that I was a rare kid who was in "both the chorus line and the defensive line." In that second year of junior high, I played football and my drumming distinguished me as I performed with the band and chorus. I was in school plays and served as manager for the baseball team. I did reasonably well academically. I was starting to show potential.

I was also showing potential to really screw up.

In the interim, I had kept in touch with Alex, and we saw each other sporadically. Whether playing hockey, going to a few rock concerts, or just hanging out listening to music, I still idolized him. At some point, we repeated the sleeping-out experiment, this time out behind his place.

As a seventh grader, I remember hanging out with Alex and one of his neighborhood friends who had stolen a bottle of rum from his father. It was a Friday during school vacation. We were out walking along a country road, taking swigs from the rum. There wasn't too much, so I drank just the right amount to catch a nice glow. My inhibitions were released, and I felt free. I laughed, and everything seemed more fun. When I got home later, I had the courage to call a girl I liked, an eighth grader. It was wonderful and awful at the same time.

~~~~~~~~~~~~~~~~~~~~~~~~~~~~

That day out drinking with Alex and the other kid was as good as it ever got. It was the perfect buzz. The memory of it is surreal, partially because the thought of inebriation is so detestable to me now. This was a once-in-a-lifetime thing. It was a euphoric state so pleasant, making such a strong memory, that I never forgot it. It likely wasn't even remotely as good as my recollection. The reason I remember it, or perhaps the reason I remember the ideal it represented, is because I unconsciously spent most of the next two decades trying to capture that exact feeling again. If there was a moment that my alcoholism was born, that was it.

~~~~~~~~~~~~~~~~~~~~~~~~~~~~

The summer of my 13th year came and went in similar fashion as the previous year, but with more partying activity. The Beach Club was the focus for this. Though I never thought much about this sort of thing, that year was the swan song; I think we joined the club the next year, but it was never the same. There was beer in our milkshake cups, and the carefree days of childhood were over.

The following school year, going into eighth grade, I was determined to play football. I had felt some regret about quitting the previous year, and I had something to prove to myself. Having confirmed I could be different, I suppose that I was also compelled to prove I could conform and succeed. That was going okay until I made a serious miscalculation that would follow me for years, in addition to sealing in the minds of many people my budding reputation as a "bad boy." Naturally, it involved drinking.

I hatched a plot to get drunk before a Friday night school dance. I stole a fifth or liter bottle of vodka from my father. The bottle was a little more than a quarter full. Having little experience with hard liquor, I miscalculated badly how much to drink, and on a full stomach besides. After dinner (great lasagna, Mom!), I went to my room to finish dressing for the dance. I managed to down the contents of the bottle, no easy feat, as I was unaccustomed to this. The effect of the substantial meal in my stomach was to slow the onset of the alcohol. My mother drove my sister and me to the dance. People later told me that I already looked out of it while I waited in line to get in. It only went downhill from there.

My notion had been that I would experience the same joy and easy confidence as that day with my two older friends drinking rum. I would easily talk to girls. I would dance really well, and everyone would think I was truly cool. What everyone really did was to stay out of my way, as I went into a blackout pretty quickly. I was told that I danced with some unfortunate young girl who made an exit at some point when she realized things weren't right. I was told that I continued to dance after the music stopped.

Seeing the figurative train wreck about to happen, my friends, Mike and Bill, got me to sit down on the gymnasium bleachers. I have some recollection of this, sitting there with my head bobbing as I was almost passing out. When it became obvious that I would be sick, my friends managed to get me to the men's room, where they kicked everyone else out. I began to vomit violently.

My only other recollection of the dance is of my favorite social studies teacher, a chaperone at the dance, yelling at me, "What'd ya have, Keith?" Apparently, he is the one who later carried me to my bed. The next thing I remember is waking up there in the wee hours of the morning, bewildered and feeling sick and terrible beyond words.

During the rest of the weekend, I was left to wallow in shame and remorse. I guess they almost called 911, but I was pumping my own stomach quite effectively. Feeling isolated, I reached out to

Mike, who filled in some of the gaps, as I had been oblivious to what happened. He said he had never seen anybody that drunk, and he and Bill were really worried. They tried to keep me out of trouble, but their efforts could obviously only go so far.

There was a meeting with the principal and my mother on Monday morning. Concerns were voiced, remorse was expressed. Even 56 hours later, I was still feeling the effects, and some remark was made as to that being a form of punishment. Additionally, I would not be allowed to attend any more dances for the rest of eighth grade.

And that was it! I was sent off to class. I walked into the middle of homeroom, and the room got quiet suddenly. I took my seat amid mixed reactions from my fellow students. Whether the other kids thought me a fool or fearless, I was getting attention. I was the equivalent of the modern-day celebrity who messes up and becomes the focus of extra media attention. In another sense, I had irrevocably taken a specific direction at a fork in the road. I was parting company with conformity, and embarking on the road of rebellion.

My next stop on that road was six or seven weeks later. It coincided with the next scheduled Friday night school dance, from which I had been banished. It was mid November. I resolved that if I was unable to go to the dance, I would top it from a rebellion standpoint. My older and worldlier friend Alex was my go-to guy.

It bears mentioning that Alex was actually a great guy, and never had any intention of corrupting me; he also had a way of looking past our age difference. I basically invited myself along for his Friday night activities. This Friday night found Alex partying with his older brother and his brother's girlfriend in a finished loft in the garage behind their house. This was about the coolest thing I'd ever done, at least in the early stage of the evening. Hanging out with older kids, listening to great music, and recreating that perfect buzz (or trying to anyway) was my twisted little 14-year-old idea of heaven.

We even piled into a car for a "packy run" (slang for trip to the liquor store), which was especially cool for me as cars and car-related activities were still years away. The frosting on the cake was that we drove right by the junior high school where the dance was just getting underway. I had to beg them not to stop there; since hearing of my escapade the previous month, they wanted to go in and start trouble. I was basking in the glorious irony of the situation. I was having this amazing time with these great, older people, and all because I got drunk at the last dance.

Of course, the other shoe fell. I was still completely inexperienced in these matters and had apparently learned nothing from my recent debacle at the dance. I quickly passed through that zone of "perfect buzz" and progressed to a state of numb-faced stupor; "wasted," as we used to say.

There were a couple of new elements for me here. We were drinking good, imported beer; what little beer I'd had before was American Pilsner-type beer. The rich and stronger German beer was deceptively powerful. Also, we smoked some strong marijuana that night. My limited experience was with much weaker pot.

I was incredibly intoxicated. I remember everyone laughing at me, and my being zombielike, unable to respond. I also had the most unnerving sensation, as if like my larynx was shattering every time I swallowed. It finally ended quite badly with me out behind the garage puking my guts out, Alex teasing me from the garage window, "puke artist."

Early the next morning, I woke up freezing on a couch in the unheated loft. For the second time in a matter of weeks, my alcohol experiment had ended badly. That long, early walk home from Alex's house stands out as one of the most miserable experiences of my young life, along with the hours following my alcohol overdose at the dance the previous month.

~~~~~~~~~~~~~~~~~~~~~~~~~~

After nearly poisoning myself with alcohol, I drank again in a matter of weeks. This is not the behavior of any rational person, age 14 or whatever. The behavior is irrational, dangerous, and, in short, alcoholic. The last chance for sanity would have been to spot the pattern after two consecutive disasters. Instead, I was undeterred. I drank at the next opportunity, having taken my tendency to vomit when drinking as a challenge to be surmounted.

An observation I made much later in life was that *normal*, or nonalcoholic, people also get sick from drinking. After all, everyone can overdo it on occasion. However, there are several differences between a simple overindulgence and my alcoholic drinking consequences. Typically, the nonalcoholic person who has a bad experience with rum, for example, would swear it off for life. If offered rum in any form—rum and Coke, rum punch, Chinese restaurant drinks with rum—the negative association would stay with him or her for life. The mere thought of rum would be enough to turn one's stomach.

On the other hand, in my case, the lifelong aversion is not valid. At some point in my drinking career of two decades or so, I got sick on just about everything. Typically, I could go back to it in a few weeks to a couple months, kind of like a statute of limitations on the aversion. For example, vodka wound up being my drink of choice, primarily because it was cheap, plentiful, and effective. And if the principle of being done with something after it made me sick applied, I probably would have run out of things I could drink long before I gave up drinking.

The point is that there was clearly something abnormal about my persevering with drinking in the face of bad, even catastrophic results.

~~~~~~~~~~~~~~~~~~~~~~~~~~~~~~

I managed to finish out the middle school years without any more serious trouble. While the dance drinking episode established me as a kid with an "edge," I still distinguished myself in numerous positive ways. As I mentioned earlier, I was well rounded and liked by my teachers. And I had grown up quite a bit in several ways. No longer chubby, I'd grown inches taller. I had made inroads with the whole social awkwardness thing; the downside was I had defined myself as… edgy. Part of it was misguided perpetuation of what I thought was mystique. It was still really rooted in insecurity, but I felt better about myself. Unfortunately, that did not appease the growing alcoholic monster inside me.

CHAPTER 3

Drumming and Growing Up Drunk

The summer before entering my freshman year in high school was transitional in many ways. I had a part-time job working for a neighbor. I had a (sort of) girlfriend. The Beach Club was still happening, but the gang of friends was starting to scatter, as we all got older and started working jobs, etc. Also, I was no longer dominating on the swim team.

I had become Alex's heir apparent when he became too old to compete in the swim league, where 16 was the ceiling. A couple of kids I knew from school, who swam on other teams, had either matured physically, practiced with the Amateur Athletic Union (AAU) team during the winter, or both. I was getting my ass handed to me. I'd had a nice run, but it was over. I also wasn't finding time to practice regularly, as I had in years past.

My job was working for the neighbor who had rescued us from the stone-wall car accident years earlier. He had horses, and I divided my time between mucking out stalls and cutting the lawn, in addition to other odd jobs. I forget exactly how much I made, but it was a few bucks an hour under the table. It gave me a little spending money.

The girlfriend was a classmate. I'm not sure how it got started really, though I am sure her parents had never heard about the vomiting episode, or I would have been off limits. She was brought up very strictly Christian, and most of our activities together consisted of my going to her Christian youth group. We would read appropriate stories, even some Bible passages, and then go out for ice cream or something, occasionally movies. At one point in the summer, she and her family spent a week at a cottage at a nearby beach community. I went to spend a day with her. We took a walk down the long beach and back into the dunes where we kissed.

There were lots of changes and new experiences, but my drums were a constant. I continued to practice for hours most days. I was bound and determined that I would soon start playing in rock bands. I did not yet know where, when, or how this would happen, but it was my steadfast goal.

Abnormal drinking was something else that happened on a regular basis. I had discovered my mother's alcohol supply and was brazenly helping myself to it with growing frequency. Goodness, I was a twisted little monkey! At the time, gin seemed to be her drink of choice, and I thought it was disgusting, but I still drank it. I figured out little windows of opportunity, and I would pour myself about 3–4 ounces and go up to my room where I would down it. It would burn my stomach, but it was a kind of familiar/good burning. Then, in a matter of minutes, the haze of intoxication would descend... I was 14 and already drinking alcoholically.

On the Sunday visits with my father, I was quite direct. I would ask for beer when we would get back to his place, now in Cambridge. I would ask for a second glass of wine with dinner. I just wanted the effect. He did not seem too resistant, despite having learned about the whole thing at the dance months earlier.

Toward the end of the summer, I reported, along with all the other school band kids, to marching-band training camp. This was daily practice for a couple hours in the mornings for several weeks before the actual start of school. The high school boasted a powerful, up-and-coming marching band, which had been built up in the years immediately before. The marching band was a priority of the school system's band director, who had taken on a kind of mentor status for me during the past four years—spanning from elementary school through junior high. By virtue of football game halftime shows, the marching band is extremely visible to the community. The band had grown stronger every year as interest grew. By this time, the band presented the best halftime show in the football league, complete with complicated marching drills, precision flags, rifles, sabers—everything but dancing bears and pyrotechnics.

I was soon disappointed with my life as a freshman in this organization. I was assigned the unglamorous role of bass drum player, actually one of three. I made no secret of my feeling that this was beneath me. The upperclassmen made no secret of their opinion that I should shut up and pay my dues as they had. And so it went.

The other thing that I did that summer was run a lot. My friend, Mike, and I would go to the high school track and do laps to get in shape for freshman football. In junior high, I had played center. It's an important position, but a lineman position. I wanted to be a running back like Mike, who was a really gifted athlete. By working on my speed and endurance, I was hopeful that I could be in line for the glory of scoring touchdowns.

Summer ended.

The first day of high school was not truly memorable. There was no Top 10 lifetime hangover, as there had been the first day of junior high school. Some basic facts of social life in high school became apparent rather quickly; there was a lot of labeling, categorizing, and cliques. While one could expend energy pondering the sociological and psychological elements behind that, it simply boiled down to pressure. There was subtle and direct pressure to declare who you were, and to which of the various camps you belonged.

In high school at the age of 14, it's fair to say that if I was not already an alcoholic, I drank alcoholically. I had that preoccupation with alcohol—drinking and just getting "buzzed"—and that influenced everything. For me, the label thing was viewed through the lens of my drinking habit. How I would choose to define myself socially was heavily influenced by drinking.

A breakdown of social grouping in the time of my high school days consisted of two primary categories—freaks and jocks. Of course, I realize that this is a tremendous oversimplification. Due to my obsession with partying, I viewed the people in my school as being like me or unlike me. *You're either with me or against me.* Freaks often smoked cigarettes, liked to party and talk about partying, and generally did not play sports. Jocks typically played sports, liked to talk about that, and did not smoke, talk about partying, or party (defined as drinking, smoking pot, or using other substances, usually to the accompaniment of rock music).

Obviously, life is not as simple as dividing everybody into two categories. There were numerous subcategories. There were people who dedicated themselves to their academics; they would later come to be known as nerds. There were band people, drama people, chess club, science club, journalism/school paper people, and yearbook people. There were also various distinctions among those who partied. People could identify with one or more of these subcategories, but it still came down to those two overall categories, freaks and jocks. Partying or not partying. Cool or not cool, at least in my narrow view.

Already, I was brazenly crossing these social party lines. I had previously taken up cigarette smoking in junior high school, and I quickly found the smoking lounge. This posed a dilemma because I was going out for football. Aside from the fact that the coaches would be pissed, I was aware of being the only "jock-ish" person out smoking. Despite consciously defining myself as a rugged individual, I was constantly thinking about these things in a self-conscious manner. I marched to the beat of a different drummer, but nervously.

A major psychological hurdle came on the occasion of the first school dance. In high school, dances were held on Saturdays and more frequently than they had been in junior high/middle school. Every few weeks a live band played in the cafeteria, and it was open to the whole school. My banishment from dances was only valid at the junior high school, so of course I planned to attend. This felt like a big deal to me because I hadn't attended a dance in a year, and also because this was, after all, high school now.

The normal thing for any kid to do before their first high school dance is to think about what they should wear, how well they can dance, or which members of the opposite sex they might want to socialize with. The foremost thing on my mind was catching a buzz. I wanted to have that perfect buzz, just like that afternoon with my friends. I wanted to feel free, poised, and euphoric. But I didn't want to get in trouble.

Drinking was probably not a good idea. I was paranoid about being scrutinized, or at least having somebody check my breath. A strange and unrealistic notion that people would pay more attention, or even notice me, was the residual stigma of my having made such a clown of myself before. I didn't know at the time, but I just wasn't that important.

Determined to alter my consciousness in some manner, I found some tincture of opium in the medicine cabinet. I had a small quantity of homegrown marijuana earmarked for the occasion, which I soaked in the liquid opium and then dried. Walking the two miles to the dance, I smoked this concoction in the woods on the way. It worked! I had no idea how well it would work, or if it would at all, but I got quite high. I smoked a cigarette to mask the smell, and off to the dance I went.

That was the only time in my life I've ever gotten high on opiates, aside from the hint of a buzz from prescribed painkillers much later in life. It was quite surreal, and I could see how people would be attracted, drawn in, and trapped by that feeling. Still, it was hardly the equivalent of smoking myself unconscious in an opium den.

It was on that occasion that I was approached by an upperclassman who struck up a conversation about music. To be more accurate, he initiated an interrogation about my drumming, during which it came out that he was a guitarist. He was on the fringe of the music clique and kind of a loner in general. He asked me about the kind of music I listened to; the Stones, Hendrix, and Deep Purple were common ground.

As it turned out, he was pretty serious about his guitar playing. He idolized Ritchie Blackmore of Deep Purple. He invited me to come to his house and jam the next day. There was a drum set there, and all I needed to do was show up. Of course, he was auditioning me. Having not yet had the experience of being with other live musicians playing amplified rock music, I was incredibly excited. I passed his audition, and started hanging out at his house when I had time.

Time was different then somehow. I juggled successfully among academic/college level courses, along with band and a choral group, freshman football practice every afternoon with games Fridays after school, and then marching band during the Saturday football games. Homework got done. Additionally, I became friendly with one of the freshman football cheerleaders and attended my class float meetings a couple evenings per week.

Each class was responsible for creating a float for the homecoming parade. If everyone who said they were going to a float meeting actually went and worked on the float, there would have been a substantial upgrade in the quality of homecoming parade floats. It was really an excuse to get out of the house. There didn't seem to be time to get drunk during the first weeks and months of high school.

As football season wound down, so did the team's roster. There was a lot of attrition due to poor grades; some of the best players had to drop out because of poor grade averages. My dreams of being a star running back ended a few weeks into the season when the coaches called me in to see them after practice one day. They gave me a little speech about how they knew I wanted to be in the backfield, but the team needed me on the line… would I be willing to become the team's new center? The sting and disappointment was eased somewhat by the fact that the center is kind of important. He calls the huddles and leads the team to the line of scrimmage before snapping the ball back to the quarterback. Sometimes after that, he gets a forearm in the helmet from the other team's nose guard. Our team record was not impressive, but I decided I would play again next year. Or so I thought.

The band director somehow got wind of this, and I guess it was not part of his plan. If I had played football the next year, I would have at least dressed for the Saturday afternoon games, making marching band an impossibility. Factored into my decision leaning toward football was something that had come to my attention—that I would be playing bass drum yet again the next year in marching band. This was because of my underclassmen status and the fact that I was physically big and able to carry the bass drum. Talent, skill, or musicianship never entered the equation.

The director cornered me in a dark, deserted hallway one day and told me that if I chose football instead of marching band, he would not permit me to rejoin the academic credit concert band at the end of football season. As I was already entertaining long-term musical objectives and had verbalized the same, this would have been tantamount to being blacklisted. If I wanted to go to college as a music major, my transcript would need to reflect exactly what he was threatening to take away. I caved. My football career was over.

Of course, that was the mid-seventies. This unsubtle extortion would probably have had a different outcome today. It would have likely resulted in a meeting with parents, principal, possibly the superintendent and even lawyers in attendance, along with an extremely warm seat for the band director. At the time, it never even occurred to me to talk to my mother about it. It reminds me that I felt so alone in the world.

Along with the threat of excommunication, he made me a promise—that I would be drum-line captain and play the prestigious triple drums for both my junior and senior years. In the moment, this lesson in the mature delaying of gratification was not apparent, unfortunately.

Much later, I talked to the band director about this. Through the miracle of social media networking, we met for lunch a couple years back. Back in the seventies, we had gotten past it, and he remained my mentor. Still, I always wondered. He retired after a long and successful career of working every Saturday in the fall for many years. As two adults, we talked about it, and he explained his perspective. It's true that things were just done differently then, and he had also looked at a larger picture.

He was well aware of my tendency to be a rogue and also pointed out that I wielded influence over others that I was not aware of. Merely by being in the band he said, I was sending a message to a cross-section of people that band was "cool." As he had worked so hard to build the organization, this type of attraction was essential. I owed much to this man: my musicianship, professionalism, and musical sensibilities were a direct result of his influence in my life. Without realizing it at the time, I really needed somebody to set limits on my doing whatever my ego wanted to do.

~~~~~~~~~~~~~~~~~~~~~~~~~~~~

Several years into alcoholic drinking and preoccupied with liquor, the difficulty acquiring intoxicating beverages was probably the only barrier between me and disaster. At the age of 15, I was unable to legally purchase booze; if I could have purchased alcohol at will, I would have been drunk every day.

With a disturbing regularity, I was stealing alcohol from my mother. I developed an amazing sense of the traffic patterns of my mother and two sisters around the house, and I had the great capability of stealth. I would seize my opportunities whenever they would present themselves. Whether the others were in the next room watching television or on the second floor, each theft was like a little secret mission. My objective: the cabinet under the sink in the kitchen. My primary target: 4–6 ounces of hard liquor, with 8 ounces of wine as a secondary target. Mission parameters were to avoid leaving signs of the theft and to avoid taking so much that it became obvious. While my mother's drinking was heavy and steady, she must have questioned the quantities of alcohol she was consuming. In reality, she was supporting two habits.

~~~~~~~~~~~~~~~~~~~~~~~~~~~~

In my mind, I was an adult. As is the case with many 15 year olds, still blissfully unaware of many of life's more severe realities, I felt I was able to manage my affairs just fine. This was a regular source of conflict with my mother. There were numerous factors at play. Obviously, I was a teenager testing the bounds of my independence, but I was also a teenage alcoholic. In addition to normal social pursuits, there was the element of the pursuit of intoxication. On my mother's end, the stresses of single parenthood were complicated by her drinking. We were frequently fighting.

Our arguments would typically concern her attempts at limit-setting being in conflict with my attempts to have no limits. I was long past the days of being sent to my room. By then, my mother's threatened consequence of choice was sending the police out to hunt me down and bring me home. They did look for me on several occasions, but never brought me back.

My musical activities with guitarist Bill started to get more interesting as the year moved on. I had become his drummer of choice, and when opportunities arose to play poorly rehearsed rock music on the spur of the moment with other musicians he knew, I always jumped at the chance. I was impressed with myself as a freshman, out jamming in clubs and bars on a school night and being paid in drinks!

I was becoming a chameleon. Refusing to observe the invisible walls of conventional teenage social order, I declined to be categorized. Wherever they were having a good time, that's where I wanted to go, and usually did. I could blend. Beyond the labels of freak or jock, beyond the cliques, and beyond the limits of things even related to school, I wanted the most from life I could get, that is, as long as it involved drinking and partying. The ultimate test of this came at the end of the school year when the seniors went into party mode in anticipation of graduation. I was quite ballsy, crashing senior parties, and not being thrown out of most of them.

I also managed to avoid throwing up at any more dances through that year. There was an interesting dance toward the end of the year where the band was unfortunately inexperienced and poorly rehearsed, not to mention young. Parents brought them to play the job. To put it bluntly, they sucked, and that was the consensus of everyone in attendance. As the evening wore on, some friends and I conspired, and we basically stormed the stage and took over. Amid the cheers and approval of all in attendance, we played the last set of the night quite extemporaneously. This was the dog-eat-dog world of high school rock musicians. I felt badly for them as their parents arrived to pick them up, only to find them watching us from the sidelines.

Bill and I had gotten serious about music, found some band mates, and rehearsed enough material to play a three- or four-hour school dance. We went out and found ourselves a job at a school in a nearby town, and we played our first paying gig. It was $100 divided five ways, after paying the U-Haul trailer rental. But at the tender age of 15, I felt like my drumming career was on track to rule the world someday.

The remainder of my high school years was devoted to musical endeavors, partying, and the opposite sex. Trite as it sounds, that translates to sex, drugs, and rock 'n roll. New musical opportunities began to take me further afield with band mates older and more experienced. I found that cliché first love in my sophomore and junior years (more about this later). Drinking, smoking pot, and experimenting with other drugs at every opportunity, my quest for the ultimate buzz continued, as did my delusions of maintaining the cool persona.

By sophomore year, I had already decided to pursue a career in music. It was my dream, and I was laying the groundwork to make it happen. My hope was to get some serious training, and I became aware that there was a famous music school in Boston, Berklee College of Music. In the meantime, I needed to get as much experience as possible. Through the school's music program, I took elective courses in music theory and history. There is a saying, that "drummers are people who hang around with musicians." This is a dig at the fact that drums are not a pitch instrument, such as guitar or piano. I was determined to be more than someone who hung around with musicians; I wanted to understand and master the underlying complexities of music.

I was in a succession of rock bands, each becoming progressively better. The band during freshman year had merely whetted my appetite. The band during sophomore year played a handful of jobs during the course of the year, including my own high school. The objective, of course, was to play every weekend.

Always looking to advance, I would occasionally audition for other local bands that were achieving more success, playing more frequently with better reputation. One of these had a "manager" who was a Christian pastor. The band played every weekend, and actually earned decent money, but I was much more interested in the steady gigging experience. I was well prepared and nailed the audition, but the manager nixed me on the basis of my budding bad-boy image.

While laying the groundwork for my "dream" with willingness to learn and do the work involved, a big part of it was based on the idea of achieving popular success. My notion was that I would be part of some successful band or group, which would be my vehicle to fame and renown. In the seventies, the music business was in transition, and I had no idea about such considerations. It was becoming just that, a serious business in which corporations (that is, record companies) were beginning to manage talented, creative artists like a resource, something to be developed and exploited for maximum financial return.

The notion that talented kids who were willing to do a little hard work could achieve greatness was a product of the seventies. Even the one-hit wonder phenomenon was a result of the "develop-and-exploit" approach, just on a smaller scale. Also, there were literally hundreds of thousands, if not millions, of kids starting to think and project exactly as I was. In a world where there was a band in every garage on every corner, I was a bit naïve in my outlook and design for the future.

Early in my sophomore year, I kept running into a girl. Jane was a junior and a few months older than I was. She was petite and cute, but more important, she was someone who defied easy labeling. She was a lot like me. More of an individual, she didn't really identify with any obvious grouping. Unbeknown to me, she was placing herself in my path. She would mysteriously appear at sophomore float meetings, or at parties that I would be likely to attend.

As a sophomore, Jane had been dating a senior who had gone away to college that year, and she was moving on in her junior year. I later found out it was mostly by her design, and her plan was to move on to me. While I hadn't distinguished myself in any particular way as yet, she must have seen some potential. We got to know each other and quickly became "steady." This meant we were exclusive, displayed affection publicly, and spent considerable time together in and out of school.

We started having sex. While she wasn't my first, Jane was my first real lover. My 16-year-old hormones were intense, and I could not get enough of this girl. I had been on the wrestling team during my freshman year, and when the season started the next year, I quit after the first week. The real reason was that I missed wrestling with my girlfriend every afternoon at her house before her parents came home.

I was becoming somewhat consumed. When Jane's old boyfriend came back from college at the holidays, that's when the trouble started. It soon became apparent that she still had feelings for him. We remained together, but there was considerable drama in our relationship.

This drama raised numerous issues for me. While it was my first experience with the emotion of jealousy, it really struck a deep chord of insecurity. The jealousy was closely tied to the abandonment I had suffered when my father left, and subsequently as my mother gradually checked out as her drinking intensified. It seemed as if people I cared about left me.

The other demon that was raised had to do with feelings of inadequacy and low self-esteem. For the first time, I had to consider certain realities of life, the bigger picture. I was a sophomore in high school, whose principal means of support was summer landscaping jobs (and it was now winter), and whose principal mode of transportation was a skateboard and a 10-speed bike (and again, it was winter). I wasn't much competition for a college guy with unlimited use of an extra family vehicle. I was also waking up to the prospect that life would be full of similar situations; there would always be the equivalent of that college guy.

These were powerful emotions, no doubt compounded by my age and tendency to isolate in my own head. I seldom confided in my friends, never to my parents. I could be quite moody and even prone to brief periods of depression. Drinking fuels depression, and depression fuels drinking. I was drunk or high, or both, at nearly every opportunity.

It was only a matter of time until I found some trouble during the summer between my sophomore and junior years, drinking related, of course. As the Fourth of July approached, plans were made for a party. This was not a party in the conventional sense; it was not intended to be a social event with friends, food, and music. This was nothing but an excuse to drink heavily. This was nothing more than a place in the woods way behind a friend's house, a keg of beer and a few bags of pretzels and chips. No one was bringing potato salad or chicken wings...

To me, this was a little slice of heaven. Doing the alcoholic calculation, there was more than ample beer on a per person basis. We were in the middle of the woods in a clearing on a rocky hilltop. What could go wrong?

Unfortunately, everyone has his or her own unique idea about what a slice of heaven entails. For some, and especially on the Fourth of July, fireworks are part of that. Here, I will paint the picture: it's the middle of the afternoon, around 2 or 3 PM. The weather is dry, sunny, and rather hot. It is the Fourth of July, after all. There are about eight or ten of us present, and we've been there going on a couple of hours. The beer is holding up, and all present are getting along well.

Then, the fireworks. The real kind. The kind that fly up in the air and make really loud noises. And those loud noises attract attention and give away location.

Just about the time I had achieved my objective of no longer feeling my face, I was lying comfortably on a huge rock (all of me must have been numb too), just staring at the beautiful sky. Every couple of minutes, some fresh barrage of bottle-rocket noise would go off overhead, but I wasn't really interested. I was really drunk, and all was right in the world.

Into this idyllic scene steps a new figure. While I am slow to notice, he is plainly not feeling the wonderful party vibe. His blue uniform is soaked with sweat from his quarter-mile-plus trek through the thick woods, as he followed the sound of the pyrotechnics. His face betrays a bit of annoyance behind his state-trooper, Carolina sunglasses, probably a result of the fact that he was not fortunate enough to follow the path to our location. Instead, he was obliged to bushwhack through all tangled manner of forest, brush, underbrush, along with poisons ivy, oak, and/or sumac... in the 90-degree heat. I was the first and only to notice him as he quietly stepped into the clearing and did not announce himself. Rather, he began speaking into his walkie-talkie radio.

Officer Smith, better known as "Smitty," was the quintessential local badass, the type who winds up either in prison or on the police force. Backup on the way, he began to make his presence known. As my cohorts became aware of him, the fireworks abruptly ceased. For me, in my drunken haze, there was a slow realization that the party was over. I think the kid who brought the fireworks ran off into the woods, but otherwise there was no resistance. We were organized and marched back out past my friend's house, forced to carry the evidence, and then put into a small caravan of waiting police cruisers. Protective custody awaited.

This was the only time in my life I had ever been in jail, even if for all of about 90 minutes. We were not booked. After all, this was a small town, and it was the seventies. The job of the police was to keep things quiet. The fireworks had been the real offending issue. I remember mouthing off badly to Smitty in the patrol car on the way to the station, and I don't think he said anything.

I was awfully drunk, but only a few degrees more intoxicated than my mother when she arrived to pick me up. Weren't we the picture of a high functioning family?! I'm sure the cops shook their heads; today they would have followed my mother out of the parking lot and pulled her right over. Back in the day, they avoided both stirring the pot and doing the paperwork.

There were vague repercussions. I was (sort of) grounded for a little while, allowed to go only to work, but eventually it blew over. The obvious issue was that I was drunk in public for the second time in about three years. Because school was not involved, my father was out of the loop, and because my mother did the same thing daily in the privacy/seclusion of her home, nothing really came of this episode.

Meanwhile, musical endeavors were starting to look up. Guitarist Bill and I had been playing together for two years, and, going into my junior year, we put together a new band. Each past effort had been successively better musically, and this new band was no exception. We had hooked up with a new bass player and rhythm guitarist from a couple towns away. The bass player was my age and pretty good. The rhythm guitarist was in his early 20s, a castoff from one of the area's top bands, so he brought with him some credibility. Our musical tastes aligned well, and we began rehearsing as a rhythm section while searching for a lead singer.

This new band-in-the-making began to open up new social opportunities. Somehow, a small entourage of... well, groupies I guess, materialized. We played our first semi-public gig at a private party in a North Shore coastal town. My girlfriend and I managed to see each other several times a week during the summer, but my hometown social circle and musical circle seemed to be on different trajectories, and they somehow never overlapped. There was a lot of partying with both sets of friends, but the musical scene seemed a little more about drinking and getting high. *I wanna rock 'n roll all night and party every day...*

If getting busted on July 4 was the low point of the summer, the party gig was probably the high point. We soon found a young (my age, 16), good-looking kid with a great voice. He could sing Zeppelin, Aerosmith, and Queen, and he was a decent front man. We were on our way!

When school started up in the fall, we were rehearsing and partying hard. We began to hustle up dance jobs with some success. We were all free to function as booking agents for the band, but I seemed to have a fair amount of success. I managed to get us hired by my high school class, now the juniors. I also got us hired by the town recreation committee to play at... the junior high school! There I was, on stage at the scene of my vodka vomiting mayhem four years prior. Sweet irony. No vodka that night, however, but the sex, drugs, and rock 'n roll train would pick up considerable speed... before it started to go off the tracks.

The band became the center of my life and my biggest priority, superseding academics, school music, and even my girlfriend. It was exactly that kind of inflated self-importance and *band-centricity* that was setting me up for a huge fall. The music was the tip of the iceberg; the band was becoming my primary social outlet, and the emphasis was on drinking and getting high.

A complicated love triangle formed, and it included me. When the summer party gig hostess returned home from private school for a month at the Christmas holidays, the trouble started. She had been the bass player's girlfriend, but made it known she was interested in me. Whether a byproduct of alcoholic tendencies toward instant gratification, or just my immaturity, I was not really capable of thinking things through. The negative consequences—for the bass player, for my girlfriend, for the band, or me for that matter—were not something I was able to connect to in my mind. I wanted what I wanted when I wanted it. When groupie girl—we'll call her Christin—made her play, I bought everything she was selling.

She was actually quite nice. She was intelligent and attended a private school up north. She was pretty and a lot of fun, and extremely... er, modern in her attitudes. I think her mother was a sex surrogate or something like that. My mother got wind of this from my orthodontist, who was their neighbor. My mother's seal of disapproval on this girl was all it took. I stayed at her house for days at a time during school vacations. I was powerless to resist, and my 17-year-old ego swelled.

I broke up with Jane. I became a pariah among her friends, and somewhat marginalized among what had been our social network, at least temporarily.

Once Christin moved on from the bass player, things in the band became strained and awkward. The bassist hated me. However, as one door seemed to be closing, another was opening. I can't remember the exact details, but a singer whose band had recently broken up visited one of our rehearsals. There was some situation with my band's singer, and we were under the impression that this guy, John, was interested in joining with us. He was really on a talent-raiding mission.

After scouting us, he later approached our rhythm guitarist (formerly of another band of renown, remember) and me to come start a new version of his last band. They had lost their keyboard player and drummer through interpersonal political squabbling (like I had caused), and their lead guitarist and bassist remained. I had seen/heard them play on a couple of occasions, and they were quite good. This situation was the kind of upward and onward move that suited my insatiable little ambitions.

From the standpoint of experience and musicianship, this new band challenged me. I realized the benefit of surrounding myself with more experienced and better players; there was a tendency to be pushed or pulled to the next level. At 17, I was the youngest in the band by far. The four other guys were in their early 20s and had jobs. They all had their own places to live except the bassist, who like me, lived at home. I was still learning to drive, being a little behind the curve with that because of being so busy with music. The band mates took turns driving 20 minutes to pick me up and bring me home after practice. Whether or not I was truly a drumming prodigy, this veritable limo service did serve to reinforce my worsening attitude.

I just kept digging in deeper. The rhythm guitarist's 20-year-old sister, Stacey, started hanging around. She was drop-dead gorgeous, had a job, a car, and… interest in me! Yikes, life was just getting so complicated. Again, immaturity got the best of me, and I just couldn't resist the option to upgrade. I upgraded my band; why not upgrade my girlfriend? What really needed upgrading was my character. I was becoming an arrogant little shit.

To further complicate matters, John, the new lead singer, was quite enamored of Stacey, and another love triangle ensued. It was just frosting him that this little 17-year-old punk drummer, who couldn't even drive, was with this total knockout. I think he had their whole life planned out, but she wasn't interested.

At some point in the early spring, my conscience asserted itself. Whether I found the common sense that had eluded me until then, or I began to realize the consequences of my actions, or both, I had a huge change of heart. I realized how shallow I had been. It was as if the pendulum swung the other way. I realized that, though both of those band-related women genuinely liked me, I had been attracted to what Christin and Stacey represented and *what* they were instead of *who* they were. Without quite understanding those insights, I felt empty and sad. I missed Jane, who I had hurt and abandoned. I resolved to try to get her back.

Jane, meanwhile, was working her way through my friends at school. She had taken up with one of my best friends, who played bass in the school jazz band, in addition to being on the hockey team. This would have been complicated, except she had just recently dumped him for one of his best friends, someone with whom I was acquainted, but not close. Oh, the drama! Finally, the world was not handing me what I wanted. Though I made my feelings known, Jane was not budging from her relationship with this other guy, Pat. They were together, and in my face on a daily basis.

I grew depressed that spring, and it seemed to go on for months. I drank at every opportunity. People grew concerned. My friend, Mike, was there for me, and he was great about trying to distract me. The band was a steady thing at that point, but a distraction at best. The singer and Stacey were together, which happened about five minutes after she and I broke up. It didn't bother me in the least; I was pining for Jane.

I would do crazy things, such as get drunk and pass out in Jane's car while she was in the school for some evening activity. When she came out to her car, I was disoriented, and someone nearly called the cops. Another time, I left school to try and see her at the train station on her way to some internship she was doing. Today people that do things like that are known as stalkers. I was going off the deep end.

~~~~~~~~~~~~~~~~~~~~~~~~~

I had fallen squarely into a common alcoholic trap. Alcohol impaired my decision-making ability; my impaired decisions had negative consequences. My principal coping skill was drowning my feelings with the depressant alcohol; my feelings of depression and self-pity spiraled down. I became obsessed. Whether this obsessive personality trait came out of my drinking, or the other way around is a chicken/egg question. The issue was more about it being self-destructive.

The spring of my junior year was one of several dark periods in my life. It has taught me that, while we all experience peaks and valleys in our mood and happiness, drinking turns normal valleys into dark abysses. At a time in my life when I needed to be developing the capacity to handle emotional pain and the ability to face the consequences of my own actions, I was instead opting to anesthetize myself at every opportunity. These experiences in this formative time in my development began to crystallize issues that would dog me for decades to follow. Using alcohol as cement, I was "hardwiring" a depressive element into my personality.

Compromised coping skills and being prone to obsession were buried in the fine print of my "contract" with alcohol, and I never understood that I was dancing with the devil.

~~~~~~~~~~~~~~~~~~~~~~~~~

I think it was sheer persistence that finally paid off. At the end of the school year, Jane came back to me. During the summer, her family moved to Rhode Island. She would attend college in Vermont in the fall. I visited her in Rhode Island, and later several times at college.

As my senior year began, my life was much less dramatic than the previous year with all its music, social and party activities. It felt anticlimactic. On my 18th birthday (18 was the legal drinking age at the time), a friend took me out for a celebratory beer... at the same bar where I had already been drinking for several years. Musically, there was no sense of moving to the next level. Efforts to get a new band going came to naught. I had a long-distance girlfriend; where I had been formerly accustomed to seeing her on a daily basis, this was much different. In short, I was bored.

Things at home became strained. My relationship with my mother was difficult for both of us on a daily basis. Her drinking was firmly entrenched; she had effectively crawled into a bottle after the divorce and remained there for 10 years at this point. She functioned after a fashion, but her attempts at serious employment in her chosen field of early childhood education had come to failure, mostly due to her drinking. She worked part-time at a local department store, and I frequently observed her leaving for work in an unfit state.

As for me, I was a teenage alcoholic becoming a young adult alcoholic, at least chronologically. In terms of maturity, my development had probably been arrested years earlier. We had a household with two alcoholics, and it was starting to get ugly. Our daily arguments were escalating in intensity. I think we both saw things heading down a bad road, and, at some point, my frustration would end in some type of unacceptable physical outburst. No longer a boy, not yet a man, I sensed the subtle ticking of a time bomb with the situation between my mother and me.

My solution was to move in with my father. In terms of my everyday life, there just wasn't a lot tethering me—no band or girl. In short, the things I defined my identity by and based my self-esteem on were not happening. It was a bit gutsy, but I decided to move on. I moved in with dad.

My father lived close to an hour away in a comparable suburb west of Boston. The high school was almost like another version of the one I had attended. I was enrolled in all the same academic classes, and the music program, which presented some new opportunities. As an underclassman, I had worked my way through all the academic music courses my old high school had to offer, so I was thrilled to discover this new school actually had a jazz improvisation course!

By this time, I had set my sights squarely on Berklee College of Music, and the new school had an active music program. I was quickly assimilated into their concert band, orchestra, and jazz band. There were a couple of serious and talented young musicians there who were immersed in the jazz world, and this influence was tremendously beneficial. I began to get my jazz chops together and studied with a good local drum teacher.

I was adopted by a clique of pretty girls. The first day in the new school, after getting lunch in the cafeteria line, as I was faced with the dilemma of which table to sit at, one of them just invited me over to sit with them. There is some unspoken social psychology behind the school lunchroom table seating, and my social future in this new school could be influenced by the mere choice of where I sat that first day. I realized that my previous social chameleon identity held no sway here. As it turned out, I hit the lottery, and remained friends with these young ladies for the duration of the school year. In no time, I was invited to socialize and party with them outside of school.

The change in location did not change my drinking. I was now of legal drinking age, and drunken episodes were interspersed through that senior year of high school. Poor dad! Talk about going from 0 to 60. He didn't have a clue what he was signing on for, taking on a wild teenager. He just hadn't seen that side of me and had no idea. One night, he observed me having a little difficulty backing his car into the garage (I was inebriated, of course). He tried to talk to me about my "drinking habit." He was a smart man, and his head was in the right place, but he had no gift for psychology, and chose the wrong time to approach me about this. I was angry and in denial. His attempts at limit setting failed utterly.

There was a classic episode where my youthful ignorance came back to haunt me. I discovered that my father was making little lines on his booze bottles, marking the labels to see if I was stealing. Thinking I was clever, I drank some Johnnie Walker scotch with the intention of replacing it later before my father, out of town at the time, could be the wiser. Unfortunately, I unwittingly thought I only needed to replace it with something brown. I restored the bottle of nice scotch to the original line with a pint of Old Granddad bourbon—I didn't realize there would be an issue. Apparently, this came to light on the occasion of my father offering an out-of-town business associate a Scotch. His guest said there was something wrong with it, and it wasn't hard to figure out what the problem was.

During Christmas break, Jane came to visit. She was growing and changing, starting to move on. She was attending a well-reputed liberal arts college in Vermont and definitely starting to spread her wings. When I went to visit her later that winter, she sent me home early, saying she felt sick. The truth was that she had developed feelings for another student in her coed dorm, and my visit to the school had brought their feelings to the forefront. This came out in bits and pieces over the next few weeks, and I took it hard. Aside from the loss of control and connection to my previous existence when I was in the midst of so much change, I really had feelings for her. She was a special and unique young woman, and we did have a strong connection. I had been completely loyal to her since the previous spring when we had reunited.

That dark depression reared its head again. I felt isolated. I had not been able to tap into any rock-band scene in my new location, and I felt stalled in my musical ambitions. I felt insecure that Jane had moved on to bigger and better things in my mind. It struck that same nerve as when her old boyfriend had challenged our relationship two years earlier. I was adrift and drowned my sorrows. One night I drank Southern Comfort, passed out in my room, and vomited. My father and his wife were horrified.

Nevertheless, I applied to Berklee. I practiced my drums, went to my lessons, and put effort into the school music program—academic courses, not so much. I somehow retained enough chemistry and Spanish to serve me later in life.[*]

My harem, the group of young women that "adopted" me, was supportive. They were really my only friends in school. I got a part-time job at a local convenience store. The school year began to wind down, gaining momentum toward the inevitable graduation. My father and his wife announced plans to go to Europe for the entire month of May. I would be alone for the last month of my high-school career. This was a huge set-up, which I thought was a huge bonus.

I was given a couple of responsibilities in their absence: to water the plants in the house, and cut the small lawn as it grew. I was left with a reasonable food allowance and use of my father's car, a 1975 Camaro.

I had parties. I somehow thought watering plants and cutting the grass could wait until the last week or so. The plants suffered from

---

[*] I credit the English department at my old high school for instilling in me a serviceable command of the language that has made this writing effort possible.

lack of attention, but I didn't really notice until I looked at them around the end of May. I had no clue about the finer points of lawn maintenance; my only experience consisted of simply pushing a mower over my neighbors' nice lawns years earlier. My boyhood home had not had an actual lawn. As I said, the lawn was small, and my father had one of those old-fashioned, mechanical, rotating blade, non-powered lawnmowers. The 5-inch lawn laughed at it. Dad was not pleased on his return home.

After taking stock of the situation, he sat me down and told me to leave after graduation. He cited my irresponsibility and drinking as the reasons. The reality was a little more about his wife wanting their quiet way of life back. They would be starting my father's second family before long, and I was really just in the way. However, there was evidence of my parties, the plants were dead, the lawn looked terrible, and I felt to blame. This was also the time my father chose to share the Scotch incident with me.

~~~~~~~~~~~~~~~~~~~~~~~~~~

Instead of offering me help, my father showed me the door. At the time, I absolutely took this to heart. I didn't like it, but did not question that I deserved this. Did I understand that I had a problem with alcohol? Not really. I defended my drinking as just what kids my age did, though I did realize it was what a minority of kids my age did. This was my version of the consequences of my actions, and it did not cross my mind that my father's vision of parenthood probably fell outside the mainstream approach. In reviewing these events in a therapeutic context much later in life, I realized that the problems did not lie entirely on my side of the street. In the words of my long-time therapist, "There is a special ring of hell reserved for your father." I think that's a little strong, but I get the point.

There were several levels here. My father's stated position was that this was about my drinking. His actual position was that he was feeling pressure from the wife and really just wanted me out. My stated position was that I didn't have a drinking problem; I was just a screw-up. My actual position was that I was not in a place to accept that my drinking was to blame.

What I was left with were more feelings of abandonment, insecurity, and depression. Never once did I look at my drinking as the root of my situation. Never once did I consider that I needed to make changes.

~~~~~~~~~~~~~~~~~~~~~~~~~~

CHAPTER 4

Hello, Cruel World

I was accepted to Berklee. Even before my father had made clear that he would not even let me live with him, he had made clear that he would not support my musical goals. He viewed them as beer-soaked pipedreams. He hinted that if I had my mind set on being an engineer, doctor, or lawyer, things would be different, but they wouldn't have been. He was effectively dissolving our father/son relationship.

I needed to earn a pile of money for tuition, and the opportunity that materialized was working at the Beach Club of my childhood. As it turned out, there was also an option to live there in a loft over the bar. This was a no-brainer, for both the right and wrong reasons. Living rent-free was good. Living over the bar was bad.

I bid my father and his wife farewell, and headed up to the coastal town near where I grew up. This was my first experience living alone. Still shell-shocked from being booted by my father, I was doing my best to pull it together mentally and emotionally, and gear myself up for starting college in the fall. Somehow, it didn't seem like this was how things were supposed to be, but I had nothing to compare to. What I had at that moment was myself to rely on, and no one else.

My job and housing came with certain responsibilities. This establishment was a family-oriented social club. It was a small version of a country club with sand and ocean instead of a golf course. While it had been a lovely experience growing up, working there was a little weird, because I had previous relationships and still knew many people. However, I had been away for a couple years, and I adapted fairly well. Because I was living at the Beach Club, I was expected to keep an eye on things. I had keys to everything, and no one was keeping an eye on me.

Life was scary, and I drank to keep worry at bay. My life now came with a ready alcohol supply, and I could get plenty to drink, as long as I wasn't stupid about it. That meant being sober on the job and when visible, because I lived there when off duty. I did manage to stay out of serious trouble, despite being anxious and stressed about my future. I tended to lie awake at night, often drinking myself to sleep. As the summer progressed, I projected that I would save about enough money for the first semester's tuition, and not much else. I pondered my options.

Figuratively speaking, my father's door slammed behind me. I had nowhere to live at summer's end. After a tremendous amount of deliberation and considerable pride swallowing, I approached my mother and put the cards on the table. We were overdue for reconciling, and it went well. She made allowances that I had grown up somewhat, and I could agree that I still had growing up to do. It's truly amazing how being tossed about by the world can help one to see the light of reason. Despite her issues, my mother still had the heart of a parent. She was proud of the things I had accomplished in my short life and, unlike my father, supported my music because it was what I loved. At the end of the summer, I moved home and started college.

Berklee was challenging. On the first day, the realization that I was going from big fish/small pond to tiny fish in the open ocean began to sink in. The place was full of the best young musicians from across the country, in addition to the world. Was I ready to fully appreciate and utilize the experience? No. While I did reasonably well in my courses, and really expanded my horizons, knowledge base, and technical skills as a musician, I was much too linear in my thinking. I would've benefited greatly from more life experience and also musical experience before setting foot in a place like that. However, it was really due to financial considerations that I bowed out gracefully at the end of the semester.

My mindset was that of a typical 19 year old, and my expectations of the college experience included some notion of an "Animal-House" lifestyle. Berklee undoubtedly ranks in the bottom 2 percent of party schools. There was about a 15 to 1 male to female ratio. To compensate, I made semi-regular visits to see my friend, Mike, who went to a state college in the middle of Massachusetts, where I met my quotient of mindless partying and debauchery.

While unable to find a permanent band, I did find transient play-ing situations, and even did some studio recording. Berklee had ele-vated my playing to the next level. I found a day job and moved to the city, where I hoped that I would find that magical band that would be the vehicle of my Cinderella story. I found a roommate situation with a house full of local musicians.

In the previous year, I had the youthful, impetuous tendency to move as the wind blew me, and in the spring of '79, I joined a travel-ing show band. Instead of using this as an opportunity to learn the art of showmanship onstage, and also learn about interpersonal dynam-ics offstage, I saw it merely as an opportunity to party in different geographic locations. Three weeks on the Caribbean island of Curaçao, working one hour a night, two hours on Fridays and Saturdays, began to swell my head. The tour groups of Venezuelan women fawning over the band didn't do much to contain my ego either. When we returned stateside, I had less money in my pocket than when we'd departed. At Caribbean hotel prices, it wasn't cheap keeping the hotel room sink full of beer on ice.

As the Caribbean tour was winding up, there seemed to be some intrigue afoot in the band, and I had an intuitive hunch that turned out to be spot on. Following a week playing a resort in the Poconos, the bass player and I were sacked. It's fair to say this was indirectly due to drinking. While my termination was not directly due to drunkenness, it was reasonable to attribute the lack of filter between my mind and mouth indirectly to alcoholic tendencies. I was openly critical of a lot of things that were actually paying my salary, little things such as our dance music repertoire and the music director's keyboard playing. And so the anticipated week home layover until the next leg of the show band tour turned into a crash landing.

My vague intuitive sense that things were not right in the band had fueled uneasiness. After it became real in the form of this signi-ficant reversal of fortune, I became bitter, resentful and angry. I felt betrayed by the music director and was consumed with resentment. I had known him for several years, and we had started putting a band together two years earlier, before I left to live with my father. This situation truly emphasizes how immature I was at this point in my life. I had no conception of how my poor treatment of this guy had resulted in consequences for me. Never did I consider the misdeeds I had done to others; my self-righteous sense of being wronged ate me up.

~~~~~~~~~~~~~~~~~~~~~~~~~~~~~~~

I was now beginning to feel the cumulative effects of alcohol on the development of my young personality. Opportunities to learn life's lessons and build a little character were "lost in the sauce." In matters both large and small, I was not inclined to choose the more challenging path, opting rather for the temporary comfort of the drink. Bad behavior leading to consequence, the inability to accept the consequence leading to more bad behavior, I was in a Groundhog Day-like situation, waking every day to face the downward spiral.

At a time in my life when I should have been developing coping skills, insight, and the resiliency to handle and solve problems, I was failing test after test. The vague intuition I had sensed about interpersonal problems in the band was a slight residual signature of what should have been coming loud and clearly through my alcoholic haze. The band mate in the show band, with the power from higher up to hire and fire, did not tolerate my bad treatment and behavior. Despite the abject lesson in humility, I had no capacity to look at myself. That kind of honest self-assessment was too uncomfortable, and I chose instead to anesthetize myself.

~~~~~~~~~~~~~~~~~~~~~~~~~~~~~~~

Landing home around the end of July was simultaneously a blow to my ego and a much-needed dose of stability. My pride was much bruised from the dismissal from my professional, fulltime band gig. It was more about just being young and able to bounce back than about any resiliency. The world-weariness I suffered from was much more an effect of alcoholic drama than anything else. I licked my wounds, sorted things out, and was able to merely relax and enjoy life without the pressure of school or fulltime work. I needed to think. I began driving a taxi locally. In the fall, I took a job as a cook at a local college.

I rekindled musical relationships with high school friends. The brief stint at Berklee and time on the road restored me to big-fish status, at least back in the local small pond. My friend, guitarist Bill, and I auditioned for an original band, my first experience with groups that played their own music. This was really exciting, and just what I always wanted to get into. They were serious, and had a self-produced vinyl recording. I joined; Bill did not. The band played local clubs and bars sporadically through the fall, and also did some recording.

As for my real passion in life, drinking, it remained ever-present. On a daily basis, I was getting by on a six-pack of "talls," 16 ounces that is, augmented with a few nips, usually whiskey. I smoked marijuana daily, as long as I could get it.

And for about a year, my life went nowhere.

In the autumn of 1980, I joined a cover band. These were weekend warriors, and they were established, playing mostly high school and college dances. They worked through a booking agency out of Worcester, and soon I was off to the far-flung reaches of the state every weekend for Friday and Saturday one-nighters. I made $100 a night with this band, decent money. For comparison, I had made $175 a week with the show band. My day job, cleaning floors at a nursing home, Monday through Friday, netted me about $130 a week. Still, somehow I failed to save any money, a phenomenon known as alcoholic hole-in-the-wallet.

There were some drinking escapades related to that cover band. We had played a Saturday night mixer for a college in Worcester, and I was so drunk by the end of the night that I could barely pack up my drums. I remember dropping my cymbals; I was a total trainwreck. I spent the night on the bass player's couch, too drunk to make it home from the unloading at the end of the night. This was something that started happening regularly. On another occasion, I drove (or rather, was allowed to drive) the band's equipment truck home on the Massachusetts Turnpike. I blew out a tire doing 80, which was quite a feat for the tired old truck. The angels were watching out for me that night, and I was able to control the truck with a flat tire.

That summer, my mother sold the house I had grown up in. She really needed to get out from under it; the taxes, heating bills, and upkeep were too much. This raised a number of issues. It came to light that my parents had agreed on a number of points in their divorce agreement, among them that my father was obligated to pay college tuition. When I heard this, I confronted him. Naturally, I was half-drunk at the time. This was only the second time I had seen him since moving out three years earlier, and it would be the last time I would see him for about 20 years.

Another issue was that my mother was obliged to set half the proceeds of the sale of the house aside in trust for me and my two sisters as part of the same agreement. It was bad enough that the home of my childhood was sold for peanuts. Situated on 10 acres of prime land in that beautiful North Shore town, the land alone would be worth $1 million today. The breakdown of what happened was that Mom and Dad and their lawyers rewrote the agreement, each letting the other out of their respective obligations toward my sisters and me. That's a screw job to anyone, but to an alcoholic who holds on to resentments both petty and major, this felt like life-altering betrayal.

The other piece was that I was obliged to move out. Wherever my mother landed, there would not be a place for me. I found a dingy apartment in Beverly with a couple of roommates. As usual, what should have been an adventure somehow felt traumatic.

The cover band, which had always customarily taken summers off, was in a state of disarray. Two founding members were resigning, and there was some reluctance on the part of the rest to continue. By the time the consensus was reached to reform the band, it was already the end of summer. The fall months were spent auditioning and finally rehearsing the replacements. I took advantage of the downtime to take a few courses at Salem State College: English composition and basic piano. The band made it into circulation by the midpoint of the school year, after the holidays. I also made a decision to attend a program to become a surgical technician the following year.

This was something I had been giving thought to for some time. I had a friend who'd become a surgical tech right out of high school, and whenever I bumped into her, I was always fascinated to hear her stories about life in the operating room. I didn't know for sure if I'd have the stomach for it, so there was a little leap of faith involved.

As the spring of '82 rolled around, something unexpected happened. The cover band disbanded, and I perused the classifieds looking for drumming opportunities. I placed a call to a local band and spoke with one of the songwriters. As was my way, I turned things around to make them the focus of the interview. I must've asked something he was unable to respond to, and he asked me to hold while he put his songwriting partner, Alex on the phone. Alex? No, could it be? He'd been connected somehow to the town that the band was from; last I saw him was in 1977 or so.

It was! My childhood friend and swimming idol, early adolescent role model and bad influence, was on the phone. Not only that, but the fates had brought us together in the context of a potential musical situation. This was an exciting development and made for an interesting summer.

Alex was back in the area, running the crew at a local estate that was home to a summer concert/theatre series. He and his songwriting partner had written and recorded a few songs together while in college up in Maine. They had enlisted a couple of local musicians to form a group, the principal purpose of which was to entertain the entertainers and in-crowd at this music festival. They were playing their own stuff, in addition to blues and British rock, on a weekly basis at a small private "tavern" on this beautiful estate. Their drummer wasn't quite up to the task, by virtue of being weak musically and strong in the beer-drinking department (oh, the irony). Everything being a matter of degree, I was acceptable from a beer-drinking perspective, and more drummer than they knew what to do with. I mean literally... I showed up the first time we played together with my oversized Sonor drums and rototoms; they were used to playing barely amplified. It was like bringing nuclear weapons to a knife-fight. I had to scale back a little.

This music was a blast! There was no pressure whatsoever. The arrangements were loose, and I picked up Alex's original songs quite intuitively. It was the complete opposite of my last cover-band experience, where the objective was to reproduce music precisely as people heard it on the radio or recordings. Reconnecting with my childhood friend was also great; we were now on a different footing as contemporaries. As the season drew to a close, there was initially discussion, then the decision to take this informal "summer" group to the next level as a perennial project.

In the meantime, I started school to become an operating-room technician. After a summer that seemed like one long party, I had a full plate. School by day, band practice a couple nights a week, and still cleaning floors at the nursing home on weekends. I managed to squeeze in plenty of drinking. One really bad hangover episode that stands out was when I showed up for CPR training at school the morning after the band played a Boston club that paid us in beer. Good thing it was just an inanimate dummy that I practiced on.

Somehow, I made the dean's list in a blackout that year. I was even elected to the student senate, which worked well for getting the band hired to one of the school's parties.

Musically, the band was muddling through. Alex wrote clever songs, and he had a lot of charisma as a performer and front man. However, the overall musicianship of the group was average, and my high personal standards and big ego fueled my dissatisfaction. This put Alex and me in conflict with increasing regularity as the year went on. About a year after this little band odyssey had begun, it ended with resentments all around. My part in that was the considerable belligerence and ego that were coming to define my increasingly alcoholic personality.

I graduated from OR tech school and was hired shortly thereafter by a large Boston medical center. Along with one of my other classmates, I commuted into the city daily. Hung over every morning on the train, my tech-school classmate would just roll his eyes. At no time in my life was it ever more apparent how much growing up I still had to do as when I was a drunken bull in that china shop.

As if there wasn't enough drama in my life that year, I had an issue with one of my organs. My heart, knowing no logic or reason, had been acting up periodically by forming crushes on a couple of women, the latest of whom was a coworker at the nursing facility. This had started in the year before I went back to school, and should have ended when her childhood sweetheart shoved an engagement ring on her finger within a week of catching us together at my place. The suspicious circumstances around that would have resolved the feelings of any sensible man, but not me. As I lamented and recovered from that lost love, another woman set her sights on me.

One of the nurses, on the unit I cleaned at the facility, had been watching the whole drama unfold with the other young woman, a housekeeper. We began to have the occasional personal conversation, and she expressed her dismay, and that she didn't understand what my attraction to this other woman was. The phrase, or something similar, "not the brightest bulb on the block" might have been applicable to the woman I'd had the crush on, but as I said—the heart knows no logic. This nurse, only in her late 20s, was herself approaching the end of the trail of her marriage to a man she had known from Pennsylvania, where she grew up. She was five years older and seemed smart, sensible, and together. She probably saw in me the potential of someone starting on a career in healthcare. Our connection strengthened, and she began to confide that she wanted to leave her husband.

The whole thing was convoluted, and wreaked of alcoholic dysfunction from my end. She left her husband, and we moved in together sometime in the winter.

~~~~~~~~~~~~~~~~~~~~~~~

At that time in my life, I had little insight into the dysfunction of my romantic feelings. I wanted women I couldn't have; I didn't want the women who wanted me. Had you asked either of the women I was in long-term relationships with during my alcoholic twenties how they felt about men who drank, they both would've said, "No way!" or something along the lines of ,"God bless him, but no thank you." Both came from Irish, working-class backgrounds with alcoholism running thick through their families. On a conscious level, they would have rejected men that reminded them of their fathers, stepfathers, uncles, or brothers, that is, the majority of the male influences or role models they had experienced in their lives.

Yet there I was at the other end of the sofa, and though I looked, sounded, and acted differently, and came from a different type of background, on a subconscious level I was exactly what they were used to and comfortable with. They gravitated to what felt familiar.

And for myself, I gravitated to women who were accustomed to and tolerant of alcoholism. In both long-term relationships in my twenties, it was as much or more alcoholism that formed the attraction than any genuine heart-based feelings or normal chemical attraction.

~~~~~~~~~~~~~~~~~~~~~~~

The next five years of my life were really more of the same, although my tolerance to alcohol increased, the minor insight I was capable of decreased, and the window of opportunity for actually doing something of significance in terms of music was slowly sliding shut.

My drinking progressed. It began to take on some characteristics of an iceberg. There was visible daily consumption of beer and the occasional festive libation—wine or a cocktail. This was the tip of the iceberg. Beneath the surface, there was a whole hidden layer of consumption. I'd begun buying hard liquor, usually vodka, and consuming that to regulate my intoxication. This would leave the visible beer drinking to give the appearance of what I thought was social drinking. Like an iceberg, the bulk of my drinking lay invisibly below the surface. At some level, I knew how sick I was. As with any habit, it became unconscious over time. My excessive, alcoholic drinking became an automatic behavior that was not subject to any critical analysis on my part.

CHAPTER 5

Drinking to Exist, Existing to Drink

If my life as a drinker had a trajectory, it was now in the phase of descent. My established alcoholism was beginning to show effects. Blackouts and memory loss, health issues, irritability and belligerence, unresolved emotional issues, compromised job performance, loss of spiritual values... a short but intense list, and I was in denial about everything on it. I was immature, overly sensitive, and grandiose. My alcohol-enhanced self-image was my ego's defense against the emptiness I couldn't face.

I didn't know what I didn't know. For the most part, I had stumbled around in my brief adult life reacting to situations. Buckling under the pressure at the Boston medical center, I sought to escape before it caught up with me and I was fired. I found a position in a community hospital in the northeastern part of Massachusetts, not far from where the nurse and I were living.

That living arrangement was getting ugly, largely on account of my drunken bad behavior. Also, our basement apartment had flooded, and the damage to our meager belongings was substantial. We found a little house to rent not far from my new job. The outcome was actually favorable; I guess that's an example of that grain of sand in the oyster resulting in a pearl. My inability to live with and get along with others was the underlying issue in our moving.

Having lacked role models, it's likely that I sought them in my job as a surgical technician. Basically, I had surrounded myself with father figures—surgeons! As a group, they are accomplished men, in charge of their immediate surroundings, which are conducive to feeding their egos. They would do fine until I became a rock star! Clearly though, I hadn't come to terms with my parental relationship issues.

Since the time of my reluctant launch out into the world a few years before, my relationship with my mother had been strained. I did not talk to her or see her often. She was starting to experience serious health issues, the results of her years of drinking. The hospitalizations began again, except this time there were serious, even life-threatening, problems. The situation became great enough that the hospital social worker was pushing for us to gain power of attorney; the possibility that she would not survive was raised. I recall feeling resentful that her problems became my problems. As during my childhood, she was like a powerful force of nature that could impact my life at any time, completely beyond my control.

~~~~~~~~~~~~~~~~~~~~~~~~~

The effect this had on me was not what might have been anticipated. More than anything, I experienced anger. I could not identify the feelings at the time, but I was aware at some level that I was not "grieving appropriately," as we say in the hospice field. Unresolved feelings about the pattern of our relationship during my childhood, in which she tended to not be present when I needed her, and being "over" present when I wanted autonomy, were the smoldering fire trap. Alcohol was the accelerant.

The other piece was almost too obvious; my mother's alcoholic complications were a roadmap to my possible future. As I moved toward my likely alcoholic destiny, my denial of that influenced my thinking. The thought occurred to me that "I will never become like my mother," even as I moved toward that outcome.

~~~~~~~~~~~~~~~~~~~~~~~~~

There I was, rocking drummer and party animal by night, respectable surgical technologist by day. If I had a master plan, it was to have that honest work/visible means of support to pay the rent and keep me in drumsticks while I pursued my conquest of the music world. My eggs were in the drummer basket. There was a succession of bands throughout this time.

At home, the relationship went up and down. The hidden part of my drinking was the wild card here. I never fully participated in that relationship; I had a mistress, and it was the bottle of vodka out in the car, under the seat. This is where my personality suffered. I started to experience instances of being a "mean" drunk, which was only a reflection of my internal sadness and insecurity. I began experiencing memory loss, blackouts, and just passing out. I would be making dinner in the late afternoon, and wake up at 11 pm on the living room sofa where I'd been sleeping for hours. With no recollection of how I'd gone from dinner prep to sofa coma, I would find the remains of the meal I'd started in the kitchen. My girlfriend had long since gone to bed after hours of watching my drunken slumber, unable to rouse me. This scenario repeated numerous times, and I had little ability to listen to my girlfriend describe it to me or comprehend its meaning.

As seemed to be my pattern, there was a coworker that I became enamored of. I never acted on this while in my relationship at that time (though I would later). What I did do was move out for a few months. I rented a room from a hospital coworker, and I was free to experience life as a bachelor. I pursued the coworker, who was eight years my senior, and got it out of my system. Then I moved back in with the nurse, same little rental house, for a couple more years.

I joined an area band that I really liked. They were an offshoot of a famous local band that had hit it big, as in record deal, national and international touring, etc. The record deal had run its course; the usual personality conflicts resulted in members leaving to form their new band. When the drummer retired to go to accounting school, I was replacing a guy who had two major label album credits.

This sums up the close-but-no-cigar way in which my music career seemed to unfold. A year earlier, I had replaced a drummer who left to seek his fortune and went on to credits with artists such as Alice Cooper, Joe Satriani, and The Tubes, among others. Finding my way into musical situations where a high caliber of talent was required, I had an uncanny knack for arriving after the fact of the album being recorded.

In the mid-eighties, I became interested in electronic percussion, a new trend in popular music. I had taken a high school course in electronic music and been exposed rather extensively to the early synthesizers of the day. Hence, I had a fair understanding and no reluctance in embracing new technology. In addition to my alcohol and marijuana addiction, my day job now had to support a growing electronic gear habit. I amassed what is known as a hybrid drum kit—half acoustic, or traditional drums, and half electronic drums. Additionally, this involved a speaker system, microphones, various programmable modules, and lots of cables. At its zenith, it took about two hours to assemble.

This mastery of a complicated array of drums, equipment, and hardware that is challenging to merely assemble, let alone coax interesting sounds and rhythms from, was part of what attracted me to drums in the first place. From both a talent and technical standpoint, I was a highly competent, even gifted drummer, on or close to the cutting edge of the art of drumming.

The stars were aligning for some more wild times. Ten years after my junior year in high school, I was destined to experience more excesses of wine, women, and song (sex, drugs, and rock 'n' roll). Quite unexpectedly, I heard from Alex, who had been teaching overseas for two years. Now returned, he was hoping to enlist me for a "one-time" reunion of our band from a couple years previous. Without benefit of any rehearsal, this effort went surprisingly well. The time away had benefited us; nobody could really remember why we had broken up.

A few months later, Alex had accepted a local teaching position, and set up shop to do some recording in the basement of his rented house. He invited me in to do some drum tracks of songs he'd written. We found enthusiasm and ease in our new collaboration, and this began to gain momentum. We discussed permanent reformation of a band, a version II of the last one. We soon began rehearsing with a new lineup and new instrumentation. Where the previous group was a standard guitar quartet plus blues harp (harmonica) player, the new incarnation was guitar-bass-drums plus blues harp and saxophone. This was a unique sound, reminiscent of, yet predating, Dave Matthews and solo Sting by a half decade.

The band rehearsed intensively and developed a respectable repertoire, which featured half original music and half British invasion-influenced rock as well as updated blues music. We had enough material to play dances and started getting ourselves booked for four-hour jobs. Our style was unique, and listeners couldn't tell whether we were playing cover songs or original music.

This should have been the ticket. We were all interested in making it as musicians. We were willing to put in the work and the potential for achieving some measure of success was really there. Egos, subtle shades of differing musical goals, and partying got in the way.

~~~~~~~~~~~~~~~~~~~~~~~~~~~~~

While a view into the world of musical performers might be interesting to some readers, I describe it somewhat at length because it became a perfect laboratory for my alcoholism to complete the fermentation process. In such a self-contained work unit, where familiarity can often breed contempt, the excesses, character defects, and general dark sides of the individuals are given fertile ground and plenty of fertilizer with which to flower and grow. During this period of my life, I was weed-like.

As I approached my late twenties, with well more than a decade of alcoholic drinking, my interpersonal skills were distinctly lacking. Opinionated, narrow-minded, egocentric, insensitive, inconsiderate, and possibly even power-mad were all accurate descriptions. In the context of a small dynamic and democratic/self-governing organization such as a rock band, my alcoholic ways made me a square peg at best. At worst, I was the turd in the punch bowl. I suffered from the inability to simply be a member of the group; I would power drive through any situation, believing I always knew best.

In short, my personality, my whole way of being, had been defined by my alcoholism. The cumulative effect of going through life while intoxicated resulted in a failure to socialize properly. The net result was that I was rendered unable to function in the give-and-take world of interpersonal relationships.

Fairly reliably, my drinking shot me in the foot. The effects of alcoholism, both understated and obvious, began to impact and ultimately sabotage my music. The drummer is the anchor or foundation in many musical settings, especially a popular music ensemble. Mild intoxication can be liberating, but drunkenness is the enemy of steady rhythm, coordination, dynamics, and arrangements. Musical collaboration is not served by the egocentric, increasingly belligerent disposition of a drunk. Arguments and tantrums too numerous to remember redefined my reputation. I was kicked out of bands because of my unreasonable behavior and poor musical performance when drunk. The consensus was great player, bad drinker.

~~~~~~~~~~~~~~~~~~~~~~~~~~~~~

My wild ride of the late eighties brought me to a new level of hedonism and a new low in my loss of spiritual values. As though repeating the cycle of my third year of high school, the musical and social parts of my life gained momentum and intensity.

The band with Alex got busy. In the way that bands do, we became focused on our musical goals, and it took on a life of its own. There was a tendency to become self-absorbed, but on a group level—the group this, the band that, the guys... overly self-involved, the focus of our energy became a little distorted, and the other areas of life lost priority. Work was somewhere I had to go during the day. Home was where I went to sleep, most of the time.

Along with the band, rolled up into it, was our recreation. While such an endeavor as a band, of itself, is considered recreation by most, this was not the case. For me, Alex, and the bass player, the music was a highly significant part of our identities and life goals at the time. However, that did not stop us from mixing business and pleasure. After all, we were in the business *of* pleasure. That frequently meant substance abuse. There was much beer consumed in the course of a practice session. I would usually make a visit or two to my vodka/mistress in my vehicle. It was not unusual to adjourn to a local pub following rehearsal. We would sit over pitchers, discussing our music, plans, and goals, oblivious to whatever basketball or hockey game preoccupied the rest of the crowd. In short, the work and play of the band had little or no distinction.

Performances (the word "jobs" almost doesn't suit) were the same, but with even more emphasis on the party component. Increasingly, the presence of a white powdery stimulant insinuated itself into band life. First associated predominantly with performing, for that extra "lift," it also gradually started to find its way into weeknight rehearsals. After all, cocaine was a phenomenon of the eighties and very much associated with the musician lifestyle at the time. The illusion of well-being and a powerful sensation that can best be described as a subtle and congenial grandiosity first tempts, then can ultimately enslave, the seeker of musical enlightenment.

Ever trying to master the domain, I viewed the increasing trend toward more partying and less music with alarm, at least as far as performances. At the heart of this, was a desire to get us to the next level of professionalism, but sometimes it felt like I was trying to herd cats. We would go on break, and it would stretch on to 20, 25 minutes. It bothered me that the emphasis was shifting away from playing, ironic as that was.

I was actually rather disciplined, in a horribly dysfunctional way. I would run to my van, slog down some vodka, grab a beer from the bar on the way back in, run to the dressing room for a dry shirt, and I was good to go. I wasn't big on the coke. I enjoyed the burst of energy, and probably would have done a lot had cost not been an issue. Unlike a couple of my band mates, who were beginning to get a little wrapped up in it, my attitude toward cocaine was, "That's nice, but now let's play music." Remarkably, I could take it or leave it.

After our gigs ended, the real parties usually began. The increasing on-the-job substance abuse was just a prelude to the all-nighters which often followed. Our harp player was part owner of a local furniture factory. This was a perfect setting for us to party the night away; it offered a central location with privacy, and no one to disturb us or be disturbed by us. We could and did make noise, drink, smoke, and snort to our hearts' content, and literally party until the sun came up. This whole lifestyle was my dream as a twenty-something, aspiring musician.

In my relentless chase for pleasure and what I thought made me happy, this period in my life saw a new low in my personal standards of behavior. It was as if my conscience couldn't stand being around me and left. In addition to my live-in relationship with the nurse, now going on four, five years, I began what can only be described as womanizing.

Obviously, something inside was missing. Unable to really examine this with a vodka-soaked mind, I assumed that my relationship was lacking. Without the conviction or courage to do something about this, it was much easier to simply chase other women. As with music and partying, this also gained intensity and momentum over time.

It started with the coworker I'd had a relationship with while broken up with the nurse a year or two earlier. I began visiting her occasionally on the way home from band practice. She was also in a relationship, so we were both cheating on other people. There was just something about that forbidden physical relationship that kept us coming back. Occasionally, our operating room call schedule would coincide, and we actually had sex in the OR a couple of times after discharging the emergency surgical patient. This was so wrong, but it was so hot! Then I would go home to the relationship that I was steadily pulling away from.

~~~~~~~~~~~~~~~~~~~~~~~~~~

By this time, I had experienced a break from the reality that my behavior had consequences. There were other girlfriends while I was in that five-year relationship. These trysts usually had their basis in drinking and partying, and I had long since stopped thinking about my behavior in any conscience-based frame of reference. That I might really hurt another human being did not compute.

The direct result of daily drinking was that my mind never seemed to come up for air. While likely still capable of weighing pros and cons, and thinking things through, the inclination was not there. I just wasn't processing that way. Instead, I thought about what I wanted and how to get it. While we think of this as a spiritual loss of values, spirituality, or the concept of something greater than me, never entered into it. It was simply a loss of values. I wanted what I wanted, when I wanted it. Unless something was going to interfere with getting what I wanted, or worse, my drinking, it really didn't enter my consideration.

~~~~~~~~~~~~~~~~~~~~~~~~~~~~~~~~

Living on such an empty and sad basis, I grew depressed as 1987 wound down. The excitement and enthusiasm of the band had faded. The reality of my spiritual and emotional bankruptcy began to dawn on me. I began to question why I clung to my relationship, and had an inkling that I was being none too fair to this woman, who genuinely cared about me. The answer to that question was uncomfortable. Insecurity, neediness, and a desire to be enabled were prickly sensations that threatened to develop into utterly painful emotions. Rather than identify and fix them, I simply took action in an attempt to make them stop. For all the wrong reasons, I decided to do the right thing. I broke off the relationship and moved out.

My descent became steeper. Now free of any restrictions on my drinking, I moved toward my bottom with ever-building momentum.

CHAPTER 6

Circling the Drain

I found a small apartment. It was located close to the downtown area of the small city where the hospital was located, a short commute to work. Utilities were included. This was my first experience living without roommates of any sort. I was now truly on my own at age 28, even though I had been alone for all intents and purposes for a decade. I moved in New Year's Day, 1988.

I was now free to drink. There was no one to observe or disapprove of my behavior. When or what I drank, and how much, was entirely up to me, free of any obligations or restrictions associated with other people. The funny thing was that I didn't consciously think about it that way. Because I was in such denial that my drinking was excessive and abnormal, I didn't change my behavior very much. There was still vodka in the car. Another bottle stayed in the closet, essentially hidden. As before, there was a supply of beer in the refrigerator. I drank in the car on the way home, had a few beers, and later usually drank more vodka out of the closet.

What did change was the quantity. Most nights at home, I drank to oblivion.

As the winter months went by, the band became busier. In addition to a monthly job at a Polish club in the band's home-base town, we had more school jobs and private parties as the weather grew nicer. Band jobs became just an excuse to party. Whether Alex was writing less new music, or because the emphasis was shifting away from being serious about our music, we weren't producing new material as we had been. Our evening's repertoire consisted of half cover music, half original. The fine line between being well rehearsed and staleness was crossed at some point. Potential for boredom made ample space for more excessive drinking and drugging around band activities.

My work in the operating room was status quo. I dragged myself up in the morning, often having fallen asleep in my clothes in the living room, and went to my job. I did the same thing I'd done for five years, except with more drinking in my outside life. Whatever degree of mastery I had attained as a surgical technologist was simply translated to doing the job automatically, and I progressively brought less energy and personal investment to the effort. Also present now on a daily basis was a new element, anxiety. I would wake up with a sense of impending doom, and only by a Herculean act of will did I get out of the car and go in to work some mornings. I was getting by, and that was about it.

My relationship with my mother had suffered steady deterioration, and by this point, I had pulled back. Ridiculous as it was, I reached a point where I'd had enough of her "alcoholic bullshit," told her off, and stopped talking to her for a period of time. Of course, my own alcoholic bullshit was half the problem in the relationship, but I was in no position to understand or accept that. This was the heyday of my alcoholism. It was in full bloom.

The band finally imploded in a muddle of misunderstanding and resentment. As our recreational extracurricular activities had continued to mount, the presence of the white powdery stimulant had become more common. Cocaine was the prime suspect in the band's breakup. Alex had started out almost two years prior as antidrug, across the board. Slowly introduced to cocaine, he enjoyed the sense of mental sharpness, especially in the context of creating music. He would often make up new lyrics on the fly, his form of vocal improvisation. Over time, his relationship with the drug escalated. My attitude toward cocaine was basically, "That was nice, but it's gone now. Let's drink a few beers and settle down." In contrast, Alex was not a happy camper at the end of the night when it ran out. Supply became an issue for him, and there were things going on behind the scenes.

From a financial standpoint, a cocaine "habit" is significant. As Alex's flirtation with the drug became first a relationship, then servitude, he became more creative in his ability to finance his nose candy. His priorities and decision making suffered. As the whole situation seemed to be getting out of hand, I made a routine trip to our music store of choice for drumsticks or something. I remarked to the owner about a lovely pair of PA speakers that looked just like the ones collectively owned by the band. "Those are yours," he replied. "Alex brought them in on consignment." Not good! Alex had gone off the reservation, essentially pawning our community property. Amid other more minor issues, this really stood out as the straw that broke the camel's back. We broke up.

Good thing I didn't have a problem like that...

Though I didn't really have any problems (outside the bottle of vodka under the seat of the car, that is) to speak of, I had a really intense bout of depression during the next year. It came and went, but I remember some black days. I went through a period of musical inactivity. My ability to "nail" auditions had gone away. I wasn't able to find a girlfriend, despite being actually available. The ironic abundance of women who had been available while I was in a relationship had dried up. I felt stuck in life. I wanted to be a great musician; I was a surgical technician who drank a lot.

The period of depression pushed my drinking to new, sadder levels. I blacked out most every night, only to wake with insomnia in the wee hours. Drinking myself back to sleep was, of course, dangerous the closer it got to the time to get up and go to my respectable job. I began to call in more. Vodka and beer consumption were up.

Sometime in the winter of '89, childhood friends introduced me to a woman, Patricia. She was tall, smart, and athletic. She worked for the state's Department of Revenue as an auditor. Besides that, she was from an Irish working-class family, and she had been around alcoholism her whole life. We were a match made in heaven, and we started seeing each other.

Patricia and I became informally engaged. I say informally because I proposed quite spur-of-the moment one drunken night during the summer. No ring, no plan, just unfiltered thought escaping through my mouth while we were in the midst of what most closely resembled joy to me at that time. We moved to a rented townhouse in the city where I lived. Her office was just a few towns away, so this worked well for her. Having an enabling girlfriend worked just fine for me.

We set up housekeeping together, and things were going okay. I had come out of my depression for the most part. I joined an original blues band, went to my job every day, and was fairly happy in the relationship. I even patched things up with Mom, because I thought I was with the woman I was going to marry, and should therefore grow up. This period of seeing a bigger picture did not include insight into my still daily drinking however. This was a plateau along the downward slope, a peaceful, but only temporary interlude before the final drop.

My drinking was well enabled in this situation. I went home from work in the afternoon and still drank vodka on the way. On arrival, I would crack a 16-ounce beer. I usually prepared dinner, since Patricia came home close to dinnertime. There would be a couple more "visible beers," and a trip to the basement for some reason, during which I would drink hidden vodka. Pleasantly numb, I would fade to gray oblivion, simply giving the appearance of being tired. I was often in a blackout. And so it went.

Life became full of the expected. In other words, it was dull.

The remedy for too much domesticity was finding a band. I took to my electronic drums and scored with a band whose music I absolutely loved. They played all original progressive rock, and I had exactly the sound they were looking for. They had a vinyl album, and it was in some sort of distribution in Europe. This was so much in line with my long-term musical goals, and I set about learning their challenging material.

Still secretly hot for my little hospital coworker, I kept after her, and we did have the occasional rendezvous. I was so conflicted. I was engaged after all. My relationship had become mundane, and I took it for granted. The real problem was that at 29 years of age, I was still not a grownup. Something about my life was uncannily similar to an earlier part of my life. Enabling girlfriend, infidelity in the relationship, band with prospects, daily work routine (less challenging than previously), and functional alcoholism. Vodka bottles in the car and in the basement.

~~~~~~~~~~~~~~~~~~~~~~~~~~~~~~

The fact that I had déjà vu about my life was well grounded. I had recreated the same dysfunctional reality as in previous years. At a subconscious level, I had been drawn to a woman whose past was thick with alcoholism. I was restless and discontent in the relationship, but nonetheless wanted the security of a caretaker. Moments of clarity were rare, and questioning myself about the lack of any real intimacy was painful. I declined to persist, choosing always the anesthesia of the bottle. The repetitious stability in my life was alcohol's defense mechanism.

My partner was also drawn to what felt familiar to her. In appearance, verbiage, and general presentation I was different; in substance, I was exactly the type of habitual drinker that she had known her entire life. For that reason, there was a comfort level, albeit an unhealthy one. In this way, the cycle of dysfunction was perpetuated.

I manifested the same experiences and relationships in a cycle that would not be consciously broken.

~~~~~~~~~~~~~~~~~~~~~~~~~~~~~~

In the spring, the band settled into a holding pattern of limited public appearances. This left me with idle "music" time, because I was not part of the creative process, that is, songwriting. I used the opportunity to find another, complementary musical endeavor. I joined a popular "bar band", playing all acoustic drums again and having way too much fun. Now I had the serious, complicated music band with long-term goals and the goodtime local performing band. I was in a state of bliss, at least musically speaking.

My bliss was short-lived. Out of the blue, I received word that my mother was deathly ill. Her doctor called to say she had a matter of days, and family needed to be notified.

My reaction was one of reluctance to believe what I'd heard before. She had been at death's door on several previous occasions, and I had trouble accepting it this time around. My sisters and I had already ridden that rollercoaster, and my reaction was to be protective of them and me. I needed convincing.

On arrival at the hospital, I was stunned. I saw incredibly sick people on a daily basis, but I was not prepared for the shell of a woman I found lying there that day. We had spent time together at the holidays, our rift mended. We had spoken a few weeks before, with no hint of any illness. Yet here she lay. Barely conscious and difficult to rouse, she wasn't lucid when she did come to. This was on a Saturday. The next day I sat with it. I wrestled with whether to tell my sisters.

My two younger sisters were both in the midst of significant life events, and my oversensitivity to my mother's old pattern of crashing into our lives, consuming our energy and attention, was making me freeze. My emotional reaction was to relive all the times through my life that Mom's alcoholism had made unwelcome demands, and it made me resistant. I struggled. Monday at work, I was completely useless. After tearfully explaining the situation to my manager, I returned to the hospital to see my mother again. She was worse, and I said goodbye for what would be the last time. I contacted my sisters.

One sister was vacationing in the Caribbean; the other was in the midst of senior year final exams at college. This had been much of my dilemma. I took it on myself to really see if Mom was terminally ill before broadcasting the news. Despite my shortcomings, I was still a protective older brother. I would inform them, and then the decision whether to come running home would be theirs. The vacationing sister booked a flight for the next morning. The sister at school, having spent quality time with mom just weeks before, decided to stay in exams with my support. There was nothing to be accomplished, and Mom was now beyond knowing anyone was there.

When I explained the situation, my sisters both understood perfectly. Fortunately, they both appreciated the way in which I handled the matter. As my sister later described it, my call came just in time for her to book the once-daily flight from the small island to the big island, where she connected back to Logan Airport. She landed in Boston at 6:30 PM, and arrived at my mother's bedside at 7:30 PM. My mother died within minutes, as though waiting for my sister. It happened exactly as it needed to, something that was not lost on me.

I was at band practice at the time she passed. I went to the hospital and sat in the presence of my mother's lifeless body, numbly absent of any kind of normal or appropriate grief.

Arrangements were made, and her ashes were scattered in the forest near where we lived for many years, in keeping with her wishes. Mother's Day fell a week later... I mourned her as best I could, but I would not really allow myself to go entirely into sadness. I kept myself intoxicated. My drinking was barely in control; I still managed to function, but it was really dysfunction. A liter of vodka and a good quantity of beers were being consumed on a daily basis, yet I continued to show up for work, band practice, and life in general. The drinking had escalated. The consequences would follow.

Vaguely in this order, bad things started to happen. Out driving one morning, a policeman observed me swerve out of my lane. Because he was coming the other way and had to turn around to pull me over, I had a chance to throw away the open beer that was between my legs as I drove. Probably because it was morning, he didn't question my sobriety, and only wrote me a ticket. About a week later, I had a car accident while drunk, swerving and hitting a parked car at a curving intersection. Miraculously, I avoided arrest for driving while intoxicated.

At work, my boss pulled me aside for a serious chat. People were concerned that I smelled like alcohol, particularly when called in at night. People were right, but my boss was uncomfortable with this, and it was still only 1990 after all. She made her concerns known, but no action was taken, as if the message was to simply get breath mints.

My girlfriend and I got into a conflict with the people in the next townhouse. They were up in arms, blaming our cats for a flea problem in their unit. The wife was pregnant, and prone to lots of screaming. The police responded on a couple of occasions, and the situation was ugly and dramatic. My drinking certainly did nothing to enhance my coping skills with this stressful disagreement.

As this downward spiral continued, my general deterioration was a source of concern to my band mates. I was dismissed from both bands within the space of a week. Ironically, the lead singer of the bar band, unbeknown to me, was decades sober. He came to my house to inform me of the band's decision, which came out of the blue. He said simply that I was "out of control," and encouraged me to get some help. I was in no place to hear that or to understand his meaning.

I became depressed again, but by summer's end, a new element was coming to the surface. Anxiety, something that I had experienced on occasion, became constant and finally intolerable. I had begun to see a therapist during the summer to cope with my mother's death. While alcohol was only discussed as it pertained to my mother, she must have been aware that I drank to excess. By leaving the matter alone, she shrewdly allowed me to succumb to all the pressures and stressors in my life and seek help. Around mid-September, I had an emotional meltdown and basically could not function. The therapist suggested a local psych facility, and I went in on a Monday evening.

I was admitted to a "brief treatment unit." The admission guy remarked "You have the gold card, you can stay up to 90 days" when he saw my insurance card. That put me over the edge. While they had a 28-day addiction treatment program, I was there because I had other problems. In my opinion, I just needed some help solving my problems... and in subconscious parentheses—so I could resume normal drinking.

Somewhere in this process, a seed was planted. It began with the admission assessment, with its many questions regarding use of alcohol and substances. There was a counselor who sent me to AA meetings and kept trying to shove a Big Book in my hand. The subject of alcohol was constantly thrust into my attention. While I knew they wouldn't be serving cocktails, I was there as a depressed psych patient, not for my alcohol consumption. The thought that I had a problem like that was, well, depressing. In reality, I wasn't yet able to face my alcoholism, because I still denied its existence. I clung tenaciously to the idea that I could drink socially, casually, normally.

I was sent to my first AA meeting, on site. The details are blurry, and other than hearing people talk about losing their driver's license, nothing stood out. My defenses were up, my skepticism set to 11 on a 10 dial, and nothing stuck. I had no comment when asked about the experience on my return to the unit.

During the course of the week I spent in the hospital, I was able to acknowledge that my drinking was "out of my control." Obviously, I was there for a reason, and my feelings of depression and inability to cope with life had overwhelmed me. I clung to the notion that I drank too much as a result of my problems and rationalized that I could manage drinking. I thought this would require ongoing support, so I decided to attend AA meetings, believing I could gain insight that would allow me to control my drinking. On discharge, I began what I look back on as an "orientation period."

The first lesson of my orientation began in the hospital. In the newspaper I had brought with me was an advertisement for a concert featuring my favorite drummer, taking place in about three weeks. I got on the unit's payphone and asked Patricia to get us some tickets, which she did. On leaving the hospital, I attended some meetings and stayed sober (though I did drink nonalcoholic beer). On the night of the general admission concert, I was still alcohol free for more than two weeks. We got a table, and I went to the bar to get us some drinks. I ordered my girl her favorite Scotch and water, and, as if somebody else's voice spoke the words, I heard myself saying, "and a Beck's, please."

I returned to the table. She said, "Thought you weren't drinking."

"I'm just having one," I said. And I just had that one, telling myself it was fine. I pushed the fact that I wanted 12 more from my mind, and told myself it was fine. Two days later I told myself again that it was fine, and that I had handled that beer well. So well had I handled that beer, that I decided to handle some more.

So started my personal experiment with controlled drinking. The concert, with its one well-controlled beer, was on a Wednesday. Friday was the end of the week, after all. Having controlled one beer on Wednesday, the next obvious step was to control a six-pack. Naturally, they should be my usual Bud talls (16 ounces or 1/3 more beer). The rationalizing that this was okay might have been based on the superficial lack of consequences. Nothing bad happened. There were no car accidents or tickets or police at the house. My best thinking allowed me to believe I had controlled that six-pack. The next step in the experiment was obvious. Sometime over the following weekend, I decided to regain control of that bottle of vodka... under the seat of the car.

At some level, I knew I was in trouble and at risk for getting back to the ugly place that had put me in the hospital for a week. I desperately wanted to drink normally, but once I started drinking, I couldn't seem to stop. The idea of that perfect buzz from my boyhood was barely a memory anymore.

In hopes of controlling my drinking and keeping my life from going off kilter again, I started going to AA meetings. There must be some wisdom, some secret knowledge about alcohol that I could analyze and abstract for my own purposes. In Alcoholics Anonymous, I hoped to find the secret to dialing back my drinking to manageable levels. Uncomfortable with going to meetings in my hometown, I began sporadic attendance in nearby communities. One day I might go to a meeting, the next I might drink. Some days I drank *and* went to meetings. On weekends, I tended to drink. Over time, the drinking became heavier. I was not finding any secret or trick to catching that so-called perfect buzz without overdoing the drinking.

The most powerful thing driving me was my fear. The foundation of my existence was cemented with alcohol. It had first weakened and was now starting to crumble. I so desperately wanted to preserve my drinking way of life. Going to the AA meetings was a double-edged sword. Instead of the golden ticket to a happy, productive way of life that included alcohol, the information I was getting continued to dissolve that cement on which my way of life was built. Fear motivated me to keep looking, but that fear only mounted as I kept getting the wrong answers.

I kept my attendance at AA meetings to other towns. I was afraid of something vague, and I believe it had to do with my insincere motivation for going to meetings. Not yet committed to actual sobriety and still guarding and defensive of my drinking, I didn't want anyone to know.

One evening, as I went up to get coffee before the meeting, the guy in front of me in line turned around and said hello. This was one of those classic awkward moments; he looked familiar, and I felt panic as I struggled to place him. He was someone from another compartment of my life, and his presence in my secret AA thing sent a wave of horrible anxiety through me. Then I figured it out. He was the hospital's director of human resources. This was tremendously unsettling, as it was exactly why I didn't go to meetings in my hometown. Worsening matters, this was one of those meetings where I had drunk before going. The whole thing was starting to feel like the sham it really was.

As 1990 moved into its final months, with the distractions of the holidays, I was lost. Drinking no longer felt right, but the idea of being sober was still completely foreign. I couldn't drink, and I couldn't not drink. I struggled with drinking and life in general. The problem was that I saw something in the Alcoholics Anonymous meetings. In the words and ideas of the people I encountered there, there seemed to be something that I couldn't quite understand. It was as if they had some insight into something, some aspect of life about which I was clueless. Witnessing people with some kind of wholeness that was decidedly lacking in my life made me feel as though I hadn't been there the day they handed out the owner's manuals for human beings. I'd always felt that way, it was just more obvious now. Here were people who talked about getting along with one another, handling life's problems, and just being happy in general. I wanted this "something" that I saw, but could not yet grasp that if I wanted what they had, I needed to do what they did.

In search of a softer, easier path, I spent a good three months on a harder, more difficult road.

The end was close, but still around the corner out of sight. On a Saturday afternoon between Christmas and New Year's, I decided to build a snowman. Sculpting out the snowman's features, I jammed the long finger of my right hand, snapping off the tendon on the back of the finger that enables it to straighten. While not even painful, this seemingly minor injury had consequences that were potentially significant. To someone who values drumming above all else, hand function and dexterity are extremely important. Not to mention my day job...

Operating room work had certain perks. I was able to have my finger seen by a hand surgeon the following Monday at work. He needed no X-rays to know what was wrong and explained that the finger needed to remain straight for weeks. The best way of ensuring success was by inserting a pin through the bones to prevent bending. He offered to do it that afternoon after work. I agreed, reluctantly. It was December 31, 1990.

In the way that we are reluctant to believe that our lives are changing before we see it happening, the realization that I would be out of work for 10 days began to slowly settle in. Most of those 10 days were spent in a drunken stupor. In the face of even this minor adversity, I had no resources, no capacity for resisting the urge to drink to oblivion. All bets were off. I would drink the way I really wanted to, while injured and out of work, and sort things out later.

Two trips to the doctor's office were necessary. The first was to check the pin at the first available opportunity after the holiday. The second was to clear me to return to work the following week. I scheduled and made both trips early in the day. That way I could be reasonably sober, but not have the visits interfere with the day's drinking. The days were a blur, one fading into the next. Aside from an early trip out to get vodka and perhaps a rental movie, I sat around and wasted away the hours. I had worrisome thoughts about the effects of my finger's injury on drumming and, looming larger, the issue of my drinking. I knew that this binge was merely postponing the inevitable. This alcoholic monster I'd been wrestling with for three months was only asleep. It hadn't gone away.

As the day of my return to work approached, my anxiety mounted. On the day before my scheduled return, I decided to go to an AA meeting. Barely able to drive, I went to the Tuesday night group I'd been going to a couple towns away. I remember finding no solace there, no relief from the gnawing feeling that my life was really screwed up. Later when I got home, I drank again—vodka in the basement. My last drink was around 11:30 that night. I passed out, more than fell asleep.

I overslept the next morning. Reporting to work after a ten-day absence, I was in no fit state. Much worse than merely being hung over, I was still intoxicated.

While the plan had been for me to work in a restricted capacity due to my injury, my manager had a new plan for me. Horrified after seeing my compromised condition, she had some strong words. In the midst of her usual morning managerial chaos, she now had to cope with an impaired worker in her operating room. This pimple on the chest of the surgical department would have to wait until she solved real problems, but deal with it she would. She told me to stay out of the way, and we would be talking. This was real trouble.

I panicked. I went to the relative refuge of the changing room and thought about my options. My mind quickly raced from immediate concerns through short-term consequences to the bigger picture. I wouldn't be working that day, possibly not ever again on that job, and I was a pitiful, helpless alcoholic. I was powerless over alcohol. I had no control over my drinking and had let my work and myself down. The last 10 days were proof that my life was unmanageable. I changed into my street clothes and snuck out the back door.

I was despondent and overwhelmed. I drove home and had what I can only describe as an anxiety attack. I paced the floor. I felt as if my life was over.

The weight of the consequences of my choices and actions crashed down on me. I could not go on as I had been. My whole way of life no longer worked; it hadn't in a long time, in fact. I couldn't continue living as I had been living, and as I paced the floor, I thought about ending my life. This scared me so much that I called Samaritans and spoke with someone for a long time. I did not want to live as I had been, but I did not want to die either. What were my other options, and was there someone else I could turn to? As I now sat, a realization came to me. I had overwhelming problems. I had desperately clung to the idea that I drank as a result of these troubles. The truth was not that I drank over my problems; I had problems *because* I drank. This realization, so simple yet so profound, represented the figurative moving of a mountain in terms of my way of looking at my life.

In my months of attending AA meetings, the only phone number I had taken belonged to a woman, and it wasn't for the purpose of staying sober. There had been numerous suggestions that I had disregarded; getting the phone numbers of guys I could call for help was but one. The easiest thing in the moment would have been to drink. The hardest thing to do was reach out and ask for help. I called the hospital and asked for the human resources department. Holding the 800-pound receiver, I waited for the man from the meeting coffee line to pick up the call.

I should not have been surprised, but he was well aware of my brief appearance at work earlier that morning. My manager had no doubt notified him of the situation when she realized I was gone. Michael's routine duties as human resources director were to be aware of the "unroutine," and I had not merely broken, but fully trampled the hospital code of conduct.

My call to a fellow AA, who also happened to be a human resources director, simultaneously solved and created problems. Obviously, there had been concern about me, in addition to concern for me. That I was safely home settled the latter, and by being in contact with me, Michael was addressing the hospital's problem. That I'd had a personal crisis and reached the point of surrender to my alcoholism presented a complicated dilemma. Ethically, he was pulled in two directions. He was duty-bound to serve the interests of the hospital on one hand. He wanted the other hand to be the figurative hand of AA, extended to a suffering alcoholic who wanted and needed help. Whether he could do both was clearly up to me and whether I was sincere.

Sincere I was. I had come to a powerful realization about my drinking and my life. All the bits and pieces of information I'd heard at meetings had filtered into my awareness, as if by osmosis. In my most desperate moment, my absolute bottom, they had crystallized into a clarity of vivid understanding. *I am an alcoholic.* In that moment, I had taken the first step. *I am powerless over alcohol.* I made a decision with an intensity and level of energy and conviction that was as powerful as any thought I've ever had. For the first time, I truly decided to stop drinking.

Michael agreed to be my "temporary" sponsor. He made abundantly clear that he would not compromise his principles or his job; my fate was absolutely in my hands. He told me to not drink and go to a meeting that night. I didn't drink and I went to two meetings.

Part II

A New Way of Being

"The cave you fear holds the treasure that you seek."

~Joseph Campbell

CHAPTER 7

The Nurse's Opinion

I was scared. I felt like I was caught between two worlds. My old world, falling apart at the seams, was clearly no longer working. The new world was completely unknown, and frankly, I couldn't quite believe it was real. And I didn't believe I could go a day without drinking.

Ah, if I knew then what I know now...

If I had known then that I could understand and know all the mysterious and elusive, yet simple aspects about life that I never grasped... If I had known then that I could be happy of myself for merely getting along with others, handling life on life's terms, and simply doing what everybody else does... And if I had known then that I could truly have a way of being in which I would not willfully alter my consciousness in any way... I would have had tremendous difficulty believing it. Why? Because that way of being was so incredibly foreign to me at that time, that I had no real basis for even knowing that such feelings were possible. Sometimes it's just impossible to see things that aren't a part of your reality.

There was something about being human that I hadn't quite grasped. It was as if I didn't get my copy of the owner's manual or something. Even though humanity comes without instructions, I felt as if there was just some major aspect of belonging to the human race about which I was especially clueless. It was as though I was absent the day the most important information was given out. Or more likely, I was off somewhere drinking when the explanation was offered.

Life was such a struggle. Maintaining (the illusion of) control of my world was exhausting. I did not play well with others; alcoholic egocentricity prevented me from seeing a bigger picture. I had little comprehension of the reality that the world was full of people who bobbed and weaved and went about their business. Empathy and the ability to walk in another person's shoes were not part of my repertoire. I staggered through my existence straining my brain just to exist. Willing the street lights to turn green as I approached took monumental effort. Interestingly, on the rare occasions when the light would turn green as I approached, I gave myself credit for it in some twisted way.

On the more frequent occasions when life's little red lights forced me to stop, coping was a challenge at best. Circumstances beyond my control felt stressful. The simplest things could make me anxious. As for life's more significant lumps and bumps, the ability to deal was a foreign concept. The word "no" was unacceptable. I had an elaborate theory and mindset about how I could not take no for an answer. In my mind, no conversation was over and no situation resolved, merely because I had been told "no."

As for living within the framework of the normal responsible adult existence, it was within the realm of possibility, but felt like a Herculean effort. Meeting basic obligations, such as paying bills and taxes or the renewal of licenses, and obeying basic conventions and civil laws deserved some kind of reward or recognition. I felt like I should get a medal and a parade for doing what everybody else just did.

Reality felt so harsh and was only to be endured, at most, for short stretches. If I'd had my choice, I would have been drunk or high or both around the clock.

Today, I wouldn't willingly alter my senses in any way. Good or bad, pleasant or unpleasant, I want to experience every moment of my life to the fullest. I live my life intuitively. I get a sense about people and situations, and trust my gut about what I should do in most instances. I trust that I will handle situations that arise; if something is beyond me, I trust that I will figure out how to find the resources I need to solve problems. The everyday anxiety that arises as part of life is not only tolerable, but a pleasant reminder that I'm okay today.

Taking responsibility for the consequences of my actions, functioning as a responsible adult, and meeting the basic expectations for a member of society are no longer things to be detested. Like anyone else, I do what I'm "supposed" to do. I seldom procrastinate. I'm certainly not perfect. Making mistakes is just another opportunity to take responsibility, learn a lesson, gain a new insight, and build some character.

The unknown world that I now inhabit, my new way of being, would have met with mixed feelings from the man who inhabited the old world. The sobriety and responsibility aspects would not have seemed attractive. The parts about feeling confident and comfortable in my own skin along with a sense of belonging would have sounded wonderful, but also like a dream. The life I have today would have sounded too good to be true, and impossible to attain.

Alcoholics Anonymous gave me all that... Which begs the question, why are we here? If Alcoholics Anonymous can do it all, why even have a discussion?

Much of what I've described is actually promised by Alcoholics Anonymous. A happy, peaceful way of living with a sense of comfort and ease, both in life and in one's own skin, is specified in Chapter 6 of the "Big Book" of Alcoholics Anonymous. The passage at the bottom of page 83 says that we will reconcile with the past and be free of negative emotions including fear and selfishness. We are told these promises will "always materialize" as long as we work for them. Great, my work here is done. Go read the Big Book. Oh, wait...

Unfortunately, those promises have a capricious nature. They are subject to change. Maybe the ideas of fast versus slow, or the concept of work is misunderstood. Whatever the case might be, if the promises were really promises, why would anyone relapse? Why would people struggle with the obsession to drink, cravings, and fear of alcohol in situations? The question then becomes threefold. How does one realize those promises? How does one attain a way of being in which the promises have permanence? And finally, how does one, without presumption or unrealistic projection of the future, attain a way of being in which relapse to drinking or drugging doesn't happen?

The benefits of working the Alcoholics Anonymous program of recovery are beyond question. They have saved my life. I had a genuine desire to stay sober, and accepted that I had to make changes in my life to accomplish that. I was willing to expend effort toward building what is referred to as a foundation in recovery. That foundation consists of knowledge combined with experience. My knowledge of AA's principles, beliefs, and steps combined with the experience of lessons learned, sometimes the hard way, gave me a solid grasp on a new way of life.

A new way of life, however, does not make a new person, but it is a necessary start! AA gave me that start, and I remain in awe of the miracle that is the fellowship of Alcoholics Anonymous. The areas of concern that I outlined above are only an honest assessment of potential obstacles and their ramifications. That's the bad news.

The good news is that the fellowship, principles, and structure of AA are the best solution for the most alcoholics. Furthermore, Alcoholics Anonymous' basic self-help formula, which is freely offered for adaptation to issues besides alcohol, has rippled outward exponentially in response to addictions and issues of all description. Recognized among the most significant cultural phenomena of the 20th century, the fellowship of AA stands strong and moving forward in the 2000s.

Alcoholics Anonymous' concept for recovery is based on the Twelve Steps and Twelve Traditions, both a philosophy and a belief system. Individually, these are inspired. The collective result is a rational and cohesive formula that emphasizes a pragmatic day-to-day approach (one day at a time) combined with a spiritual perspective. Rooted in the notion that there are no atheists in foxholes, the spiritual component is the jewel in the AA crown. By feeding people's minds, they experience change; by feeding their spirits, they are transformed. Spiritual change and growth are the hub of recovery.

AA works. It worked and continues to work for me. After what I have come to regard as an orientation period of some months, I have stayed continuously sober. I adhered closely to basic suggestions. I availed myself of a sponsor, allied myself with certain groups while attending meetings almost daily, became involved and worked at the twelve suggested steps of recovery. Aside from the obvious—being continuously sober—other external and visible changes happened within a matter of months to a few years. I successfully returned to music, setting my sights on and landing a position with a serious original rock band. I quit smoking cigarettes. I began running, cycling, and working out. I returned to school, at first working toward a nursing degree before matriculating into a challenging formal nursing program. In the middle of that, I bought a house. I withstood upheaval in my employment situation to work fulltime while eventually earning my degree.

Net result: at the end of my first five years in recovery, I was alcohol, drug, and nicotine free with a healthy, toned, and muscular body, living in my own house with a newly earned nursing degree, about to begin a new career. It sounds so amazing; I have trouble believing that, as I read it back. So again, why am I not saying "thank you Alcoholics Anonymous," and writing "The End"? It's not as simple as that. Not remotely.

I stopped thinking about drinking as early as the first year. I didn't ponder this much until later, but I really stopped thinking like an alcoholic. At the meetings, the topic often comes up that we alcoholics have a certain way of thinking about alcohol. Alcohol is just part of contemporary life; depicted on television, in the movies, and aggressively advertised in much of the media; we see it all the time. This everyday observation of alcohol registers differently with the alcoholic than the nondrinker. Examples: Mmmm, doesn't that look good? I'll bet that tastes... boy, wouldn't I like about 20 of those? At some point early on, not only did I stop identifying with that kind of thinking, I simply ceased thinking that way.

Not only did I stop thinking about drinking, but I soon no longer experienced cravings, or even the desire, to drink. Again, I wouldn't have thought anything of this, except that I heard others sharing about their struggles on almost a daily basis. I was constantly being reminded that the plight of the vast majority of recovering alcoholics is to continue to experience the desire to drink. The battle rages on for most, even years into recovery, whether frequently or infrequently.

Why not me? The preceding section documents the fact that I was an alcoholic, well on my way down the road of hopelessness. Impaired in every way, I simply could not go a day without a drink. Physically, mentally, emotionally, and even psychically, I was addicted to alcohol. The following anecdote is a fast-forward one year to the day from where I left off in the previous chapter:

On my first-year anniversary, 365 days sober, I found myself in an odd circumstance. It was January, 1992. Music having been a significant part of my life, I had returned to playing the drums a few months prior. After getting my "chops" up (musician jargon meaning to sharpen one's skills), I answered an advertisement seeking a drummer for an original rock band. To that point in my life, I had dreamt of achieving success and making music my livelihood. This was just such an opportunity.

This advertisement was really serious. It sent a clear message: don't respond unless you're a rock n' roll *god in waiting*! More than 100 responses were received. There were 40-plus interviews conducted, and 17 were auditions held. I got the gig. Quite the rigorous process, but I had the talent, experience, and motivation. We went into rehearsal mode, and then began playing publicly in area and regional clubs.

So, on the occasion of my first anniversary in recovery, we were performing at one such regional club. It was about 50 miles from home, and located on the other side of Boston. Boston traffic being unpredictable, particularly around commuter hours, I left a comfortable margin of travel time.

I traveled alone, and arrived comfortably early... So early, in fact, that the club was locked up tight. After several minutes of pounding on various doors, my persistence was finally rewarded. The fellow who eventually unlocked a backstage door was apparently the bookkeeper, working upstairs in some office. He was good enough to grant me access so I could begin hauling my gear in, then disappeared back to work, leaving me alone. I surveyed the scene, which consisted of the club itself with tables and dance floor, the stage, and... the bar. The bar caught my attention. It would've caught anyone's attention, as it was rather impressive. Centrally located, it was probably 25 or 30 feet long, but the thing that really stole the show was the 20-foot long fish tank elevated behind it. It must've held thousands of gallons of water. Rows and rows of bottles were organized at the base of this truly impressive aquarium.

Then I was struck by the thought that there was a certain irony at work here as I began carrying my drums into the building. In drunken musical days gone by, there would have been something coming back out to my car with each successive trip. It would have been drums go in, bottles go out. Not to mention the fact that I would have quite likely helped myself to too many cocktails before anyone else even arrived. In the old days, this would have been a recipe for a drunken disaster. One year sober, this was not the case. I had not only attained a neutral attitude toward alcohol, but I had no inclination or desire to do what would have come naturally—to drink any available alcohol. On further reflection, I was not being the person who instinctively behaved that way. I was in the process of becoming someone else. In fact, I was already being someone else.

My experience in the fish-tank bar on my one-year anniversary was the tip of the iceberg. Effortlessly, I could be around alcohol. This seemed to be another huge hurdle for many alcoholics, and the vast majority of my fellows spoke about avoiding situations with alcohol. I would attend work and social parties, weddings, events, and all manner of social functions where alcohol is normally an integral part of the festivities.

"How can you do this?" a high school classmate, who had known me to be quite wild in the day, asked. It was about 2 AM at a party following our 25th high school reunion. I didn't have a ready answer, because I just didn't think about how or why I could feel right at home while everyone else was well lit with beer in hand.

I didn't know exactly how I did it, but I was becoming more curious almost by the day. I began to think about my experiences in AA and outside. I have taken the Twelve Steps, embraced them to the best of my ability. I built what is referred to as a foundation, but most everyone does that. Beyond that, I have embraced certain ideas. I have opened my mind to these ideas, because they seem to be intuitive, scientifically valid, or both, and just plain self-evident. There was no great effort on my part, just a deliberate open-mindedness. This information simply came to me in my everyday travels, one piece leading to the next. Other than a desire to be more peaceful and enlightened, I undertook nothing overtly intentional. All I did was want the best recovery possible.

How then did I realize the promises in my life? Answer: I worked the recovery program of AA and an additional layer of effort after the fact and on top of the Twelve Steps.

How is my new way of being permanent? Answer: my daily recovery has taken on a certain quality. It is SUSTAINABLE.

And last, how will I avoid relapsing? Answer: I became a person who will not drink again. In other words, my new way of being was such a profound change at such a depth that I am no longer the man who could not go a day without a drink. If I continue to do what I'm doing, it's reasonable that I will not drink again. Why would I?

I'm not making any promises. I can only share what's worked for me, in the hopes it will work for others. This is a leap of faith for me as much as someone reading these words. For myself, I'm still a work in progress, but I know something extraordinary has happened to me. As someone who has received this profound gift, I am merely compelled to share it.

I absolutely advocate to anyone with a desire to stop being alcoholic or addicted that they build a strong foundation in Twelve-Step recovery. Despite minor shortcomings, I highly recommend AA. This was the basis for my recovery, and so a huge part of what has worked for me. In the coming chapters in this section, I will discuss how I have approached that and offer as much insight as I can, at this point in my personal journey. That means it is my opinion. Beyond that, I will share as much as I can possibly explain about my added layer, which I believe is the catalyst for the change that has made me a different man.

I call what I have today a sustainable recovery. It is like a machine that drives itself, a layer above, beyond, and in addition to conventional recovery. It does not rely too heavily on any one aspect. Meetings, fellowship, books, mentoring, prayer, and meditation... they are all part of my recovery, yet no one aspect is relied on more than any other. However, if I had to choose one aspect of this sustainable recovery that sustains it more than the others, I would have to say that it lies in the nature of my relationship with a power greater than me. To truly recover, I had to come to terms with spirituality. So at this point, I will resume my narrative the day after my attempts to return to work, the second day of my recovery.

CHAPTER 8

Withdrawal

The next day, I did not exactly wake up with a new lease on life. I had that ugly, anxious feeling of unresolved problems. I was in trouble. I'd been out of work with a legitimate injury before, but now I was in some vague unexcused-absence situation, with drunkenness on the job involved. My job was in jeopardy, and I had that nagging uneasiness about the situation.

The other reason I didn't wake up to greet a new day full of promise was because I was detoxing. Thursday morning, January 10, I was about 36 hours away from my last drink of vodka. My body was panicking.

My system had grown accustomed to a significant quantity of hard liquor on a daily basis. How I managed to function in that state is somewhat beyond me today, but people do it. Never indefinitely, but people do it for a while. The human body is amazingly adaptable, and does its best to maintain a balance of all its systems at all times. As soon as something goes off kilter in any one area—circulation, breathing, digestion, as examples—the body goes to work trying to restore order to the system.

By putting alcohol into my system on a daily basis, I forced my body to adapt. My liver got better at breaking down the toxic alcohol, or detoxifying my body. My metabolism got better at using the available nutrients, minerals, and vitamins to repair cells damaged by the toxins. My circulatory system got better at carrying the broken-down poisons to the kidneys, which got better at flushing them out of my system, etc. And my poor central nervous system struggled to counter the sedative effects on my level of consciousness, or alertness, and also maintain my other bodily functions, such as heartbeat, blood pressure, breathing, etc.

The abrupt elimination of alcohol after the body has worked so hard to adapt to its effects does not immediately restore order to the system. Far from it. It's like driving down a steep and winding mountain road. The car (the body) wants to accelerate (respond to its environment), but the brakes (alcohol) are applied and the car is put in a lower gear. A comfortable speed is maintained (adaptation). Withdrawing alcohol abruptly is like an instantaneous failure of the braking system. Not only is the car starting to roll faster downhill, but now imagine that the car responds by popping itself into high gear (the body is used to compensating). As that car is now at risk for crashing, so is the body when alcohol is suddenly taken away. Alcohol withdrawal is potentially lethal.

The situation depends on the individual. How much he drank, for how long, the long-term damage done to the body, and a person's underlying general physical condition are the factors involved with a detox. Physically, most people experience elevated pulse, blood pressure, sweats, headache, stomach cramps, diarrhea, nausea, and marked tremors, or "the shakes," among others. Difficult sleep and general restlessness and anxiety are common secondary symptoms. In more severe cases, the above are more intense, and the blood pressure might become dangerously elevated. The anxiety might range up to feelings of panic. There might be odd, disturbing sensations in the skin, described by many as "skin crawling." The above would describe a mild to moderate detox with basic withdrawal symptoms.

In worse situations, all of the above symptoms might be present along with agitation, bad tremors, and changes in consciousness. At first confusion might give way to disorientation; someone will not know who or where they are, or even what day it is. The confusion might manifest as outright hallucinations, both visual and audio. Remember the old stereotypical pink elephants? While I've never seen anyone describe these, I have observed people claim that all manner of nonexistent people are present and speaking to them, that they are in locations other than where they are, and involved in nonexistent activities. I once observed a man who thought he was making an elaborate meal in a nonexistent kitchen. As this progresses, it is referred to as delirium tremens, or DTs.

The part of the central nervous system that functions automatically to control breathing, heartbeat, and other essential bodily functions—driving the car, as it were—goes out of control. Basically, this is because the body's response to alcohol was to stop producing certain chemicals, called neurotransmitters, which served the function of controlling the figurative car. When alcohol is taken out of the equation, those neurotransmitters are still missing. The resulting imbalances are responsible for all the various symptoms.

Of particular concern is the high blood pressure and the risk of stroke that goes with it. Seizures might occur in people with no history of any type of seizure disorder. People with seizure disorder are at much greater risk during this time. A seizure could be characterized as a temporary electrical storm of the nervous system, resulting in loss of control of muscles, coordination, and bodily functions. The only good part is that there is seldom any memory of the event.

Net result: it felt like my body was freaking out. At the time, I did not know all the information I just listed. While not anticipating a pleasant experience by any stretch, I didn't take into account that my previous detox had been significantly assisted by close supervision and medication as was indicated. The nurse gave me some pills, which didn't seem to do anything, or so I thought at the time. I realize now that they had done a lot for me during that previous detox. I had minimized the benefit of hospitalization, and though I did not know it at the time, detoxing myself at home was dangerous.

As I had entered this whole proposition with a clear decision to stop drinking, my mind was made up. However, over the hours and days to follow, it was as if my body started to develop a mind of its own—in other words, it wanted to be the mind. The rational thinking part of my brain had weighed the situation and knew what needed to be done. I needed to stop drinking. The problem was that the brain was writing a check for the rest of my body to cash... It was as if my body decided to start a conversation with my brain. It went something like "Hey, moron, what were you thinking? Stop drinking? Are you insane? How can you do this to me? I gave up producing neurotransmitters for you! Now we got a situation down here, send down six ounces of vodka, stat!"

I spent the next two or three days and nights on the couch. The best I could do was to sleep for 10 or 15 minutes at a time, and I would repeatedly jolt awake, feeling like I was bouncing five inches in the air out of the middle of the fitful sleep. I ate next to nothing, was hot one minute, cold the next, but sweating regardless. It was really brutal.

My girlfriend did not know what to make of this. I honestly don't know what she thought, though I gather she just assumed I was sick with the flu or something. When she finally asked, I told her I was quitting drinking (again). She asked "what's up with that?" or some such.

"It's just time," I responded.

I scraped myself off the couch and went to a meeting that morning.

Friday was the same. The couch. Feeling like crap. Two meetings. Fitful sleep.

Saturday, I felt better. I had turned a corner, but did not feel normal by any means. I had worked my way up to merely feeling lousy. My body was finally starting to settle down.

The urge to drink never left for a minute. Even after passing beyond the point of physical discomfort where I thought a drink would no longer help, I still wanted to put alcohol into my body. Part of that was force of habit; the rest was the addiction, pure and simple. This was white-knuckle sobriety in its truest sense. I had no coping skills and no real power over drinking. The rational part of my brain was just holding on out of stubbornness, and only in response to fear of consequences. My body was traitorous, and even the lower, more instinctive part of my brain was not to be trusted.

There was a good snowfall overnight Friday. I had decided on a Saturday morning meeting in the next town, and had to do some digging out. The blizzard having not quite wound down, it was a bit of an adventure to go somewhere. People hadn't really dug out and resumed normal activity as yet. I made it to the meeting, along with six or seven other brave souls, many of whom were to become dear friends. It was a nice meeting, more so because I felt so welcomed. I even won the raffle! Within about three months, I would be the secretary of that group. That meeting would become what I considered my "home group" for better than 10 years. In time, I came to think of myself as Mr. Saturday Morning. I have no particular recollection, but I assume I also went to another meeting that evening.

The next morning, Sunday, I had selected another meeting that I would attend for the first time. It was located in my home town and was listed as an open meeting. As I was getting ready to go, I was also thinking about something that had been on my mind for a while. It had come up during the meetings of my orientation period, and it seemed to come up at every meeting since I had actually stopped drinking.

~~~~~~~~~~~~~~~~~~~~~~~~~~~~~

One of the most unnatural things in the world is for an alcoholic to stop drinking, or for any addict to stop using. I talked about some of the bodily conditions in play with alcoholic drinking. In addition to conditions, there has been lots of conditioning. After years of drinking or using, addictive behaviors acquired over time have become a part of the person. After they are established, it is extraordinarily difficult to go against them.

In my case, drinking and all the associated behaviors that went with it became as deep within me as any other instinct. It could be said that I had an alcoholic way of being.

What does that mean? I have basic instincts. I have the instincts for survival—to procreate and defend myself and those I care about—and I had the instinct to drink and defend my drinking.

How did this come about? It started out as an acquired skill. It took a lot of practice. At first I thought about drinking and acted on those thoughts of drinking. I had to give it thought; it didn't come to me naturally. Next, it became a habit, something I did more naturally. Then it became part of me—I became a drinker. Thinking about drinking, to drinking habit, to being a drinker. Drinking became my way of being.

I liken it to learning to drive a car. I first get behind the wheel, and everything is foreign. The steering wheel, the pedals, the controls... I have to think about every step from putting the key in the ignition to the actual mechanics of driving. The steering, the foot on the accelerator or brake, and the traffic! When I started driving, I had to concentrate on every step, every aspect. After a while, it became less foreign and more natural. I could get in the car and go somewhere, and while still thinking about the process, I was driving. Now, years later, I climb in the car and the next thing I know, I'm arriving somewhere. It was so automatic, I didn't really think about the driving unless something unusual happened. At that point, I AM a driver.

Over time, I became a drinker. I unknowingly learned behaviors that went with the territory. Without consciously thinking about it, anything that threatened my drinking was dealt with appropriately. No matter what else was going on, there would be adequate opportunity, time, and supply. These things were a given, and automatically became part of any situation or circumstance and the choices around them. I developed an instinct for my drinking's survival.

Furthermore, as with driving automatically, all this instinctive drinking is being done with a different part of my brain than the part that makes conscious decisions. These unconscious instinctive drinking behaviors live in the same part of my brain (the back and bottom) that runs all those automatic bodily functions. Those are the same bodily functions that get all screwed up when the alcohol is taken away. Therefore, the conscious decision to stop drinking meets the violent opposition of what has long since become the alcoholic's natural way of being, or instinct.

The battle is on. The problem is that time is on the subconscious and body's side. While I was kind of poking fun with my example of what the body would say to the brain in the throes of withdrawal, it's really not far off the mark. How many conscious thoughts do we have in one minute? A lot. Typically, stopping drinking would seem like a great idea at six in the morning. Hung over and dragging myself out of bed, head pounding and worse, I would consciously analyze the situation and think, "I need to stop." A scant few hours later, my body has taken control of the situation, commanding the arms to turn the steering wheel as the car pulls into the liquor store parking lot. The brain acquiesces, "What was I thinking this morning?"

"Stupid brain!" says the body.

~~~~~~~~~~~~~~~~~~~~~~~~~~~~

Now, back to Sunday morning…

CHAPTER 9

A Personal Miracle

Something had been weighing on me for several days. I'd given the matter thought in the preceding weeks and months, but now it was more important. It was life-and-death, actually. I sensed that the stakes were high. I needed to come to terms with the idea of a higher power.

Because I was thinking in real terms of getting sober, I was thinking in real terms of what I needed to be doing. I just didn't know how to stay sober. My fevered brain never stopped analyzing, and it became increasingly obvious that there would have to be some reckoning with "this God thing."

For one thing, God or a higher power was a real mainstay in the AA literature. The concept was woven all through the steps, and in the first section of the Big Book. If the steps and Big Book were the directions, the directions definitely involved God.

The other piece that I really noticed was that people at meetings often spoke about God. Praying to God, seeking guidance from God, surrendering their will to God (using the expression "turning over"), etc., were recurring themes that people mentioned frequently. Better still, these references to God always seemed connected to something favorable. Things such as handling life on life's terms, getting along with others, and just being happy were constantly being connected to people's experience with this higher-power concept. It sounded as if the people who were succeeding at staying sober, and life for that matter, had worked out this higher-power thing. I kept hearing people say that they got on their knees and prayed to God. They asked for help to not drink on that given day. I also heard people say it worked.

Here was a huge stumbling block. Growing up, there had been no religion, no spirituality, no God. As a little boy one Sunday morning, I had asked my parents if I could play with a neighborhood friend. "No," I was told, "his family's at church." I asked why we didn't go to church.

"That's something you'll make your own mind up about someday," they said. The matter was put to rest for a long time. Later in life, I dabbled in a Christian youth group, getting born-again, and some reading of the book of Revelation in the Bible. The youth group and the notion of accepting Jesus both came as a result of association with women who were involved with those things. The attempt at Bible reading was out of curiosity. In any event, nothing really took. My experience with religion was fairly limited, and, more significantly, I had no real ideas about spirituality.

God was a word. It conjured the image of a wise, but powerful-looking old man with long white hair and beard... like Charlton Heston playing Moses in *The Ten Commandments*. Sitting on a throne in some cloudy domain, he oversaw the day-to-day operations of the universe. That was the image, but it didn't attend any solid or valid belief in my mind. There was no association. Though open to possibility, I didn't know what God was, and doubted if anyone really did.

Yet here were these AAs sounding so convincing and painting an attractive picture. I wanted that whole "handling life on life's terms, getting along with others, and just being happy" thing. But more important, I wanted to be sober. I had been bludgeoned by alcohol into a state of reasonableness, and my mind was now wide open. Relationship with a higher power seemed paramount. I needed to make some kind of beginning, some movement in that direction.

So it was Sunday morning, and I planned to attend a local open-speaker meeting for the first time. I had been thinking hard about the spirituality question and resolved that I would try something new and different. After getting dressed, I went in the bathroom and closed the door.

I got on my knees. Out loud, I said something close to the following: "I don't know if there is anything or anyone there, but if there is, could you please give me some kind of sign so I know you are there?" I said this solemnly, but not too loudly. My girlfriend was around...

Lightning didn't strike. The world continued to turn. The sun was still somewhere in the sky. I got up and left the bathroom. My girlfriend did give me a look. I went to the meeting as planned. The meeting was held in the cafeteria of a local Catholic school. This was the largest meeting I had attended up to that time; there were more than 200 people in that cafeteria. I found a seat, and the meeting got underway. The format is known as open speaker. This is where a series of 10- to 20-minute talks are given by members of a visiting group. Sometime during the previous or following week, the members of the local group would reciprocate by visiting today's incoming group. This is known as a commitment exchange. The meeting was an hour and a half, and there was a short break in the middle.

The third person who spoke looked familiar. She was a youngish, nondescript woman. As she introduced herself and began speaking, I distinctly remembered having heard her tell the same story on a previous occasion. In fact, I was so sure of recently hearing her speak that I thought about stepping out for a cigarette, but decided not to as I was trying to be dedicated. I would sit and listen to this "rerun." I even remembered details of her story: that she was painfully shy until she drank, then became the life of the party; teaching ballet to the football team; having her friend ring a neighbor's doorbell as a decoy, while she snuck in his back door and stole his booze when he answered the front door; horror stories of fights with her mother; drinking at the Laundromat; her general self-loathing; her alcoholic bottom; and the gift of her finding recovery. I remembered these significant and specific details from the previous occasion as she told them *again* that morning. Then the meeting adjourned to the break.

I was glad I had stayed and listened. On my way outside, I crossed paths with the woman who had just spoken. She was with another young woman. I said hello and thanked her for speaking. I mentioned that I had recently heard her speak elsewhere, but liked it even more this morning, or something like that. She looked at her friend, and then looked at me strangely. She asked when I had heard her speak. This was a little fuzzy to me; I could not pinpoint exactly where and when this had been. I told her where/when I thought it might have been, obviously during the previous few months when I had been going to meetings. She looked at her friend again and at me even more strangely, and said this morning was the first time she had spoken in over six months.

Well, about that time I was wishing I could turn invisible. I felt like something really weird was happening. Awkwardly excusing myself, I continued outside. I pondered what happened for the rest of the meeting, and then for the rest of the day.

My experience of listening to the young woman at the meeting, secure in the knowledge that I had heard her before, only to find out that was not possible was profoundly moving. More, it was earth-shattering. As the significance of my morning began to settle in on me, it was almost like the world slowed, then stopped. All I could think of was that something clearly amazing had taken place. And I could not stop thinking that I had asked for it.

Behind that simple gesture, though actually a huge thing for me, was a genuine desire to be shown something. I had been shown something that was so unexpected, so out of the ordinary, that my ideas about what's real were shaken. Getting on my knees and asking for a sign, while perhaps an everyday occurrence for many, at least in AA, was as incredibly out of the ordinary for me as the results which came.

Growing up, I had always enjoyed science fiction, fantasy, and stories about the supernatural, etc. My disbelief in such things was solid however. As the guy who had figured out the whole Santa Claus thing at such an early age, I was onboard with the conventional, scientific way of understanding the world. If you couldn't see it, hear it, smell it, taste it, or feel it... it just wasn't.

Then I had that experience that was... who knew what? Uncanny? Eerie? Supernatural? Paranormal? The expression déjà vu, meaning already seen, came to mind. The strong sense of having already experienced something was not exceptional. What felt so extraordinary was that detail. I knew this woman's story. I was sitting there thinking, *Okay, now she's going to tell the part about...* The whole event had just been profoundly powerful.

During the rest of the day, I did little but think about the experience of that morning. I tried to go about my business, but could not. It was as though the world had changed. Clearly, I could not continue as I had. I now lived in a reality where an attempt to communicate with the divine had received an answer. The experience defied intellectual reason and was clearly outside reality as I had understood it.

I was going to need a new reality.

One of the things I did that day while trying to wrap my head around that new reality was to attend to another detail that had been weighing on me. Though I had not smoked since the last day of my drinking, I had a decent stash of pot hidden somewhere. Where I think some unconscious reservation about my sober status kept me hanging on to it, I suddenly felt like I had no need of it. In fact, I had a strong desire to rid myself of something that defied my new sobriety. That afternoon, a couple of ounces of marijuana were thrown out with the trash for the next day's pickup. This was a significant shift in my thinking at a fundamental level. This was heartfelt desire and willingness to do the footwork and sacrifice necessary for sobriety.

~~~~~~~~~~~~~~~~~~~~~~~~~~~~~~

A mystical experience can be defined as an experience that is beyond normal consciousness; it encompasses knowledge, insight, or revelation that defies the intellect.

Throughout history, the course of people's lives has been altered by such events. Even the course of history itself has been influenced. Moses, Joan of Arc, Mohammed, and Joseph Smith are examples of people who had life-altering, mystical experiences that in turn influenced events and people.

This experience allowed me to arrive at a new reality. While I am not comparing this experience with the mystical experience that resulted in the founding of the Mormon religion, I cannot minimize its significance for me personally. Mystical experiences are spiritual. While the course of history remains unaltered, the course of my personal history changed that day. I know this was a spiritual experience.

What must be emphasized is that this experience had to happen for me. I needed to have my cage rattled. I can look back and realize that, at five days sober, I was poised at a fork in the road. I was in a critical window where I needed to be nudged in the direction of recovery. My sobriety in those five days prior could only be described as "white-knuckle," an old AA expression meaning hanging on by sheer determination in the face of wanting to drink. Willpower would only take me so far. I knew this at some level, so therefore my desperate willingness to try anything, even prayer.

The results of that prayer resulted in the most amazing and liberating shift.

That my prayer was answered does not mean I am somehow special or exalted. Again, it was what I needed at that moment. The factors—that my intentions were good and honest, my willingness genuine, my motivation true, and that I had made myself ready—all played a part in this minor miracle. What I accomplished, I would compare to successfully tuning in a radio signal on the dial. While the radio signal is always there waiting to be tuned in, I need to have a radio, turn it on, switch it to the proper function (AM, FM, CD, etc.), decide which station to listen to, and then tune in the right frequency... After doing that, I began to understand that the radio signal had been there all along; I knew that there had always been a God or a higher power. I had just never invited it into my life. If my alcoholism was born that day around age 13 when I caught that perfect buzz, it began to die that Sunday morning when I got on my knees.

~~~~~~~~~~~~~~~~~~~~~~~~~~~~~~

That evening, I went to a meeting and told one acquaintance about this experience. He was somewhat incredulous, but not unsympathetic. Based on his reaction, I kept this to myself for years to follow.

What I did continue to do in the moment was to allow this amazing experience to wash over and through me. I gave myself to this. I believed in it wholeheartedly and felt tremendous gratitude. This was real! I now understood, all at once, much of what I had been hearing throughout my *orientation period*. I now had the basis for belief in a power greater than me. The challenge that lay before me was to reach an understanding of how to define that power greater than me.

CHAPTER 10

Deconstruction

The period that followed in the days, weeks, and months after my experience at the Sunday morning meeting was like a dawn after my dark night of the soul. It was the calm after the storm. As the figurative clouds withdrew and my horizon brightened, I jumped into the program of Alcoholics Anonymous with both feet, as they say. But first, there was a little wreckage to clean up...

I had left a bad mess at work. I had presented myself for duty in an unfit state, been called right out on it, and had fled the scene. I had several things going for me at this point. First and foremost, I had done the hardest thing I could do—I sobered up. Not only that, but I had taken serious action toward working on my underlying problem. Surrendering my will by getting on my knees Sunday spoke volumes about my attitude. Though not something that could be appropriately discussed at a disciplinary meeting, Mike E. knew this.

The situation was not black and white. As a human-resources director, Mike had a duty to the hospital. As a member of the AA fellowship, he saw a bigger picture, and I know this posed a dilemma for him. He carefully explained to me that he was bound by his obligation as the administrator who made decisions on such matters, and that things had to be done by the book. That he was privy to the all the details of my situation actually made his job simpler in one way, but he was ethically bound to do things a certain way. That certain way entailed my facing the consequences of my actions. There would be no free pass from a fellow AA member.

A meeting was set up. In attendance were Mike and the operating room manager, the one who had called me out on my drunkenness the previous Wednesday morning. This was eerily reminiscent of the meeting with the principal at the junior high school, following my drunken vomit rampage in eighth grade.

While Mike offered me some reassurance going into this, he made clear that the outcome was entirely up to me and my willingness to take responsibility. Basically, he told me what I needed to do to succeed. This was not a problem. I admitted everything, my drinking problem, my bingeing while being out on injury, and my intoxication on return. I took responsibility and apologized. I meant it. I accepted and signed some sort of written discipline measure, which I'm sure spelled out that I was a cat with no more lives. There would be no other chances, no further tolerance.

The important thing was that the underlying problem, my alcoholism, was out in the light of day. There was no turning back. Nor did I want to now, in view of Sunday's revelations.

I returned to work the next day. It was awkward. The reception was not warm, but not hostile. I don't know what my coworkers had been told, but it was a small department with few secrets. Horrible enough to cause me to contemplate ending my life at the time, the passage of time would eventually make this episode water under the bridge.

I turned my attention not toward the future, but toward each moment as I was in it.

The first hurdle to overcome was a daily routine that had involved drinking after work. Every afternoon, somewhere between the hospital and my home across town, the vodka bottle under the seat of the car would emerge. While the vodka bottle was now gone, its memory remained. Home alone at 3:30 in the afternoon, the evening's AA meeting still hours away, my resolve was tested. This is the sort of situation where human willpower eventually fails.

While challenging, those early days were made so much easier because I had absolute faith in what had happened that Sunday morning. There was something real, some unseen yet undeniable force that I was excited to know about. I had faith that it would reveal its secrets, and that it was worth staying sober for. Those first days were hard, but it wasn't about white knuckles anymore.

I began going to meetings daily, and two on Saturdays and Sundays, morning and evening. As I became regular at meetings night after night, week after week, I noticed something that I had never noticed with my previous sporadic attendance. The same people were there every night. I started getting to know people, and more important, letting them get to know me. I soon developed a kind of weekly schedule of meetings that involved a "healthy" variety of meeting formats. As in diet, where one should not eat the same food constantly, variety of meeting types is suggested.

It was told to me that the speaker meeting, the original format dating back decades, could be a tempting overindulgence. Meetings that focused on the Big Book and Step Book should be included in a weekly rotation, in addition to discussion meetings that encouraged people to develop their ideas about recovery. Rounding out the meeting diet, there should be various other formats, in addition to one or two speaker meetings.

Mike E. had consented to be my temporary sponsor, the emphasis as much on temporary as sponsor. Looking back, I understand that, had I not made it, Mike could've had a big mess on his hands with me. Over the years, I've seen situations like the one I was in turn out much less favorably. There is no predicting anyone's chances for success, unfortunately. I needed to find a permanent sponsor.

My first real sponsor was working a good program at the time. I say "at the time" because that situation changed, but not for a few years. Unfortunately, there is no real guidebook or set of instructions for the whole concept of sponsorship. More on that later.

Chris D. was five years sober. I had seen him occasionally at the meetings I attended a couple of towns over during my orientation period. He was five years sober when I was negative days sober, which is a fair experience base, especially for sponsoring somebody brand new. His sponsor was one of those old-timers who everybody looked up to.

Chris seemed to be at a lot of the meetings I went to. He later 'fessed up to purposefully putting himself in my path. It was several weeks before I finally asked him to sponsor me, the answer being predetermined. Chris knew the program and also the steps. He also took sponsorship rather seriously. He was able to teach me things that made a huge difference in my recovery down the line; he taught me a code of conduct and a code of ethics in addition to the workings of the AA program. Our relationship was a nice balance of student-teacher and cohort. We were about the same age.

~~~~~~~~~~~~~~~~~~~~~~~~~~~~~~~

While length of sobriety is a loaded topic, it's a relative thing. That is, five years' sobriety is a lot to someone with five weeks. The gap or difference in experience, knowledge base, and ability to stay sober is huge between anyone with a short-term recovery and some-one with even just a couple of years. Beyond five years, it becomes a matter of quality as much as quantity. Someone who has applied themselves for five years in recovery can easily have a recovery comparable to someone with ten years, or even surpass them. Again, it's about the quality.

Has someone become comfortable in their own skin? Have they done the work? By done the work, I mean have they dug deep and really done the steps? Have they taken that really hard, unsparing look at themselves? Yes, there is often significant discomfort in that process, but the results speak for themselves. As it says in the prom-ises on page 84 of *Alcoholics Anonymous*, the ability to intuitively handle situations comes. What someone puts into the effort equates to the benefit they get back. So, it's not exactly measurable in black-and-white terms, which translates to time in recovery being more about the actual quality of that time.

~~~~~~~~~~~~~~~~~~~~~~~~~~~~~~~

After a couple of months, it soon became apparent that there was a disconnection between my recovery, which was beautifully on track, and my home life. There was actual disconnection between my girlfriend and me. Whatever the basis of our attraction had been, it was following close behind my dissipating alcoholic tendencies. Part of it was simply a matter of time. I wasn't spending much at home. I was attending a meeting every night, usually tying up the prime wak-ing hours of the evening.

At some point this became formalized. We officially went from couple status to roommate status. I don't remember which happened first, whether she announced that she would be moving out, or my taking up occupation of the second bedroom, but both things oc-curred. The whole thing happened in a mature and cordial way. There were calm discussions, as opposed to arguments. I don't re-member any significant disagreements, but if there were any, they were handled quite civilly.

One thing I was rather insistent on was that the two cats would remain together with me in the house they were used to. Aside from that, furniture, finances, and timetables presented no serious source of contention. I started coming home with things that I would need— a vacuum cleaner, dishes, a CD player. The major decision had been made for me, and I was adjusting reasonably well.

In fact, I was adjusting so well that I made a new friend.

This is an anecdote that I share from the podium, or even from my seat at a meeting. Depending on the group and my delivery, the response might be somewhere between a few chuckles all the way up to boisterous laughter. In either case, it is more a response to identification as opposed to any comedic value. I succumbed to a common pitfall of early recovery.

At one of my regular meetings, a holdover from the two-towns-over days, I made the acquaintance of a woman about my age. She was blonde, pretty, and quiet. When she did say something, it was usually clever. We'll call her Linda.

Linda and I struck up an acquaintance while outside having ciga-rettes during the meeting break. After chatting on a few occasions, we went together to have coffee after the meeting. It bears mention-ing that the two meetings where I would routinely see her most like-ly became cemented into my schedule as regular meetings on the basis of her attendance. It also bears mentioning that the phenome-non of "talking at the break" leading to "coffee after the meeting" leading to something else is a valid one.

My situation at home, essentially roommate status, was a gray area to be sure, but in our conversations I put more emphasis on my feeling blue about it. Linda was both sympathetic and responsive. Coffee after the meeting led to a phone-number exchange, which led to an impromptu Saturday evening call, which led to a visit, which lasted until the next morning.

My naïve perception was that anyone who was already estab-lished and regular at meetings when I first started going had to be okay. When I had seven days' sobriety, someone with two months walked with Jesus, in my eyes. When I started seeing Linda, I had about three months. She was a regular long timer... with about nine months! In the big picture, nine months is barely enough time to stop vomiting, but my newbie perspective was much different. The point is that I thought she was solid in her recovery, and I put some faith in this.

We started to see each other regularly outside of meetings. One late afternoon, I was at her place and we were making dinner (read playing house). It dawned on me to call my sponsor, who on hearing where I was asked, "What are you doing?"

"Making dinner," I replied.

"No, I mean what are you *doing*?" His tone and emphasis on *doing* clearly implied that I had not answered his question, and that he was not interested in our evening's nutrition. This interrogation was intended more to make me think about my actions and their potential consequences than to enlighten him. He pressed on. "Keith, you're in a relationship, and it's not a good idea right now. You're playing with fire," he said.

We agreed to disagree, and things went on as they had been... for a while anyway. But Chris was right; the situation was a fire hazard. Without being exactly combustible, I was like that frayed, unshielded wire, or the overloaded circuit that would eventually spark and finally ignite. In the end, the house would still burn down.

My problem was quite simple really. I was the same person I was before, just not drunk on a daily basis. The previous Keith had developed no usable relationship skills, unless selfishness, stubbornness, and an inability to see the big picture were assets. Compounding the issue was the fact that the Keith who had created the problem was not capable of solving the problem. Simultaneously, all that great forward momentum of my recovery seemed to sputter and stall... I became sullen and irritable in the ensuing days and weeks.

The result of this was that Linda, going to different meetings, began talking to someone else at the break... which leads to... well, you get the idea...

When she unceremoniously tossed me aside like a used candy wrapper, I had a meltdown. Still being the previous Keith was most inconvenient right about this time. The combined lack of coping skills and absence of alcoholic anesthesia made me one big raw, exposed nerve twisting in the wind, just as that fire Chris had warned me about started getting mighty hot. My first little crisis of the heart proved vastly amplified by my newly sober status.

I kicked and screamed. I acted like a 17 year old, possibly a 13 year old, because that's the approximate age when I started drinking and stopped the normal process of growing toward adulthood. The memory of my behavior, attitude, and reaction to what should have been a minor bump in the road is of itself painful. It was a huge lesson that took a long time to absorb. The experience was another painful bottom of itself. But at the bottom lies opportunity...

This miserable lesson in humility, this dour reminder of the impairment caused by years of drinking, this vivid illustration of my deficiencies served as a veritable work order for all the things I needed to transform about myself. The previous Keith needed an upgrade.

Apparently, merely stopping my drinking would not be enough.

This is where Chris became more than a sponsor. He became a life preserver and a priceless commodity. Not only had he anticipated this turn of events, but he was there to prevent my capsizing the boat or worse, diving headlong back into the sea of alcohol.

~~~~~~~~~~~~~~~~~~~~~~~~~~~~~

This story is mine, but it's not unique. Variations on this theme have happened to countless others, many with less favorable outcomes. The mere fact that I did not drink in the face of the worst emotional pain of my adult life is itself a favorable outcome. Drinking had been my only real coping skill to that point in my life.

It was explained to me that my life up to that point had been commandeered by my drinking. The approximate age when I began drinking alcohol, 12 or 13, is the approximate time when many components of my psychological development ceased. Specifically, my ability to tolerate emotional discomfort (pain), my ability to comprehend and face the consequences of my actions, and in general, my ability to negotiate life's lumps and bumps as they came were all ruthlessly compromised.

In short, every time an opportunity to face a little adversity, build a little character, and grow up a little presented itself, I was faced with a choice. On the one hand, I could do what was expected of me and what everybody else mostly did, or on the other hand, I could drink. I always opted for the other hand; that hand held anesthesia, arrested development, and self-destruction.

~~~~~~~~~~~~~~~~~~~~~~~~~~~~~

From the ashes of that sick relationship came something wonderful. I began to rise, phoenix-like, and started to take that much needed hard look at myself. Though I didn't recognize it at the time, I was making lemonade from the sour lemons of my broken heart. I was responding to events, rather than reacting, perhaps for the first time in my life. The previous Keith needed to be disassembled and deconstructed before a new one could be created.

"Maybe it's time for you to start writing out that fourth step," Chris said. The dreaded Step Four! *Made a searching and fearless moral inventory of ourselves.*

Having come to terms with Steps One, Two, and Three, I had procrastinated with Step Four. Frankly, it gave me the willies, and I don't think I'm alone. Facing up to my character flaws, interpersonal recklessness, and general selfishness felt frightening. Now, caught between the proverbial rock and hard place, it seemed like the only thing to do. The pain behind me was worse than the fear in front of me.

I began writing.

I discovered some things about myself in the process. In doing this writing and searching my mind to uncover the fuzzy events of my misspent youth, I found I had the capacity to be diligent and thorough. Not only was I going back over events, declassifying, decoding, and exposing them, but I was also examining the feelings and motivations behind those events. In a word, fearless.

I was actually doing it! I had one of those 11-inch yellow legal pads, and I took it with me everywhere, careful to keep it close and safe. I would go sit on the beach for three hours after work or in the living room for hours into the evening with music playing. I was alone now; Patricia had moved out. My life became work, meetings, and writing Step Four. As it neared completion, the writing had swelled to about 45 pages on that big legal pad.

As my sense of purpose gained momentum, the throbbing broken heart feeling began to subside, first to a dull ache, then finally to an intermittent itch. I had successfully channeled energy born from lack of acceptance and agitation and turned it into something that would potentially benefit me. However, to realize that benefit I needed to take all the information I had uncovered and begin to apply it. The next step in this process was doing a formal Step Five: *Admitted to*

God, to ourselves, and to another human being the exact nature of our wrongs.

My sponsor, Chris, seemed like the obvious candidate to hear my inventory. We had bonded over the last few weeks, and he had helped me tremendously through an extremely difficult time. So, on an evening in late June, somewhere between my fifth and sixth month of sobriety, I did my fifth step. I told Chris things I thought I would never tell anyone. It really did take courage to expose things I was deeply ashamed of and embarrassed to even think about, let alone discuss. I knew that the purpose was twofold: to be free of the burden of those things from the past, and to find and demonstrate the willingness to go through with the whole thing. It was an exercise in courage, as it is meant to be. It was also a rite of passage for my recovery.

~~~~~~~~~~~~~~~~~~~~~~~~~~~~

This whole timeframe in my recovery was critical. Had I not rolled up my sleeves and started to begin the process of self-examination, the entire trajectory of my recovery would have been different. I understand today that the course of my recovery was set in those early months. Why it is that we so often have to wait for a painful, ego-puncturing experience to motivate us, I'm not sure, but it is quite often the case.

Later in my recovery, I observed others doing things differently. They did not apply themselves to the steps, especially Four and Five. Perhaps they didn't even have a sponsor. When that inevitable time of loss of momentum and stagnancy arrived for them in the early going, they responded not by stepping up their game, but by simple acceptance. So often I have heard people ask, as their "pink cloud," or honeymoon phase, evaporated, "What happens now?"

I think the answer lies in our own willingness to take some initiative and chase recovery. Asking myself, "What more can I be doing?" What was I doing to have the best recovery I could have?

That I had a galvanizing experience that pushed me onward and upward was my individual circumstance. Like the day my first prayer was answered, it was what I needed at the time. And also like that prayer, which I chose to interpret as having been answered, the outcome of my experience with Linda was the result of my choosing to gain something from it.

Things happen in life that we really don't like at the time, but whether something is good or bad might not necessarily be ultimately determined in the moment. If I'm able to learn a lesson or gain an insight that I can apply to some situation down the road, then I have not made a mistake or wasted time. Where character building is concerned, I must not be hasty in my judgment of an outcome; what I think is the conclusion might not be the final outcome.

~~~~~~~~~~~~~~~~~~~~~~~~~~~~~

Five hours after we began my fifth step, I was saying goodnight to Chris. It had been a long evening; I was tired, but I felt good inside. I felt a sense of relief, and although it still hurt to think about Linda, I knew that I would get over it. As an aside, she and the guy who she dumped me for married within a couple of years. They live in New Hampshire, and I see him once in a while. I heard that she stopped going to meetings; it's really none of my business, and it's all water under the bridge.

Before Chris left that night, he made a suggestion that didn't really sink in at the time. He suggested I read two little paragraphs in *Alcoholics Anonymous.* On page 76 in the fourth edition, Steps Six and Seven are concerned with the disposition of my character defects. I had finished inventorying them, now I was supposed to become ready and work to be rid of them. Whether I didn't really hear him, was too tired and meant to do it later, or ignored the suggestion... I don't recall. I did not immediately turn my attention to Steps Six and Seven. As things unfolded, I would be spending a lot more time yet in the company of my character defects.

CHAPTER 11

Reconstruction

I was building what is referred to as a foundation in my recovery. It had several components. I had a weekly schedule of daily meetings, two a day on weekends. These consisted of a variety of formats and locations. I had a sponsor whom I spoke with or saw almost daily. He frequently instructed me on some aspect of the recovery process, which could include the history of AA, a code of conduct and ethics, and the steps or insight into chapters of the Big Book. I was active in my home group, functioning in the capacity of secretary.

In keeping with a strong suggestion that new people not speak "from the podium" for three months, I waited the requisite 90 days. My sponsor briefed me on the basic goals of an AA talk, to discuss "how it was, what happened, and how it is now." I went on an "outgoing commitment" to a southern New Hampshire group with a couple of other guys, and spoke for the first time. Despite having the best of intentions, I figuratively vomited on the collective shoes of the group for about 45 minutes. There were a couple of old-timers from one of my local groups there, and it was much later that I understood their amused smiles. Whatever I said that night was undoubtedly toxic sludge from the bowels of my still twisted little mind, and I had much to learn about "carrying the message." After me, they should have changed the suggestion to six months until newcomers could speak, but the horse was already out of the barn. I resolved to do better, and learned from my first experience.

As far as speaking at meetings, I did not exactly get with the program right away. "Sharing at meetings," as it's called, is a personal experience committed in a public way. There are several approaches and philosophies behind this. While my sponsor had given me some guidelines—honesty, brevity, and sticking to the subject at hand if there was one—I had a tendency to share from my head more than my heart. I was always thinking critically and analyzing the concepts of recovery. Not critical thinking in the sense of negative criticism, but rather in the sense of digging toward a deeper understanding.

I also had a tendency to intellectualize with liberal use of ten-cent words. The result I began to observe was that people often had problems with their eyes when I spoke. Two things seemed to happen. Some people lost control of the little muscles that keep the eye facing straight forward, causing the eyes to roll back momentarily; this happened when I said something that made perfect sense to only me apparently. The other problem people had when I spoke was a glazing-over effect, again centered in the eyes, and that happened when I spoke too long or just said things that didn't interest anyone but me.

~~~~~~~~~~~~~~~~~~~~~~~~~~~~~~

I began the ongoing process in early sobriety commonly referred to as "clearing up." As I began to learn and understand the ideas and concepts of recovery and the Twelve Steps, I started to raise my hand and speak at meetings. It takes people a while to find their voice and comfort zone in this regard. I wasted some time trying to sound smart, and my vocabulary and attempts to intellectualize, what were, for the most part, simple concepts, did not serve to resonate with others. It took me a while to grow past that.

As I began to understand the bigger picture, and to speak from the heart more, my ideas did not always reflect the mainstream of prevailing opinion. Depending on the particular situation, I sometimes received some negative reactions from people. Eye rolling was the least of it. People might get up and leave. They might feel compelled to start a conversation with someone next to them, or in some other manner make obvious their disinterest in listening to me. Sometimes they would go as far as to rebut. This type of reaction only gave me more cause to look at what I was thinking and saying, and to question for myself why this was happening.

It was that type of scratching beneath the surface that drove my opinions, and also my pondering what it all meant in the bigger picture. I was thinking outside the box. I was becoming a little bit of a paradox. My traditional, even fundamentalist, approach to my recovery was nonetheless yielding nontraditional ideas. By adherence and observance to the suggestions of AA recovery, I was a poster boy. By thought process and disposition, I was anything but.

~~~~~~~~~~~~~~~~~~~~~~~~~~~~~~~~~

As time began to pass, the changes I had made in my life would begin to insinuate themselves into my feelings and behaviors. My thought process was shifting. However, before the new can really enter, the old must be reconciled... I had a huge lesson to learn about music, and the role music had played in my life.

I defined myself as a musician before anything else. Since my mid teens, drumming and music had been a consuming passion. Automatically programmed to "be" a musician, I planned my reentry to drumming. I had sublet a rehearsal space nearby and began woodshedding, or building back my rusty drumming "chops." Drumming, in the modern North American tradition, that is, the drum set, is a physically intensive proposition. Like golf or tennis, one needs to be "on your game," so to speak. The act of repetitive physical practice hones the coordination and fine-tunes the mind-body connection that is required for making something musical come out of a drum set.

As illustrated in an earlier anecdote, I passed an audition and began playing with a regional original rock band somewhere around my ninth month of sobriety. We played several times a month, usually at clubs from Manchester, New Hampshire down to Boston, and out as far as Worcester. We also made the finals of a Boston radio station band competition sometime during the winter.

One night on stage in front of about 500 drunken revelers, I had a little epiphany. As though someone had simply turned a switch, I realized that something had changed. Playing music was much different now, and it wasn't just about being sober. Previously, it was unusual for me to even sit at my drums while clearheaded. With significant effort, I had worked through the whole "being comfortable" thing; I was at ease on stage, loose and able to find the groove. What had formerly required some form of lubrication, I could now do naturally. What dawned on me was a profound insight about why I was there. I understood that I had been seeking something for much of my music-playing life.

I had spent untold hours, days, and years questing after the "ultimate note." My music, drinking and substance abuse had all melded together at some point. In some misguided manner, I thought that altering my consciousness would unlock some mystical and universal secret. Playing music while intoxicated was seductive. It's an age-old experience dating to when grapes were first crushed, I suppose.

In modern times, the scourge of the contemporary musician is drinking and drugging; from the birth of American jazz to the psychedelic 1960s on, the quest for the ultimate note has littered the musical landscape with casualties. However, like so many young people, terminal invincibility defined my attitude. The false sense of musical well-being, the illusion of telepathy with other players, and an intangible feeling of resonance with some larger, cosmic vibration served to feed an addiction within an addiction. For a time it was unclear which addiction was within which, but ultimately alcohol asserted itself.

Clearly, I was looking for something. I was searching for the answer to a question that I never knew how to ask. With no formal religious upbringing and no clue what God or spirituality was, I was looking for spirit in the silence between the beats, the vibration of the cymbals and the synchronization of the rhythms.

My quest for the ultimate note had been a search for spirituality. I came to understand that it would not be found on stage before 500 people in pursuit of their own ultimate something. Music was part of spirituality, not the other way around. I gave notice and withdrew from the band. I was completely comfortable letting go of drumming, for the time being anyway. No longer feeling the need to define myself as a musician, there was room in my life now for other things to enter.

Almost uncannily, a sequence of seemingly unrelated events occurred, which set my life heading in a completely new direction. Within a matter of weeks of finishing with the band, I would be enrolled in college courses, which would ultimately lead me to a nursing program.

Someone said the right thing at the right time. A temporary nurse anesthetist was working in our operating room, as I did my job as a surgical technician. "I've been watching you," he said. "You can do this job in your sleep. Why don't you get off your ass and go to nursing school?"

He was right. Since getting sober, I had stepped into a new level of confidence and competence in my job as a surgical technician.

The man who had once sat in the parking lot, almost paralyzed by anxiety and afraid to go inside to work, now met each day as it came. It was as if I'd had one hand tied behind my back, figuratively speaking, during the whole time I'd been trying to function as an alcoholic.

I started thinking about what he'd said. Then, almost as if by magic, the hospital announced that they were participating in a program with the local community college. Hospital employees interested in furthering their careers in healthcare could take free medical-related courses. It happened so fast that it made my head spin, but I was enrolled and beginning Anatomy and Physiology I the next week.

Returning to school for the first time in 11 or 12 years took a little getting used to, but I managed. I also found a couple of things to be remarkably different. It's true what they say about adult learners; we tend to have a more serious approach than in our youth. The other difference for me, naturally, was being sober. Though I had somehow managed to make the dean's list a decade earlier at the operating room tech program while in a virtual blackout, I was well aware that this time my being present, alert and unadulterated was a profoundly different experience. Get use to it I did, and my final grade for the course was A-.

I set my sights on being accepted into the community college's highly competitive registered nurse program. This would prove challenging, as it came to my attention that there were approximately 500 people trying for a total of 90 seats (combined in the day and evening programs). The evening program was my obvious choice, because I would have to continue working fulltime to support myself.

The program looked at candidates' qualifications in terms of how much prerequisite course work was done, in addition to academic performance. As far as I knew, my previous clinical experience and years of related work counted for nothing. I next enrolled in Anatomy and Physiology II and Introduction to Psychology for the fall semester of 1992.

Beginning to hit my stride, I earned A's in both courses. At the end of the fall semester, it was time to make my formal application to enter the nursing program in September 1993. Months later, I would be accepted.

There were more courses in the spring and the summer: microbiology, more psychology courses, and sociology were all requirements of the nursing program. I was able to utilize credits from Berklee and Salem State College for other requirements and electives. I still hadn't met the English requirement, so I challenged that. I took a test in English composition. Passing score was 450. After writing the test, I thought I did a fair job. If I failed, I would try it one more time before taking the time and expense of taking English Composition II. My score came back as 650! To this day, I'm not entirely sure how I came by my moderate level of ability at written communication, but I'm exceedingly grateful for the gift.

I had been living alone in the rental townhouse since Patricia had moved out. My notion had been that I would let the dust settle, clear my head a bit and then find a roommate to split the expenses. My income was the same as when I drank, but without weekly expenditures for beer and vodka, it somehow seemed to go further. Imagine that!

Another weekly expenditure was cigarettes. I had seen my habit change after I quit drinking, alas increasing. At the time, just about everybody in AA smoked, and with the exception of some church meetings, smoking during the meeting was still prevalent in the early 1990s. I went from half a pack daily, smoking only on the way to and from work, breaks and lunch (and never inside my home!), to a solid pack per day with a heavily used ashtray on my coffee table. I had gone from buying a pack every few days at a convenience store to buying cartons almost weekly at the wholesale club.

There was an odd mental disconnect that I started to become aware of. I might spend the morning assisting the thoracic surgeon in the removal of a diseased lung. Then I'd head out the back door for a smoke, not making much connection until I began thinking about addiction in the larger sense. The knowledge that smoking cigarettes didn't lead to blackouts or arrest at roadblocks did not change the fact that it was just another addiction gaining ground in my life. I quit smoking in April 1992. I began to run and cycle.

~~~~~~~~~~~~~~~~~~~~~~~~~~~~~

In fewer than two years, I had undergone huge changes in things I did, and also in the way I defined myself in my own mind. Quitting drinking and smoking were the most significant. However, from the standpoint of my personal self-image, letting go of my perceived need to boost my ego by playing music, thereby sending myself a subconscious message that I was "in the game," represented a monumental shift in how I viewed myself and lived my life.

This was not part of any master plan. This was merely me making choices on a daily basis that came naturally. The result was that, outwardly, the things I did and how I might have appeared to an observer were morphing. Inwardly, I was letting go of old ways of defining myself, while beginning to assume a way of being that would actually work in a long-range way. On reflection, I realized that during my late 20s I had been unable to envision life in my 30s. I likely would not have survived had I remained the previous Keith.

~~~~~~~~~~~~~~~~~~~~~~~~~~~~~~

I began to investigate the possibility of buying a house. Without the ball and chain of bad habits constantly siphoning from my bank account, I was finding to my surprise that I was financially stable. I had also received a small inheritance sometime after my mother passed. I had gone momentarily crazy—new drums and a new (used) vehicle. I was being sensible, and a down payment on a modest home seemed like a good investment. After realizing the tax and long-term financial advantages, I persevered and found a place not far from where I'd been living... after looking at about 35 or 40 houses. The timing worked out well, and I closed on the house after the end of the fall semester. I was moved in by the end of 1992.

Nursing school started in the fall of 1993. While I had adjusted to the rigors of balancing studies with work, and more importantly my recovery, this was a new level. During the first days, there was much indoctrination to the idea that we must put nursing school before all else, making it top priority. I was completely serious about my goal of becoming a nurse, to be sure, but as I listened to the boot camp speeches of the nursing instructors, I knew that my being there was only possible because I was in recovery. I would need to balance my priorities; nursing school and sobriety would need to coexist.

My life became work, school and clinicals, meetings, and studying. Time management became the challenge. There was always something I needed to be doing, something that was coming due, or some impending test requiring adequate study. No longer able to attend meetings daily, simply because I went from work to school until 9 PM, I was still doubling up over the weekends. I had settled into this routine over the first two months when life, as it has a way of doing, decided to give me some help with time management.

I was fired from my job! In all the years when I barely functioned in an alcoholic state, I was terminated only once. This dismissal would be the first of several in sobriety, and would be the first hard lesson in my long, stormy relationship with healthcare administration and its functional sorority, or sisterhood. The local hospital operating room had come under the directorship of a new manager, and there was valid speculation that administration had given her a mandate. She was supposed to be a new sheriff who would "clean up Dodge City." Hospital administration specifically had their eye on one of the RNs who happened to wield a strange and unsanctioned power, by virtue of personality, influence, and history. After she proved too smart for the new manager, and hence unmovable, the manager turned her attention to more movable targets.

The manager and I did not get along well. Much of this was due to my immaturity and character defects, in addition to my significant naïveté about how these things worked. Sadly, I was clueless about departmental politics, especially as it affected me. While this woman gave me absolutely nothing to respect her for, she was also recently divorced, and even went so far as to compare me to her ex-husband on one occasion. Combined with my as-yet-unresolved history of maternal competency issues around my mother, this was a recipe for interpersonal disaster. She began compiling documentation and progressive discipline actions against me. Most of this had little validity and was prejudicial. However, when I gave her some real ammunition in the form of a childish prank backfiring, she had enough in the tank to have me terminated.

This started a tough period of character building. This was the first in a series of related life lessons having to do with my relationship with work and authority. Of course, I did not immediately recognize how necessary this part of my growth was in the bigger picture.

I also failed, at least at the time, to recognize it as an opportunity to integrate all the new elements in my life. Of course, my security was threatened financially and emotionally. I was a wreck. However,

I was collecting unemployment and managed to get by okay. I had time to go to more meetings. I began going to the gym. I found a music situation that fit into my schedule, playing at a weekly jam night with my childhood musical friend, guitarist Bill. Except for the doomy, pessimistic thoughts that I would never find employment again, life was actually going okay. Most important, I found recovery to be sustaining through this difficult period, and never once thought about picking up a drink. That was incredibly significant!

After almost four months, and holidays that were rather gloomy, I found a new job. This new position as a surgical technician was at a larger general hospital in a nearby city. I was afforded a wider range of clinical experience, which would only benefit me in my educational process. Having those months without fulltime employment had really helped me settle into the school routine, and now in the second semester, my balancing act was able to reincorporate fulltime employment.

As my routine became established, my weeks were often 80 or 90 hours, with 40 hours of work, along with at least one night of "on-call" per week and every fourth weekend. School was four nights a week between lectures and clinicals, plus studying. I still managed several meetings a week, plus a few trips to the gym. I had incorporated all these elements into my weekly routine and reached the point where I was constantly in motion. I got by on less sleep and just had the mindset that I was always supposed to be busy.

In addition to meetings, the gym became something that sustained me. I had become increasingly more enthusiastic and focused on leading a healthy lifestyle since quitting drinking, and later quitting smoking. I went from gym novice to gym rat in a matter of months, learning at least the basics of working out. I began to see results as my muscles first toned, then developed. More important, it gave me a sense of well-being that really helped to sustain me during that insanely busy time in my life.

My AA program was well maintained, but just that, maintenance. I kept my serious approach, but usually made only four or five meetings, about half my weekly attendance prior to nursing school. There was nothing wrong with five meetings, but I did not feel the same sense of intensity and forward momentum that characterized my first two years. I changed sponsors in this time frame. After a transitional relationship of about two months that did not pan out, a man named Vince became my second permanent sponsor.

Vince came with conditions. He required me to read an entire story from the first section of the Big Book on a daily basis. This proved beneficial, and I soon discovered this was time well spent. This went on for the first 90 days of our relationship. Vince was a self-described "Step Nazi," and had much valuable insight to share. Realizing that I had more-or-less stalled after my fifth step, I worked at steps six through nine. As best I could at the time, I sat with my character defects, particularly impatience, selfishness, and my tendency to obsess. I explored humility and looked hard at my lack of that quality. I first became ready, then contacted or approached a list of people that I had wronged. This was done in the context and intent of Steps Eight and Nine.

Nursing school, while my daily and weekly focus and task, did become more than a routine. Somewhere in the process, I became enthusiastic. The education I was receiving was more than job training. Nursing training is like an in-depth orientation to health, proper function, and troubleshooting problems for the human body and living. In addition to the body and its function, the focus on the interrelationship of everything around health, the psychosocial category, was tremendously enlightening. The thought occurred to me that everyone should know these things. The emphasis on critical thinking and problem solving is key; nurses, by inclination, think out of the box and don't give up until something is resolved.

My initial objective on completion of nursing school had been to enter the psychology field in alcohol rehabilitation. Early on, I had viewed the training as a kind of condition I had to meet to do what I wanted to do. As I progressed through the process, I gave myself over to it. I realized the value in it and opened my mind to the possibilities. By the time I graduated, I was interested in building a foundation in general nursing and open to the possibility of spending a year or so as what's known as a medical/surgical nurse—the nurse who does general duties on the hospital floor.

Then came the cold shower of reality. I was entering a cyclical job market at a very low point in the cycle. Nursing goes through shortages and gluts. Economic, social, and healthcare business factors had all conspired to make 1995/1996 a 10- or 15-year low in the need for nurses, especially new ones. Starting with the hospital where I was employed as a surgical technician, the only available positions were for experienced nurses.

Undaunted, I made a rather courageous decision. After graduating from nursing school with honors on schedule in December 1995, I decided to resign my position as a surgical technologist. The hospital had made clear that there was no opening for me there as a registered nurse. With enough money in my checking account to either take a vacation or pay my bills for a while, I opted to prepare for the challenging nursing boards and devote my time to a nursing job search. I took and passed the boards in January 1996.

Something else happened in January 1996. I celebrated five continuous years of sobriety.

As I no longer had the weight of my school responsibilities, I had some time to reflect on things. How different my life had become! Five years earlier I was at my wits' end, the absolute end of my rope. I could not go a day without a drink, and there was an open bottle of vodka under the seat of my car. Five years later, as I sat in front of the same group that I had first attended on a snowy Saturday morning on my fourth day of sobriety, I had some inkling of the significance of all this. First, that I long since had stopped thinking about drinking. Second, that my needs (not necessarily my wants) had been met every moment of that five years. I had a new fit and muscular body, a home that, along with the bank, I owned, and despite the minor obstacle of a transient down cycle, I had a bright new career ahead of me. How amazing was all this?

CHAPTER 12

More Lessons

My first few years in nursing were full of lessons, both good and bad. My desire to work in general nursing unfortunately did not materialize. The realities of the job market initially dictated the path of my fledgling career. I was diligent in my resume preparation and in honing my skills in interviewing and presenting myself. I searched out opportunities and knocked on many doors. The ones that eventually opened were those of operating rooms. As I marched forth bravely to seek my place as part of the healthcare assembly line, I naïvely thought that my education was behind me. I couldn't have been more wrong; it was only beginning.

In terms of the technical, bureaucratic, and ideological reality of the way our society promotes and maintains optimal health, I was on the same level as any layperson, except for understanding the language. Two-plus years of nursing school were little more than a procedure-based, politically correct exercise in how to successfully participate in and perpetuate a system that often fails to work in the highest interest of those it purports to serve. Despite being idealistic and analytical, I had not really begun to question the propaganda content of the programming I had received in training. This would come later, as I observed the differences in how we were taught to do things and how things were really done.

The other piece of education that was only starting as I entered the workforce related to my growing up in recovery, and how I would navigate the many subtleties of human relations. Despite my recent experience in politics, hierarchy, and organizational drama, I was still an absolute babe in the woods. Ignorantly thinking I was entering a realm that was a level playing-field, I found medical organizations and the nursing profession to be complex political and interpersonal mazes that I was ill equipped to handle. Despite being in my mid-30s, I had no idea how immature I really was.

If nothing else, I was idealistic. In searching for my first nursing job, I made a beeline straight toward my heart's desire. I wanted to work with and help people suffering from addictions.

Next down the list, I was pragmatic. I looked at the job market in the area, and reconciled in my mind what was available with what was in my best interest. I remained open-minded to working as a medical/surgical nurse on a basic hospital floor.

In addition to my job search activities, I kept busy in the meantime. Looking to bolster my meager resume, I became a volunteer at one of the nearby hospitals where I eventually hoped to work. I was the surgical services waiting room liaison, updating relatives of surgical patients. I also started the first Nicotine Anonymous group in my hometown after responding to a notice I saw on the gym bulletin board. I was used to being busy, after all, and felt the void that having no fulltime work left in my life.

My first opportunity came in the form of an interview in the psych department of the hospital where I was volunteering. They had two mental health units on two different floors, and two positions available. I interviewed hoping to get a fulltime position; that job was filled by an internal employee transferring from another department who just wanted to give psych a try. I was hired in a per diem capacity. This meant I had no set hours or benefits, and was offered shifts that were left over after permanent staff members worked when they preferred or took time off. It was a proposition in getting my foot in the door and paying dues, plain and simple. I started there in March of 1996. By April, I paid my bills by the skin of my teeth.

The job search continued. I accepted a second per diem position at a small private psych hospital. This place was much different from my other position, which was a busy community hospital that was also a Catholic hospital. The small place, also in a nearby community, was a freestanding facility specializing in substance abuse and general psych, with a 2/3 to 1/3 ratio accordingly. It was not meant to work out, as they tended to ask me to work on short notice, without fail calling me for weekend second shifts when I was already booked at the other place. After the orientation, I don't think I worked a single shift there.[†]

As my search took me farther afield, I heard about a southern New Hampshire hospital looking for med/surg nurses, and went to apply. I heard back a short time later from their human resources department that they were interested in interviewing me for an operating room position, not a med/surg position. Intrigued, I met with them. On seeing my experience as a surgical technologist, they had forwarded my resume to the operating room manager, who was looking for... a per diem nurse. Despite wages that actually made me choke a little when I heard them, I accepted the position. I was quite determined. Even if it meant stringing together a bunch of per diem work, I was going to get into that difficult job market. I was stuck in that Catch-22 situation; they didn't want me without experience, and I couldn't get experience if they didn't want me.

The operating room position was on the day shift, weekdays. After they oriented me, I was working three or four days a week, and, along with the mostly weekend shifts I was getting at the Catholic hospital's psych ward, I was getting something resembling fulltime hours. As summer approached, the operating room offered me a permanent four-day/32-hour position. This was part of their business model, to keep a huge buffer between me and overtime, which they paid only after 40 hours of work. When I was on call, I would work from seven in the morning until well into the evening shift, or beyond, just completing the day's schedule. Again, I was paying dues to get experience, but I also knew they were taking advantage of me.

~~~~~~~~~~~~~~~~~~~~~~~~~~~~~

Something that negatively impressed me about that southern New Hampshire hospital was its emphasis on appearance. Management was obsessed with it. Not even in so many words, but it was emphasized in numerous ways that patients needed to be made to perceive that their care was good. Mandatory attendance at "customer-service" trainings, and meetings with the CEO, in which he outlined his "plans for market domination," became routine. The market-domination stuff seemed absolutely over-the-top. While I assumed that there was a place for that corporate-type stuff, as a care-

---

[†] Until 16 years later.

giver, I was disinterested. This was merely part of my continuing education in the business of healthcare, but was my first cause to stop and ponder that bigger picture.

~~~~~~~~~~~~~~~~~~~~~~~~~~~~~~~~~~~

After a year and a half, I moved on to a better position. Closer to home in a lovely seaside community, I felt like I had hit the lottery with my new 40-hour position in a busy operating room where I was acquainted with some of the surgeons and staff from my surgical technician days. Unfortunately, this quickly turned into a nightmare. The events are difficult and painful to recall. The turmoil around this new job could also have been an omen. What happened led to a dark time in my life and recovery, and I was challenged on several different levels. My mental and emotional well-being was tested to the limit. While I could not know at the time, the message the universe was sending me was that the path of normal, everyday, and run-of-the-mill was not the path in life that I would ever be on. The universe just had other ideas for me.

The simple description is that I was fired from the new job. This happened during the typical probationary period, and no actual reason was given. I was totally blindsided by this.

The reality, which did not become apparent for months, even years for some details to emerge, was that there were people who had it in for me before I set foot in the place. Not to say that I didn't go skipping into the situation with a kind of dopey ignorance that helped set me up for the fall. Obviously not stamped from any typical cookie-cutter, I had no clue that this was a place that expected everybody to be from a certain mold. There was a culture of stodginess that certainly wasn't me, and my only real crime was being a visibly free spirit. Individuality was not welcome.

There was no incompetence, no mistake, and no legitimate behavior that would have warranted termination with the prejudice that took place. I could've benefited from guidance to be sure, but there was none. Aside from the absence of any warm, fuzzy acceptance, I was completely surprised when I was brought to the manager's office. She actually yelled at me, and I was totally shell-shocked. I changed clothes, cleaned out my locker, and walked out to my car, someone from security discreetly shadowing me on the way out. I felt like I had been fed through a meat grinder.

This happened in early November and in some ways felt reminiscent of my experience years earlier as a surgical technician, but the stakes felt higher. I was now a nurse and had been fired as a nurse. I wondered if this would follow me forever, or if I would even work again. Initially, I accepted the message the universe seemed to send me without question. I was a worthless piece of crap.

Within a few weeks, I was contacted by a woman I had worked with at the seaside community hospital. She had watched this entire drama unfold, from weeks before I even arrived at the hospital, through the couple months I was there, to my being shown the door. She told me she was horrified and explained why. Before my first day, a nurse anesthetist who had worked at the community hospital where I had been a surgical technician all those years earlier had started what could be described as a smear campaign. The reasons for his malice could only be known to him, but envy and insecurity are likely, if not obvious, motivators. He was morbidly obese; I was blessed with a healthy, fit body. He'd had a crush on the nurse who I had the torrid, illicit ongoing affair with. Whatever the reasons for the deliberate and petty character assassination, it happened, and the small operating room department had a negative opinion of me before I even arrived.

I was in a dark place emotionally. I felt that I must have been to blame and deserved what had happened. The thought of applying for unemployment hadn't even entered my mind. Painful as it was, I had to reprocess all the events of the past couple months. I began to put things in a different context. Things began to make sense.

I applied for unemployment. The hospital attempted to deny my claim, and I appealed. This was all stressful and I didn't want to face going to the hearing. The days and weeks leading up to it were horrible. I was depressed, fearful, and generally miserable. When the hearing date came around, I was a wreck. The hospital sent the head of human resources and an attorney. I went alone.

The unemployment department arbitrator seemed amused at the issues presented by the hospital. The director of HR was in the unenviable position of saying that people said I said things (that I never said). That was all they had, and that none of those people were present spoke volumes. No incompetence, no mistakes, no insubordination, in short, there was no valid reason to terminate me. The arbitrator said, in effect, that it was "wrongful termination." I don't remember the attorney saying a thing. I left the hearing knowing I had won.

While my pride and self-esteem had been bolstered, my career was still on the rocks. The holidays came, and I was battling depression. I went to meetings, stayed in touch with my sponsor, and stayed sober.

Financially, I was getting by, but I was insecure; I had a mortgage, after all. The fact that I was alone in the world, out there without a safety net, really hit home. I had no one to rely on, no one to reach out to if it all fell apart, and it started to. The engine in my car blew.

Still, I kept it together. I figured it out. I took care of the car. I kept applying for jobs and was hired in an operating room at a community hospital about 40 minutes from home. As this dark, scary time drew to a close, I looked back on the approximately four months. I had never wanted for anything, and my needs had been met every minute. I had learned huge and scary lessons about human nature and my relationship with the bigger picture. I had also seen firsthand that, though I had no problem looking at my side of the street in issues, the fault was not necessarily as much mine as I had been so quick to assume. Most important, I had never thought about getting drunk.

CHAPTER 13

New Information, New Experience

When I bought my house in 1992, I had fantasies of marital bliss replete with white picket fence, and the 1990s equivalent of my parents' "standard 1960s model 2.3 children that made the average household."

Whether in the back or front of my mind, this influenced my decision-making process. The house itself was large enough for a family. Though not part of any larger development, it was in a growing neighborhood and in a community with decent services and schools. Even the appliances I purchased reflected the notion that I would also be "installing" a wife and kids just down the line. I was settling down, marriage-minded even. Build it, and they will come. I just assumed nature would take its course, and I would become only a minor statistical outlier by marrying in my early- to mid-30s.

If you want to make God laugh, tell him what *your* plans are.

During my 20s, I had been in two significant relationships where an outcome of marriage would have been a reasonable expectation. Alcoholism was the basis for those relationships, but also the reason they didn't progress naturally. My brief and heartbreaking relationship shortly after I quit drinking was different from those previous relationships only in duration and the fact that I was physically sober. That I had not, as yet, attained mental or emotional sobriety doomed that relationship from the outset.

~~~~~~~~~~~~~~~~~~~~~~~~~~

I'm glad I did not marry either of the women I was involved with during my alcoholic 20s. My romantic life since sobriety has been marked by some great relationships, some not so great, but all learning experiences in any event. As my spiritual life has unfolded, the challenge has been to be true to that and to find a partner who is at least tolerant of, if not able to share, my perspective. One significant difference between dating and relationships after I got sober was the ability to remain friends with women after it became apparent we were not perfect romantic matches. The notion that things did not have to end badly was a revelation at first. Simply understanding and acknowledging that we were two nice people who were not compatible in that big picture way was definitely a new way of being. Many people I count among my friends today are women I met initially in a romantic context.

~~~~~~~~~~~~~~~~~~~~~~~~~~~~

One of the prime suggestions floating around out there for early recovery is to stay out of relationships for the first year. I actually entertained that... briefly. Another suggestion is not to date within AA. I took that one, but had a tendency to break it every six to nine months or so. While I never set out to use AA as a dating pool, in the early years I had a tendency to investigate possibilities of women I found attractive. I had a number of involvements with women in recovery in my early years. There were no major train wrecks, but there were a few bumps and bruises along the way.

On my quest to settle down, there were a number of significant relationships. Two and a half years, one year, a few times six months or so... But nothing had gone the distance as I came to my 40th birthday.

Shortly before the end of the century (late 1999), I met a woman in the gym. The circumstances were quirky. There was an elliptical machine that I preferred to use, and she was on the one next to it. When I got on the machine, she told me that she had watched someone attempt to use it, only to have it malfunction. She had warned several people away. I said I would take my chances. The machine worked fine, and we had a long conversation as we did cardio.

She told me she was a massage therapist and personal trainer. Her arms and upper body were quite impressive, and I was instantly attracted to her beauty and fitness. She had long, light brown hair and compelling eyes. Her name was Vanessa.

She also began to tell me about being a student of an "energy healer." I was intrigued with that, as I was with this woman in general. The whole conversation was memorable and left an impression on me. Unfortunately, she was married. We seemed to have an instant connection. In that first conversation, she felt the need to tell me that she planned to leave her marriage.

Our paths crossed numerous times in the weeks that followed, and we had some great conversations. She was quite knowledgeable about alternative and holistic medicine, and also this energy healing she was learning. She had studied something called Polarity Therapy and was currently learning the techniques of a remarkable sounding woman from California. Being an operating room nurse, I was fairly hard-core Western medical approach in my training, ideas, and beliefs about healthcare. My training and practice was based on the technical, mechanical, and chemical approach that doctors and nurses are taught. We cut out the broken or rotten parts, stitched the good parts together, and threw chemicals on top for good measure. She had some different ideas, and I was curious.

There was a gray area in our acquaintance. She was the most interesting woman I'd ever met; otherwise there would have been no issue. We would have been friends, and her marital issues would have been irrelevant. Even in our first conversation, she said she had been remaining with her husband because he was struggling with health issues. She knew she was leaving the marriage. Nevertheless, the fact remained that I was becoming involved with a married woman. The 800-pound gorilla in the room was an attraction that went beyond friendship.

We went for a walk one day. We had probably known each other four or six weeks; it was sometime in January. We met at the local park and walked the trails, resuming our ongoing conversation about energy, and she was describing Polarity Therapy. We were walking along the trail when she said it would be easier to show me rather than to describe it. We stopped. She asked me to close my eyes and just stand there. I did as she asked. A few seconds later, I felt myself first leaning forward, then being pulled forward off balance. I opened my eyes. Vanessa had her hands in front of my solar plexus, one over the other, as though she was manipulating an invisible object, four to six inches in diameter. It was as though she was tugging on something connected to me. She had moved me without touching me. This was quite extraordinary. I was completely at a loss for words.

Extraordinary didn't even describe it. As had happened on a January morning nine years earlier, the world and reality as I understood it had just changed. I had just had an actual Carlos Castaneda moment, and Vanessa was Don Juan.[‡] This was amazing! What do you do when the world changes? Not yet realizing the full ramifications of how my world had just been altered, I attempted to ask more questions.

Polarity Therapy is an alternative healing modality that is concerned with the human energetic system. It came as news to me, but apparently in addition to our physical, anatomical systems, we have a "subtle" energetic system. Vanessa learned all this at massage school. She had integrated this type of energy healing into her everyday massage practice, which was, incidentally, extremely successful. She often did 30 treatments a week, a lot for a massage therapist, and she was booked a couple months in advance. The theory behind Polarity Therapy is that we exist and function within a universal field of energy, and, in addition to our physical bodies, we have an energetic anatomy. When problems occur on this energetic level, they will likely manifest ultimately as physical problems. In principle, physical disease is rooted in energy problems. I was fascinated.

~~~~~~~~~~~~~~~~~~~~~~~~~~~~~~~

I didn't realize it, but that day of the walk was a fork in the road that would change the entire direction of my life yet again. The simple yet definitive demonstration of energy at work, and that it was actually part of me, would change my way of being. As I would slowly integrate the knowledge that witnessing this phenomenon firsthand would bring me, it would affect and change my ideas about my recovery and what I did for a living. Most of all, it would change my ideas about Spirit and the concept of a power greater than myself. That day on the trail actually began the journey that brought me to my life's work as I understand it. It is certainly what ultimately brought me to the writing of this book. It would make sense of and

---

[‡] Carlos Castaneda was an anthropologist and author of a series of books based on his alleged apprenticeship with a shaman of the Meso-Americans tradition, Don Juan. Don Juan exposed Castaneda to a series of experiences that were completely outside his perception of the way the conventional world is commonly understood, forcing Castaneda to adopt this new reality.

give context to many ideas I already held, and also present me with a whole new set of challenges in the realm of everyday living.

~~~~~~~~~~~~~~~~~~~~~~~~~~~~

So, I did what any man whose whole worldview, personal reality, and way of being had been irrevocably altered would do. I went home and thought about the amazing woman who had come into my life. In the weeks that followed, Vanessa did leave her husband. I supported her as a friend, but it seemed a foregone conclusion that we would be together.

Our budding relationship was challenged from the start. While Vanessa had grieved, processed, and otherwise moved on in her mind well before her second marriage ended, she wisely knew she had work to do. She needed to think things through and define what she wanted, in addition to the woman she was becoming. Hers was an amazing story. A happy-go-lucky stoner who sought to escape deep emotional pain, she married a jerk after being date raped (resulting in the loss of her virginity) shortly before they met. She had thrived and moved on in every way imaginable. She had redefined herself as a successful businesswoman and gifted healer. She had clearly outgrown two limiting relationships and was coming into the prime of her life. While simple logic dictated that she should be on her own for a while, the problem was that we had a connection on many levels that was genuine. The heart knows no simple logic.

As things progressed between us, I utilized the lessons, experience, and personal transformation of my nearly 10 years of recovery. I stepped back and looked, as objectively as possible, at the situation. No longer that previous Keith who had lacked skills and insight, I viewed the relationship as being poised at a tipping point. I felt that I still had the option of sensibly stepping back; if I continued to fall in love with this woman, it could end badly for me. Despite my new lease on life, I did not relish the idea of having my heart broken. I had a serious talk with my sponsor (no longer Vince, but my current sponsor of nearly 20 years), laying out the situation. He shared a similar experience from his own past and counseled me to "run." I thought it over and decided to follow my heart, taking a huge chance and willing to accept the consequences. My reasoning was that if I didn't take a gamble on love, I would always have to wonder, "What if... ?"

There was a fair amount of drama in our relationship—and not just because I was in it. For the first two years, she swung back and forth, pendulum-like, between desiring a relationship and being alone to focus on herself. She "ended it" more times than I can count, but we always got back together.

My operating room nursing had taken me beyond permanent affiliation with hospitals; I was working as a temporary contractor, doing three-month assignments at facilities in the region. After working six months at a lovely community hospital inside the Route 128 belt, I decided to apply to return to the hospital in my home town that had discharged me about 10 years prior. The old issues seemed to be water under the bridge as I put out feelers. The hospital was being acquired by a private owner after being city-run. I was hired and given a start date to follow three wonderful weeks off in the beautiful New England month of September.

As my time off wound down, I received some bad news from the hospital. My position was "frozen." The explanation I received from the HR specialist was that the facility had lost so much staff in the transition that there were only 17 inpatient beds, hence surgery was way down. No further information was forthcoming. This was plausible, but it was strange that the trail seemed to end there. No plans to move ahead in the future, no other information. When I called back a week later, it was suggested I "move on," which sounded totally bizarre. I later found out that a surgeon, on learning of my imminent return, had gone out of his way (as in down to HR) to prevent it. Apparently he succeeded, though I didn't hear about this for a year or two.

In the meantime, I needed to find some work, a situation that was becoming all too familiar. Temp-work options were not all that desirable. There had been a mini-boom, but that was passing. Then, from Vanessa of all people, I heard about a nursing opportunity. She had a client with a special needs son that required nursing. The family had taken to recruiting directly, so dire was their need.

This was a job I never would have dreamed of seeking out, but somehow it had found me instead. I met with the family. While the last thing on earth I would have looked to do was caring for seriously sick children, this came about in an unexpected way. I was already well established as an operating room "specialist." If you want to scare an operating room nurse, tell them they are "floating" to the nursing floors. They'll get hives and try to go home sick. The same applies to a med/surg nurse. The thought of working in the OR would strike fear into their hearts. The jobs are all nursing, but the duties are totally different and specialized.

I met with the parents and met the boy. I saw the routine of his care and realized I was perfectly capable of doing the work. It just required a different mindset and flexibility. And I had to check my ego at the door. OR had a certain prestige that pediatric homecare lacked, in title anyway. So began my career in general nursing. As a security blanket, and to balance out my work week, I found a per diem OR job one day a week.

It was at this operating room job, one day in January, that I imposed on an orthopedic surgeon with whom I'd been long acquainted for a quick "hallway consultation." I'd had pain in my right arm for weeks, and it didn't seem to be resolving. My doctor friend urged me to come to his office, and not just because I was hitting him up for a freebie (professional consideration such as this is common for nurses). He was concerned that this was more than just a strained muscle. I didn't know it at the time, but that was the last day I would work for about six months.

The next day at the doctor's office, a tug-of-war ensued. This injury seemed to be work-related, as part of my everyday duties had continually aggravated it, and likely caused it in the first place. If that was the case, it was workers' compensation, and my insurance was no good. The doctor's office needed a claim number and other details, but I still didn't even know if I was injured at that point. Only because the doctor knew me personally did he intervene and direct his staff that we would sort the billing issues out later. After examining me, he diagnosed my problem (correctly as would be borne out by an MRI) as a partially ruptured biceps tendon. In other words, the "strap" that held the big muscle of my arm to the bone was failing. He put me in a cast for four weeks. I started what rapidly turned into a fight with my employer about the work-related status of the injury.

The arm required surgery. The workers' comp issue required litigation. My surgeon and lawyer were both excellent. There was a bit more to it than that, however. Initially, I was in a confusing maze of exclusionary circumstances. My employer was acquired by another agency; hence I was on leave from nothing and worked for... nobody, on paper anyway. While the workers' comp dispute was pending, I fell through a crack in the system and had no medical insurance, because there wasn't even a company to acquire COBRA benefits from. My surgeon buddy had referred me to a specialist, who felt surgery was indicated, but wouldn't do it until workers' comp was resolved. It was frustrating and scary, and there were days when it looked really bad. It seemed there was no way out of the stalemate.

When my arm came out of the cast after four weeks, the muscles had all shrunk, and in addition to the still-present pain of the tendon, the whole arm was stiff and painful. There were some dark days emotionally, with a useless arm, and no clue about how the situation would resolve. Through sheer persistence, I found out that my old insurance company actually had a department that handled bizarre, out-of-the-box situations like mine. I contacted them and arrangements were made for coverage pending the outcome of my workers' comp claim. I had the surgery on my arm.

As with most things, there are several ways something can be done. My surgery was no exception. The specialist I saw had performed about 150 such repairs, published his results in journals, and used a rather involved procedure that was more extensive and entailed longer recovery time than alternatives. The benefit was there would be no metal pins or screws in my arm as a result. The first night, the pain was excruciating, and the prescribed medication mostly ineffective. I had to take strong medicine for a couple days, which was difficult. I hated the way it made me feel; there was a hungover quality about it.

My state of mind had suffered through the weeks, now stretching into months, that this process was dragging on. I found an attorney, and the appeal process was officially begun. Again, this had required perseverance. There had been no resources to explain how to solve my situation. There was a range of possible outcomes. If the finding was in my favor, I would receive back pay (I was running through reserve savings quickly just to pay the bills), and all medical and legal expenses would be paid. If the finding did not favor me, I would be responsible for some fairly significant medical expenses. Of course, I had way too much time to ponder the possibilities. I was feeling overwhelmed and stressed and became quite depressed.

This was a perfect storm of negative life events. I had stepped out off the proverbial ledge by leaving the operating room, and had not yet solidified my new nursing identity as a pediatric nurse. Only months into my new endeavor, my livelihood was in serious jeopardy; I was unemployed with no job to return to. I had the most debilitating physical problem I had ever faced; my arm had wasted away, and I suffered daily from pain. I had a legal dispute. Then, to complete this picture, Vanessa felt the need to first distance herself, and then exit our relationship. I had gone through some tough stretches in the past, but this was truly my dark night of the soul. It was the spring of 2002, and I never felt more alone.

I went to meetings. I sat in the back and spoke to no one. My sponsor, friends, and acquaintances grew concerned. I was in a state that could best be described as desperate, despondent, and hopeless.

~~~~~~~~~~~~~~~~~~~~~~~~~~~~~

I thought about drinking, but not as in wanting to drink. It was a different context than thinking about picking up a drink. I thought, *My circumstances must be the reasons that people decide to relapse after sobriety.* Being so overwhelmed that you think your head is going to explode, and then being even more overwhelmed...

In the moment, these times in life feel terrible. I could see no benefit, just pain, both emotional and physical. This was a bottom in my life, just as significant as the one that brought me to recovery. Reaching this point left me nowhere to go but up. Therein lay opportunity. The big picture of my life was destined to change, and only by coming to understand that I had become as spiritually debilitated as I was physically could I become willing to embrace the change. Again it took a crisis to really get my attention.

~~~~~~~~~~~~~~~~~~~~~~~~~~~~~

Time is always a factor in any healing. However, after my tangle of depression and being overwhelmed gave way to self-pity, I did not merely wait to move through it. I made a conscious effort to ask for and seek help. There was a turning point where I mindfully shifted my attitude and started to pull myself up and out of the ditch. I began to fix my broken life on every level. As soon as I got the go-head, I began physical therapy. Slowly at first, I began to condition and build back what had become a scrawny, wasted arm. Eventually graduating to the gym, I must have been quite a sight with one bulky, muscular arm, and a skinny stick of an appendage on the other side.

My workers' comp hearing loomed. I did my part, following my attorney's instructions. He sent me for an independent evaluation and had me get portions of my medical record. After doing everything I was supposed to do, it was out of my hands. On the day of the hearing, I was present, but had fairly minimal participation aside from answering a few questions. It quickly became apparent that it would turn out in my favor. The attorney for the workers' comp insurer even apologized for my trouble after learning the details of the case. About six months after I presented at the doctor's office with a painful arm, the matter was finally resolved. After putting me through the ringer, the system ultimately worked.

During the dark months of my injury, Vanessa had to step away from our relationship. Knowing how sensitive to people's energy she was, I understood this at some level. She was also working through her own growing process, raising her children, and moving forward professionally. Over time in her life (and forward to the present day), steady growth and personal transformation defined her; that was always part of my attraction to her. In the year plus that we had known each other, she had become my best friend. I struggled through a period of figurative kicking and screaming and finally began to resolve the loss of our relationship. I still cared deeply about her. I still loved her. I had to let go of her.

As I mindfully shifted my circumstances and began to heal on all levels, I did finally release Vanessa in my mind and heart. As my body and mind got better, so did my spirit. Likely, it was my spirit that actually began to heal first. I walked or rode my mountain bike every day during the spring of my arm's rehabilitation. I began to shift my focus from survival mode up the scale, back to the bigger picture. Finally beginning to put too many hours of idle time to some constructive purpose, I made some decisions about where I wanted my life to go.

After I had made a physical and psychic shift and had come to a place of acceptance of my circumstances, something unexpected happened. Vanessa, who had spent weeks, months actually, wanting nothing to do with me, came back into my life. I had changed, or perhaps I had been changed. Whatever the case, we began anew and built on the foundation we had started. I was tremendously grateful for the profound learning experience and felt she had come into my life to teach me things.

As my arm healed, I had to next consider my options for returning to work. I had stepped outside the comfortable specialization of the operating room, but had not established myself, at least in my own mind, as anything else. I could have run back to the security of what I knew, but chose instead to continue on the path I had started when my injury interrupted me. I went back to pediatrics, applying to the company that had absorbed the one I worked for previously. This took me places that I wouldn't have imagined only a year prior.

As earlier described, nurses like the security of their specialty. There is a reassuring safety in the drudgery of routine. The confines of the comfort zone are the rule, not the exception in medicine. So, if I had been told (as an OR nurse) that I would one day be caring for a premature infant on a ventilator after he was transferred home from the ICU of Boston Children's Hospital, I would not have believed it. In some other universe, maybe... but that's what I was doing by the following summer.

I spent several years doing pediatric nursing, moving from case to case, child to child, family to family. This was a tremendously beneficial experience that changed me, not only as a nurse, but also as a man. For the families I worked with, nothing had gone according to plan. The arrival of a child with an obvious birth defect, or manifestation of a serious disability early on, meant life as they knew and expected it would be changing forever. Witnessing the dynamics of families as they handled varying degrees of adversity, the tribulations of a special-needs child, taught me things that my upbringing had not. I came to understand that unconditional love is normal for a parent, not exceptional. This cast a new light on my past.

Vanessa and I had been through a lot, and as we were together for a couple years, we began to invest some serious effort toward mending our often turbulent relationship. Things became so calm in fact that I proposed marriage around Christmas 2003. Unfortunately, the mere absence of turmoil did not mean we were ready to tie the knot. Our engagement and relationship unraveled in fewer than five months. Though her kids were just not ready for her to marry for a third time, the fact that she'd never really had time to be on her own seemed the heart of the matter. The few months apart while I was injured weren't a substitute for a significant chance to process and heal herself and her children from their previous decade. It was more about timing than compatibility. Within a couple of months the spark was gone. She told me what I already knew—that we couldn't get married.

I was really depressed for a time. I threw myself into my program and my fledgling exploration of alternative healing. It was during this timeframe that I went to a shaman. Shamanism is healing in a spiritual context and common to many different cultures worldwide. This shaman was a woman who could have been anyone's next-door neighbor, except that she had studied tribal medicine in Central America for several years. Initially, I went to her to heal. I continued out of desire for enlightenment. She instructed me to read and write on certain subjects and to eat certain foods, sensing my deficiencies. She also did meditative processes with me, and told me things about my "soul" that made sense of so much of my life to that point. She told me that I am, among other things, a "storyteller." The thought of writing a book first came to me in this timeframe.

During the next few years, I dabbled in other areas of nursing. My breaking out of the OR mold had set a precedent. If I could do basic nursing with sick kids, what else could I do? I sampled working with dialysis and IV therapy. After about five years I returned to the OR, big city, medical-center style. However, the OR had lost its luster, so it was back to working with kids. After trying something new, I tended to go back to something familiar. Next was nursing at an outpatient methadone clinic. There I learned more about the mainstream medical perspective on addictions, and that mainstream medicine was not interested in fresh perspectives. While sad, this was a useful experience. I wasn't happy about it, but it was important to know where things stood.

I moved on to tenure with a facility-based hospice that recruited me based on my now broader experience. This seemed to bring me full-circle from the realization that I had a huge capacity for empathy, which had moved me toward nursing in the first place. Caring for patients and families around the time of death is both a privilege and a challenge. Hospice is a calling in which the clinical nurse is a combination of all relevant disciplines, in addition to being a bottomless well of compassion. To be effective in this specialty requires critical thinking on numerous levels simultaneously and a diverse knowledge base encompassing everything from gerontology to wound care to cardiology to pain management. The effective hospice nurse is not usually a fresh-faced kid right out of nursing school; experience in both nursing and life is requisite. Hospice also further educated me to a bigger picture of service-based reimbursement, the true driving force behind our healthcare system. Later with this same company, I moved to an administrative position in a quality assessment/performance improvement role. In essence, this made the company my patient, as I was responsible for auditing and reporting on all patient-centered activities.

In the following years, I continued to move around, still dabbling. I had been through a brief and distasteful experience working in the state mental health system, a brief and distasteful experience working for a large home-health company, and a brief but positive experience teaching at an established career school. After returning to special-needs children for a year, I was recruited by the same small, private psych hospital that specialized in addictions/rehab that had been unable to schedule me as a per diem 16 years prior. After 16 years in nursing, I felt like I had found my home! My now considerable and diverse experience, alternative perspective on health care and recovery, and my personal recovery had prepared me well for this opportunity.

If my life and experiences were routine, conventional, or ordinary, this book would end here. After pulling myself out of the sea of alcohol, making my way in recovery and life, and resolving some of life's larger questions, I had found my true calling—working with people struggling with diseases of addiction. Unfortunately, what initially felt like a happy ending proved otherwise. My personal recovery since my 10th anniversary had plateaued. No longer driven, no longer hungry, I experienced an insidious self-satisfaction that was indistinguishable from complacency.

Categorically, I still never thought about drinking... but other more subtle forms of rot began to undermine my foundation. Meeting attendance slowly dialed back, and I turned into a critic at some point. I judged what I heard and the people who said it. I ceased to identify with the disease of alcoholism, and addiction in a broader sense. Though I had somehow become a different person than the one who drank, this person was a man I am not proud of. The self-absorption returned. The air of superiority based on insecurity returned. There was a new self-righteousness. In short, I developed new character defects, or old ones came back. I lost touch with my sponsor for weeks, even months at a time. We literally did not connect, even on the phone, for three months in the winter and spring of 2012, the timeframe that I started at the psych hospital.

The outer world had sent me the message that I had paid my dues and had finally arrived. Or, that's how I chose to interpret it. I had my dream job, and after a couple of months, I felt comfortable with my new routine and responsibilities. A sense of entitlement was now added to the aforementioned character defects. What I lacked was a sense of purpose, a compass. Where I had once been dedicated to a way of being that revolved around something greater than me, I was becoming more and more Keith-centric. Through the summer, my meeting attendance declined precipitously.

The last straw came in August in the form of a beautiful redhead. I saw in her only what I wanted to see—the woman of my dreams. While she initially sent mixed messages, I received only the ones that suited me. Widowed for less than a year, she deserved the benefit of the experience and sensitivity of which I should have been fully capable. Instead, I utterly failed. It was like both my common sense and my hard-learned knowledge had been deleted. First, I failed to understand what should have been obvious; she was confused. Second, I failed miserably as a gentleman. I became first demanding, then badgering. Eventually, she called me on this in no uncertain terms, a brutal and total rejection.

Again, and for the third time in about two decades, I needed a catastrophe (or what felt like one) to get my attention. It was like a mirror had abruptly been held up for me to see the monster I had become. It was about much more than a woman's rejection. She was merely the catalyst for a long-overdue gut check. The natural compassion, empathy, understanding, and selflessness that I had worked so hard to develop and enhance in early recovery weren't even running on vapors. The tank was utterly empty. At least I could admit it. I saw it clearly, and it felt devastating. I was profoundly distressed, and deeply disappointed in myself.

So, I made a decision. I made a decision with as much intensity, power, and energy as my decision to stop drinking 21 years prior. I decided to change.

I started with my sponsor. I went to see him for the first time in months, and I told him everything. I was absolutely ashamed, but I had to be honest. I left nothing out. Not only did I begin going to meetings daily, but I brought a completely different attitude. I was attentive and focused, while humble and receptive. I returned to the psychologist I'd not visited in more than a year, seeing him numerous times in a matter of a few weeks. I was openly asking for and accepting help. I was thinking differently and doing things differently.

More than ever before, I realized I had a choice in how I lived my life. On an almost daily basis I meditated. In these meditations, I released my pain, shame, and suffering. I began to rewire my thoughts, attitudes, and beliefs. Slowly I became the change I set my mind and heart on. There could be no going back. In the course of hundreds of meditations, I steadily became a different Keith. While I had never fully reverted to the man that drank, I began to recognize those negative emotions, character defects, and old behaviors in the moment. I would stop myself in real time, and choose to be different, consciously becoming an upgraded version of myself.

The people in my life began to observe this. My sponsor observed this. The psychologist observed this. My spark returned. My passion for recovery and life was evident and stronger and more intense than ever before. I began to seek out and draw new experiences, and my energy grew more positive. My recovery program became supercharged, and I attended workshops on personal transformation and healing. I began to eat, drink, breathe, and live recovery. My work was all about recovery, and I focused intensely on passing on principles for change that I have come to believe in supremely.

Since that third bottom, I have worked unceasingly. On a daily basis, I work my basic AA program. Just as important, I mindfully practice an intentional form of personal transformation, an additional layer, which more than enhances my recovery. It sustains that recovery. I have so much to be grateful for. I was a man who could not go a day without a drink, and today I don't even think about drinking. I have meaningful work that feels completely in tune with my real life's purpose. I draw on my connection to everything at the most fundamental level as a source of strength and guidance, and also as the energy that perpetuates and makes possible ongoing change. Change is the most important thing in my life today, and I want to improve constantly. My recovery is now like a perpetual motion machine, and I strive daily to make that recovery continually more sustainable.

My recovery continued to inspire me, and inspired me to continue. By the summer of 2013, it was finally time to sit down and write.

Part III

Old Worlds, New World

"All truth passes through three stages. First, it is ridiculed. Second, it is violently opposed. Third, it is accepted as being self-evident."

~ Arthur Schopenhauer

CHAPTER 14

The Three Worlds of My Existence

I was a man who could not go a day without a drink.

While this way of life carries a severe price physically and emotionally, the spiritual cost is potentially fatal. Though more subtle, the spiritual price is no less significant. Because such things are less tangible, they might seem less immediate. The broad category of spirituality, encompassing that part of us that is the domain of mind and consciousness, ultimately influences and controls every aspect of us. In the context of recovery, it cannot be ignored. Though much of our daily experience suggests to the contrary, every part of our physical and emotional selves is controlled by what we believe. To truly recover, we must come to terms with spirituality.

Let's not automatically equate spirituality with God, religion, or anything remotely rigid, structured, or cumbersome. For the moment, all I'm saying is that there is a bigger picture than everyday life would suggest. If I'm trapped in a box of addiction, eventually, I need to look for out-of-the-box solutions. At a basic level, alcoholism and addiction are about me and the world. Just as I looked to something from the outside world to change my inner world in my state of addiction, I needed something outside me to recover.

As I sought escape from my world that alcohol afforded, I had slowly painted my life into a corner. A long series of choices and consequences, each one leading to the next, changed my life into something I never intended or wanted. I didn't see or understand the small changes from one day to the next. Like a snowball rolling downhill, gathering more weight and momentum as it travels, my life tumbled toward the inevitable result. My drinking brought me to a bottom. However, what seemed disastrous at the time ultimately made me a profoundly different and much happier man.

Taking a drink or using any mind-altering drug changed my experience of the world. It not only changed how the world felt in the moment, but also changed the external world. Whether intentional or not, controlling the world within me and the outside world around me had the same result. My mood, level of consciousness, and awareness were altered. The short- and long-term impact on my environment (and the people in it) was negatively affected whenever I introduced a chemical substance into my system. My health was negatively affected. My spirituality was most certainly negatively affected, because it never even developed. I went way beyond the point of any kind of harmless or benign social drinking.

Like most people, it took a crisis to get my attention. My survival had to be threatened before I would become willing to make the necessary changes. In the beginning, fear of consequences was my prime motivator.

I continued putting one foot in front of the other, doing the work, and learning the lessons of recovery. As the figurative paint of that corner I had painted myself into began to dry, it seemed as if options in life began to open up. I began to change my inner world. As a result, the outer world also began to change. I worked the Steps. First gaining knowledge of them, and then reinforcing that knowledge with experiences, I slowly attained something resembling wisdom in some everyday areas. Over time, I started to develop insight, but the revelation that the outside world responded to my inner state did not immediately register.

The changes in my world began to present as opportunities. My general desire had been to work in service to others, and that took the form of nursing. As these opportunities were manifested, one leading to the next, two things happened while I wasn't even paying attention or thinking about it. I began amassing knowledge and insight into healthcare in a wide variety of areas. This practical knowledge related to how people get well and stay healthy on an everyday basis. I became entrenched in that Western medical healthcare model. However, I was also on the front lines of a delivery system that I was starting to look at from a new perspective. As recovery became the driving force in my life, my livelihood became subject to the larger questions that my recovery continually raised. In short, I was becoming accountable.

Those larger questions, sometimes referred to as the perennial questions, had been coming up almost since the day I got sober. Why are we here? What is my life's purpose? What is the true nature and real meaning of being human? Where do we come from? Where do we go? How did all this get here?

Occasionally waxing philosophical at meetings, I found that most people wanted to "keep it simple." My verbal meanderings, shared at meetings in the form of thoughts relating to the larger questions, drew little visible identification. The response felt more negative, varying from the snarky "keep coming," right up to laughter and, sadly, mockery. This was discouraging, but I persevered. In fact, some of the negative reactions I encountered stimulated incredibly valuable growth experiences. Pondering issues such as the need for approval versus integrity to my own feelings and personal process had tremendous worth, as did sharing these things with my sponsor and some personal mentors. As time passed, I realized that I was onto some things that fell out of the mainstream of Alcoholics Anonymous.

As I initially became interested in alternative healing, I gave myself to the learning process. Quite uncharacteristically, I seldom questioned the background of the knowledge and skills I was acquiring. I was usually all about analysis. The concepts seemed to have no relationship to my "day job." I earned my associate's degree in Polarity Therapy, took seminars in Extragenesis, Quantum Touch, and Reconnective Healing, and spent months seeing a shaman of the Mesoamerican tradition every few weeks. Looking back, disregarding my natural inclination for analysis was of benefit to integrating a holistic approach into my way of being. The questioning would have interfered with the doing.

Along with the studies of healing techniques came exposure to new philosophies and belief systems. Polarity therapy endorses a universal energy "circuit," emanating from a "source," and moving through space in a circular shape that I inferred was more or less toroidal, similar to a doughnut. Later, and independent of my polarity training, the idea of universal energy as a torus was reaffirmed by numerous other sources.

The powerful work of psychiatrist Dr. Brian Weiss states a compelling case that we are indeed eternal beings. Whether we use the term consciousness, spirits, or souls, the idea that we are more than the brief human lives we lead made sense to me. The work of medical intuitive and educator Dr. Caroline Myss gives further definition to us as spiritual beings with a life's purpose of learning spiritual lessons within the framework of karma. With the shaman, I explored the history and specific archetypes of my own spiritual journey, shedding much light on some of the quirks of my personality as well as a context for the way my life had unfolded.

These were some interesting ideas, but I was not sensing any particular relationship. The different areas of my life including Twelve-Step recovery, mainstream medicine, and the notion of humans as energy-based beings with greater spiritual circumstance seemed linked only by virtue of my interest in them. Otherwise, there was nothing binding these divergent and even mutually exclusive subjects. There was no logical interrelationship. And, of course, my notions made for dinner conversation that could cause a date to start looking at her watch halfway through the meal.

I was trying to organize my worldview, and the missing ingredient in this stew of ideas was something to bind them. Numerous books on alternative-related topics ranging from revisionist history, prophecy, consciousness, mysticism, and even quantum physics enlightened me, but failed to provide the unifying overview I wanted. Finally, I stumbled on spirituality and science researcher Lynne McTaggart's *The Field: The Quest for the Secret Force of the Universe*. There was something absolutely compelling about this work, and not just the Star Wars-sounding name. It was a fact-based, journalistic case for the existence of an all-encompassing matrix of energetic reality; we exist within this and are part of it. Abstracting the ideas this book puts forth, the miraculous becomes explicable. The book details scientific discoveries, often inadvertent, that defy the conventional understanding of the way things work. When viewed as something not yet fully understood, the miraculous becomes part of the possible, less inexplicable. Things beyond that which can be measured, classified, defined, and otherwise explained within the framework of our five-sense reality became part of the fabric of my belief system. The different and opposing worldviews, indeed the different worlds I was simultaneously living in, began to work together. Not only did they merely work together, they created synergy. Together, these different worlds of my understanding were greater than the sum of their parts.

The world was different than I had believed it to be. My amazing recovery, transformation, and way of being were the products of my combining three different worlds, indeed three different models of reality. The old, standard model world of our common understanding and agreement was home to the "previous Keith." In that world, I drank to the brink of destruction and spiritual bankruptcy. The spiritual world, with unexplainable faith and power greater than me, was home to the highest ideal of me, the Keith of my dreams. To bring the Keith of my dreams from the spiritual world to the real world, I needed to pass through the third world, which is the world of infinite possibility. In that still largely unexplored third world, nature and the universe support both the spirit and its energy, which manifests as our earthly reality.

In this third world lies sustainable recovery.

We are not really people who are divided in thirds, each one living in a different world. Think of each of the three worlds as an idea about how things work. Each person has his own way of being; his particular allocation of emphasis to these different worlds defines him. Many people live entirely in the first world, because that's how we're brought up to believe things are. People with deep faith and/or religious beliefs live in both the first and second worlds. Sometimes the two worlds don't fit well together. More people are starting to acknowledge and embrace the third world. I like that it explains how the other two worlds can both be, but most of all, I like the idea that I exist in the third world as not insignificant, not all-powerful, but just as a part that is connected to everything else. By thinking in terms of three worlds, I organize my understanding of the big picture, especially as it affects recovery.

The First World

The Real World: Seeing Is Believing

This is the purely physical world. We were born into it, schooled in it, and conditioned to it. This is the world that makes sense, where everything fits together. We believe things in this world because we experience them with our own senses. From our earliest memories, we are oriented to the environment through our five senses, and to experience this world, we see, hear, feel, taste, and smell it.

First our parents, then later society condition us. We are socialized, then educated, and then socialized some more. We are assimilated and become members of society. We learn how to be human
beings by watching other human beings, and by doing more or less
what they do. From a young age, we are compelled to get onboard
with the program of how the real world works. Young children are
encouraged to develop their imaginations with "make-believe." Implicit in the mere idea of make-believe is the condition that it's not
real, but rather an indulgence the world allows young, developing
minds. Children must be taught the difference between make-believe
and the real world. How else could they function (in the real world)?
At a young age, we are instructed that there is no magic. We are
taught that magic is something magicians do with smoke and mir-
rors. Their tricks are simply well-protected trade secrets. There is no
Santa Claus, Easter Bunny, or tooth fairy; they are fictional contriv-
ances for the amusement of children and adults alike. Ghosts, haunt-
ed houses, the supernatural, UFOs, the Loch Ness monster, and Big-
foot are also fictional.

On the upside, we usually know what to expect, so our expectations are frequently met. The superficial sense of well-being that accompanies met expectations works for many people much of the
time.

On the downside, it is a sad fact that we are pressured both subtly
and unsubtly to conform to, rather than question, authority. The authority structure in all its manifestations, from family to institutions
to governments, both local and national, is a built-in part of that first
world. We are part of an authority structure where people basically
know their places. We are members of families and communities, we
live in neighborhoods, we work for organizations, and we know who
we are and where we stand in relationship to all these things in a
kind of hierarchy. In the areas without this kind of structure, we run
into problems, quickly moving from the laws of society to the "law
of the jungle."

The concept of "normal" is heavily encouraged, deviating from
the norm discouraged. The nail that sticks out is the one that gets
hammered down. Though authority generally comes from above, we
also police ourselves laterally. How do we treat our rugged individuals, those who march to the beat of their own drum? We make it
tough not to conform. Consider the person who chooses to be a little

different from the majority. As an example, a young man might choose to express his individuality by wearing spiky punk hair, perhaps bright orange in a Mohawk cut. Perhaps he likes piercings and tattoos and dresses in leather with studs and jackboots. As this young man walks down the street, some good old boys driving by in their pickup truck roll down the window and share with the young man their opinion of his appearance. They insult him. This kind of negativity discourages nonconformity. It takes courage to be a "rugged individual."

In the above illustration, most alcoholics would identify with the young individual. It matters not whether we agree with his fashion preference. The whole concept of our addiction brings us into a type of underlying opposition with the rest of the world. Before we even have our first drink, we exist every moment as individuals constantly bending our wills and desires to the realities and rules of the real world. This relationship is often at the root of our drinking, as we give ourselves the illusion of control by altering our perception. Something outside us to control what's inside us... Unspoken and unacknowledged, the effort of existence is a moment-to-moment challenge, and we seldom even think about it. We become so conditioned to reality that we don't question it anymore. Drinking, alcoholism, and addiction in general are often the side effects of a desire to disengage from this real first world.

In this world, we are focused on "stuff." We like our stuff solid (although liquid and gases are acceptable), observable, and measurable. We are materialists. No, not in the sense of wanting bigger cars and houses, but rather by focusing on the material surroundings in which we exist, that is, the real world. Thinking about stuff is okay, but touching it is better.

How did we come to be this way? Our whole way of looking at things in the physical world is owed largely to that pioneer of science, Sir Isaac Newton. If you have enough information, that is, mass, velocity, trajectory, opposing forces, etc., everything can be explained and predicted based on its physical properties. What has come to be known as the Newtonian Model defines the modern world.

Newton applied observations of the world around him to formulate principles and scientific laws that seemed to apply to the world and universe beyond. Using a telescope and a new type of mathematics, both of his own invention, Newton discovered the true nature of our solar system, and also a conception of the universe that was accepted until theoretical physicist Albert Einstein modified it 300 years later. Newton's ideas about motion, gravity, optics, and celestial mechanics became the paradigm for science as we still know it today. He's the one you can blame if you ever took calculus. Our understanding of the world and everything in it is based on chemistry, the foundation of which is the Newtonian Model. Our understanding of the human body is based on genetics, which is based on chemistry, which is based on the Newtonian Model.

In this Newtonian Model–based real world, we are the products of our genetic codes, which were inherited from the combination of our parents' genetic codes. This tells me that since my mother died of the ravages of alcoholism and was unable to get sober, and my father was nearly bald by his mid-30s and emotionally abnormal, that I am doomed to drink myself to death in the next five years (I'll need to hurry), should have a shiny head (nope!), and lack emotional intelligence (okay, depends on who you ask). Our genetic destiny should be our life's destiny.

In this first-world concept, we are only machines of flesh and blood. We are switched on at birth, switched off at death. We come from nothing but our component chemical compounds, and in the end we go back to our component chemical compounds. This is the strictly materialist perspective. There is even a special name for the philosophy of the Newtonian Model: scientific materialism.

Around the Newtonian Model have sprung the current ideas about medicine. I refer to our system as the Western medical pharmaceutical/medical device/insurance-based industrial complex, because it has become a massive, self-perpetuating entity. Modern medicine, in what we call the civilized world, emphasizes a chemical and mechanical approach to health that is based in the first-world concept of cause and effect. Some disease or injury "causes" a problem, or "effect." Modern medicine provides some type of intervention, or another effect to cancel, negate, or repair the bad effect. This usually involves a pharmaceutical substance, a chemical, to solve the problem, or a mechanical correction, or both. A mechanical correction would involve cutting out or excising the diseased part, or physically modifying something, like setting a broken bone.

The miracle of modern fracture management aside, the chemical/mechanical approach has the major limitation of treating something that is a symptom, or effect of something else, something underlying. In other words the horse is already out of the barn, so to speak. Think of a broken leg as a side-effect of skiing...

Modern healthcare uses Newtonian principles of chemistry and physics to restore optimum health in a material sense. So, as materialists, we want to define things by assigning them properties. We want things to have measurable physical characteristics, such as dimensions and weight. Things should be located somewhere in our physical space. And things need to exist in a timeframe, be it past, present, or future.

Don't get me wrong. There is much about the material world to love, and I love much about it. Our modern age is wonderful, and a lot of what we take for granted would seem miraculous by the standards of any bygone era. It is only through the blessings of the modern age that I am able to move beyond the level of survival, or subsistence living, to ponder those larger questions that I mentioned earlier. The answers to those perennial questions lie outside the material or real world. I cannot find answers to questions that lie outside the material world, if I limit myself to thinking like a materialist.

Before scientific materialism, there was religious monotheism. There was a slow transition from one to the other, as religious monotheists had a tendency to burn scientific materialists at the stake for disagreeing with them. Initially, the materialists were deferential (terrified). They said they would only concern themselves with the material world, or that which could be seen, heard, felt, smelled, or tasted.

The religious establishment was, of course, concerned with matters of God, the spirit, and the unseen, and churches ran the world for centuries. As the paradigm shifted, religion was grandfathered into the real world and occupies its own small box, which is kept in a dark corner. It doesn't go away, but the materialists, remembering how mean religion was to them early on, wish it would. While it's tolerated, it has been meticulously excised from governance in the majority of civilized nations under the provisions of separation of church and state. In the academic sector, the highest echelon of scientific materialism, personal practice of religious freedom is tolerated, but any leakage of faith into the professional arena is not tolerated today. The mention of creationism, for example, can get a scientist blacklisted.

It was in this first world that we became addicted, and against this backdrop that we come into recovery. The real world has trained us that we need something in our environment, something outside us, to change how we feel inside. In order to break the cycle of addiction, we need to move beyond that real-world conditioning. We have the innate capacity within us to bring about change and move beyond what we've been led to believe our limitations are. The epidemic of alcoholism and addiction is a real, material-world problem. We set out to control our mood chemically, cause and effect. The long-term damage—physical and emotional dependence and their consequences—are also the result of cause and effect. It is not possible to reverse that addictive cause-and-effect relationship from within the addictive state. Just as we put something external into us to alter our state, we must look externally to solve our addiction problem.

The mind that creates a problem is not capable of solving it, so that mind must become greater. The mind that became diseased with addiction in the real world needs to look beyond for answers to basic and larger questions. The principles of cause and effect no longer apply, and merely seeing is not enough to believe.

The Second World

The Spiritual World: Believing Is Believing

At the end of a busy day of sensory-based, cause-and-effect activity in the real world, there is nothing better than coming home and:

A. Flipping on the TV and being passively entertained by reality-based singing competitions with celebrity judge panels, or reruns of *Friends* or *Seinfeld*.
B. Chemically altering my mood with alcohol and/or drugs in a futile attempt to suppress that sensory-based, cause-and-effect world, avoid processing emotions, and postpone dealing with my problems.
C. Both A and B above.

D. Ponder the nature of my infinite consciousness in relationship to the larger questions, that is, what is my life's purpose, the nature of existence, and how did we get here?

If you answered A, B, or C, thank you for reading up to this point. You might find this book useful as a door stopper or for propping open a window. Please remember where you left it, should you ever decide that you want an amazing life, completely free of the ball and chain of addiction. If you answered D, please continue reading about the second world we inhabit, the world of the spiritual, religious, and other beliefs.

The spiritual world ultimately is the place we go seeking answers to the larger questions. What is our true place in this unfathomably immense universe? Where do we come from, and (more important) where do we go? What happens when we die? Is this all there is? And if so (and if not), what was it for? These are the issues of religions, belief systems, and of broader, general spirituality. These matters are not measurable. They don't have dimensions, locations, weight, or (finite, at least) timeframes. These second-world things are only ideas. However, they are ideas connected to experience and strong emotions to the point where they become something greater. These ideas have become beliefs, and therein lays the power of this world. The second world of belief is absolutely as real as the measurable world of cause and effect, the first world.

The predominant belief system and driving force in the second world is called religious monotheism, the belief in one god or deity. In three major religious traditions, a god named Yahweh is thought to be the supreme being and creator of the universe and everything in it.

Judaism, Christianity, and Islam all share the same god, but do not observe the same way. Each has distinctly different perspectives about history, practice, and the relationship between God and man. They share the idea that that we are created in the image of our god. Furthermore, God is a paternal or fatherly figure.

My early notions of this supreme-being God were of a powerful man, definitely appearing older than me, who had a fatherly presence. For some reason, he also had long hair and big beard, kind of like Charlton Heston in *The Ten Commandments*. He sat on a throne in the clouds, overseeing the day-to-day operations of the universe.

Our "one god" culture was preceded by the idea of polytheism or multiple gods. The civilizations of the Roman, Greek, and Egyptian empires believed in many gods. These gods also had purposes: the god of war, the goddess of love, etc. Going back to the beginning of recorded history, gods were on Earth, part of everyday life. At some point they withdrew, and as they seemed to "consolidate" into one god, the hidden/supernatural element became part of the notion of God.

The idea of faith is primary to religion. Faith is strong belief, loyalty, and trust in one's god. Worship is a big part of religion, and with it the idea that we are small and God is big.

Central and common to religions and some spiritual belief systems is the notion that they are supernatural. That is, that there are invisible forces beyond the five senses of the observable universe responsible for the workings of the religion or belief system. We don't know how it works, but it does. That's where faith comes in.

What place does religion occupy in the lives of the religious? And what purpose does it serve? In our Western culture, there is a wide range of levels of devotion. To my parents, for example, their religious affiliation was little more than a label, identification with a larger group. They were nonpracticing. To others, religion is a part of their everyday lives, in addition to being a source of inspiration and strength. This is the highest ideal of belief, and the true meaning of the second world in our lives. Wouldn't we want that second world to somehow enhance our lives? To make the first world feel warmer? Wouldn't we want it to give our lives in the five-sense, cause-and-effect world something akin to a sense of meaning? As entertaining as *Seinfeld* reruns can be, don't we want something more at the end of the day?

We do. We want those larger questions answered. Where do we come from, and where do we go?

The current top religion, Christianity, and the up-and-coming Islam both endorse the notion of an afterlife. For living by faithful observance to the religion, believers will be rewarded by spending the rest of eternity with God. This, of course, is subject to interpretation, and the promise of salvation was historically leveraged toward living an obedient life within the existing power structure (that ever-present first-world aspect), especially with Christianity.

Separation of church and state is contemporary. It's a relatively new idea that government and religion should not be enmeshed. As the Christian church of Rome transitioned through the early centuries AD, monarchs with the "God-given right" to rule maintained close relationships with the church. Through history, life was often difficult for the masses, and unless you were part of that small percentage born to nobility, there weren't a lot of options. Really, the only possibility for upward mobility was through the church. The resulting relationship between the church and leadership was about maintaining the balance of power. The general public was heavily encouraged to love God, be loyal to the king, and pay taxes. And tithes (church donations).

The word of God was transmitted from scripture, through the church, and ultimately reached the people. Prior to the 15th century and the advent of printing, no one had a personal copy of the Bible. Scripture, and written works, were not for the masses. The relating and interpretation of scripture, of "God's word," was exclusively in the hands of the clergy, essentially middlemen, who were part of the power structure. Hence, maintaining the status quo was certainly served by the living of a good Christian life. Eternal salvation was the carrot dangling on the stick. Eternal damnation was the penalty for failure. The big limitation was that you had one life, one chance.

Two major Eastern religions, Hinduism and Buddhism, believe in reincarnation, the concept that after physically dying, the soul or spirit moves on to another existence. More recently, many Western people have started to think along these lines, and the idea is part of the so-called New Age philosophy.

This belief system supports the idea that we are eternal consciousness, or spirits or souls, having a transient human experience. One aspect of this is that our earthly lives are a kind of spiritual kindergarten in which we are learning lessons and gaining experience. The real test lies in the fact of our unawareness of the bigger picture, that the human situations we negotiate and resolve are just that, tests. A sort of firewall exists between the conscious memory of accumulated experience and the current incarnation's personality and life. When push comes to shove in our human existence, we might not handle things the same way if we knew that it was just another day in soul school. The true test and real lesson comes from what happens when we believe we are playing for all the marbles.

Karma is the second-world's version of cause and effect, that what goes around, comes around. In the context of reincarnation, our behaviors and actions, both good and bad, have effects throughout our lives, and even from one life to the next. Particular and strong emphasis is placed on the taking of life, and the notion of living and dying "by the sword." If I take another's life, my life will eventually be similarly taken, even if it's in another lifetime. These beliefs give a strong emphasis on self-preservation to the Golden Rule: Do unto others as you would have them do unto you.

As eternal spirits incarnate as human beings, it stands to reason that the lesson, or challenge, might be to come to some state of grace with these larger questions. The latest thinking, and even research, would have us choose the lives we come into on the basis of the challenges the lives will manifest. You don't like your life? Too bad, you chose it. So, if the older, wiser souls choose the more challenging lives, it starts to put those special-needs children I've worked with into perspective. They are the oldest souls in the room, having chosen to experience lives locked inside crippled bodies that are wracked with numerous seizures all day long.

Through much of history, religious experience has been about conflict. Sadly, much of man's inhumanity toward man has been rooted in religious differences. Human nature at its lowest denominator, as opposed to highest spiritual ideas, seems to win out. In today's world, there are many incredibly complex problems rooted in history and social/political/economical issues, but the real bottom line is that someone thinks his or her invisible friend is better than someone else's invisible friend. The second world is absolutely real all right. Anyone in the Middle East or Northern Ireland will tell you.

For me, the second world became real the Sunday morning in 1991 when I had that extraordinary, inexplicable experience at the big AA meeting. Then it took me years to sift through the possibilities, ultimately arriving at my personal belief system through experience. The information that I was given reached me in just the manner it needed to.

Understanding that I fell into the category of *spiritual, not religious*, I felt it only right to modestly educate myself about the religions I was essentially ruling out as, pardon the expression, gospel. Having done so from a place of objectivity, my faith has become firmly based in something not religious, not gender-based, not the conception of the human mind... but rather something more nature-based and elemental. Looking beyond the first and second worlds for a source, and for a place where these worlds can exist together coherently, I needed something else. I was comfortable in believing, but I needed more than simple belief for its own sake. I needed more than merely seeing, definitely more than merely believing. To answer those larger questions, I was going to need a whole other world to believe in.

The Third World

The Quantum World: Believing Is Seeing

After the material world of our everyday lives and reality (the real world), and after the world of religion and belief systems (the spirit world), what's left? Those two worlds would seem to account for everything. The cause-and-effect foundation of everyday living that we rarely ponder is where our needs, basic and otherwise, are met. As soon as we do begin to ponder the questions of our origins, destiny, and general existence, the seemingly limitless bounty of spiritual perspectives is where we move to. The options are kind of "either/or"; we're in one world or the other.

The standard Twelve-Step model of recovery, as with life in general, suggests that I integrate those two worlds. By incorporating a spiritual basis for everyday living, I can stay sober one day at a time. Reliance for guidance and strength from the second world keeps me sober and reasonably happy in the first world. But...

There are limitations, conditions, and exclusions. As with the fine print in a contract or the list of possible side effects with a medication, the promises don't come with any guarantees of a successful intended outcome. The biggest stipulation is that recovery is time-limited, or contingent on the maintenance of a spiritual condition. In other words, I'm the same person, different day. I could start each day with the same untreated alcoholism as the previous day. I need to say my prayers and ask for help (spiritual world), go to a meeting and call my sponsor (real world), and basically do things differently than I did when I was in the throes of addiction. The operative word is "do," doing something different.

What I'm proposing, and what's worked for me, is to "be" someone different. It naturally follows that if I am different, that I will do different things. I'm not talking about "fake it 'til you make it." I'm not talking about the power of positive thinking, and I'm not just talking about mind over matter. Well, maybe a little mind over matter, but it's really much, much more than that.

There is one more "world." Unlike the previous two worlds discussed, this world is inclusive of the others. The first world and the second world are mutually exclusive, more or less, oil and water at best. You need to shake things up to make them go together. This third world, not a reference to underdeveloped nations, is actually the world in which the other two exist. This world is the raw building material of the first world. In this third world, the miraculous and supernatural of the second world are rational, even commonplace. This world is the fabric of our reality; in it resides the creative intelligence that is the essence of all life and all nature; this world is the underlying, invisible foundation of the entire universe.

Yes indeed, this might come as a bold revelation. It wasn't on the six o'clock news. We didn't learn this in school. It's not common knowledge. Remember, it doesn't fit into the scheme of the first world. The first world is part of the third world, not vice versa.

There is an all-encompassing, energetic field, matrix, or medium that makes up the basis of everything we know about reality. Through this field, everything is connected. Everything! Because of this field, and the fact that everything is connected, the notion of space, particularly distance, is not what we were taught. As it applies to this field, the concept of time is not what we are accustomed to, that is, past into present into future. And very importantly, the state of matter—the physical material (including us) that everything is made from, is not the finite, concrete way it appears. Rather, everything is only one possibility from a limitless set of possibilities. The world, indeed the universe, is not remotely what we have been conditioned and accustomed to.

So the idea occurs to me: if I can recover in a reality that is free from the limitations of time and space, where I have limitless potential, wouldn't I choose that world over the one where I am subject to endless cause and effect? The single most profound aspect of this world is the apparent relationship between it and our consciousness (spirits or souls). There is a curious, mystifying, even paradoxical element at work here. Either our consciousness is a part of The Field, or The Field exists within our consciousness. Either way, there is a profound chicken/egg relationship at work.

Unfortunately, I'm not a physicist. I'm just someone who has read a few good books, and listened to some brilliant people explaining some complicated things in a basic way. The principle that works for me is that I don't have to completely understand how something works in order to benefit from it. The Apollo astronauts were not designers, engineers, technicians, or builders. They were pilots. They didn't conceive, design, engineer, or build the spacecraft that took them to the Moon and back. The point is, they didn't have to be able to build it to use it. By the same principle, I don't have to be an expert on quantum mechanics to utilize and benefit from this little understood, as yet, part of our reality. Neither do you. Remember in math-class tests, the teacher always used to say, "Show me your work"? With this, I don't have to do the math.

There are a few things that are helpful to understand. First, that Newtonian Model, with its finite concept of space and its linear concept of time, is not so much wrong as incomplete. It's kind of an outline that looks a certain way until you read further into the smaller details. Centuries ago, the old model worked just fine for explaining things in the everyday macro, or big, world. But once scientists started to examine how things worked on a microscopic scale, the scale of atoms and subatomic particles, the old model failed to explain what they were seeing. So, that old picture of the atom, with its nucleus in the middle and little electrons in close, neat little orbits around the nucleus is no longer valid.

The reality is that if an atomic nucleus the size of a golf ball was sitting on the 50-yard line of a football stadium, it would have electrons the size of a grain of sand orbiting in the cheapest seats in the house. That means the atom is mostly empty space. It's 0.0000001 percent stuff, and 99.9999999 percent space. The reason that it can appear solid is because those electrons are in something called quantum superposition; they are everywhere at once—that is until they are observed. Then they collapse into the position in which we observe them. When those electrons are everywhere, they are waves, just like light. When they are observed, they are particles, or matter.

That begs the question, if we are made of those same empty atoms, why are we solid? The answer is because those atoms have their own mini fields of force—that's right, force fields. These force fields bond those atomic particles and atoms together into groups called molecules, which in turn are held by force into groups called compounds and chemicals. The cells of our body are made up of these chemicals, and hence we have the appearance of being solid. We are really made of waves like light!

Another significant property of subatomic particles in The Field is called quantum entanglement. Once associated, objects become connected, or entangled. This means that they have a special relationship that can never be undone. This means that the effects of action on one object are experienced by the other entangled object.

Furthermore, this is felt instantaneously at a distance by the other object in the relationship. This immediate mutual action is another important principle called non-locality. Regardless of the distance separating two distinctly separate and different objects, their connection via The Field is instantaneous. Tests have shown that it is not just some really fast communication between the objects, but literally simultaneous. Einstein called this "spooky action at a distance."

As for time, it's merely an agreed-on system for structuring our reality, which is simply one big "now," not the linear past-becomes-present, present-becomes-future concept that we perceive. We are programmed that we can remember the past, act in the present, and by our actions thereby influence and/or change the future. But what if we could "premember" the future? What if we could act in the present and influence the past?

Remember the Apollo astronauts. While I don't have to know everything about the quantum model of physical reality, having a basic knowledge makes it real enough for me to work with. So, getting back to the notion of actually being someone else as opposed to simply doing what someone else would do, knowing the following is useful:

A. At the smallest levels of organization, we are energy that appears as matter when observed, therefore—
B. —what happens every moment comes from infinite possibilities in the quantum field, therefore—
C. —my consciousness observes my reality into existence.
D. And since everything is potentially connected (entangled) by the quantum field regardless of distance (non-locality)—

E.   —it is possible for my consciousness to become entangled with a possible "me" of my own choosing ahead of the actual experience (in essence, remembering the future).

What's possible in the third world differs from what's possible according to the rules of the first world. The most important thing for me to bear in mind, as someone in recovery, is that my belief is crucial. I can use my conscious mind to realize possibilities of my choosing. I can literally move toward and become one of unlimited possible Keiths.

Therefore, in this amazing third world, what my consciousness knows, or believes, is what I can experience with my senses, as in the first world. In the third world, believing is seeing.

My personal experience with this phenomenon happened before my knowledge and understanding of it. It's true that I did on a daily basis the things that a different Keith would do. In that first world, cause-and-effect way, I slowly moved toward my objective of living a sober life. With persistence, I eventually arrived at something resembling the desired outcome. Over time, and with luck, I started to "be" the contented sober person of my dreams. I intuitively did this. However, as my alternative belief system developed, I came to understand that the standard model of recovery, the Twelve Steps, was a vague set of directions. Kind of like—drive past every liquor store until you are rocketed into a fourth dimension. The directions aren't really specific, nor is the destination.

The destination, the objective, is a sustainable recovery as characterized **by no desire to drink, a harmonious balance in the elements of recovery, and a secure knowledge, a belief, that if I continue doing what I'm doing, it's reasonable that I will not drink again.** To achieve this desired outcome while living happily in the first world as I've described it, I must move beyond that first world through the second world and into the third world. It is in that third world, embracing and learning to live by the quantum model, that I gain the knowledge I need. Bringing my new understanding and skills to my everyday life, I attain the sustainable recovery of my dreams.

CHAPTER 15

Evidence for the Third World—What's All This Energy Stuff?

In Part II, I described how my perception of reality was challenged and changed on two occasions. The first had to do with my experiencing knowledge that I shouldn't have had. The second was a demonstration of a physical object (me) being manipulated without physical means (being bodily touched). It's difficult for most people, especially without some personal experience, to grasp or believe such things are possible. After all, such occurrences are the stuff of science fiction and hokey TV drama. We are so conditioned to a conventional reality based on the known, the five conventional senses, and cause and effect that it's challenging to accept something outside what we "know" to be real.

Going to the other extreme, we who grew up on the *Twilight Zone, Star Trek,* and Stephen King novels can experience something quite extraordinary without fully appreciating it. That day in the park when Vanessa demonstrated her energy work to me by manipulating my third chakra, the energy center in the middle of my body, my life went on. I was somewhat impressed, then went home, made dinner, probably went to a meeting where I said nothing about it, returned home, probably watched TV, and went to bed. Even though I had seen firsthand evidence of something greater than my present reality, it was just another day in the life.

So then, what is all this energy stuff, and why don't we all know about it? Is it supernatural? And most importantly, how do we know it's real?

My understanding of reality did change that day. The experience in the park built on the experience I had five days sober when I knew that girl's story before she told it. The first experience was the planting of a seed. The second experience was water on that seed. Though I didn't sense my life to be profoundly, immediately different, the course of my sobriety, and hence my life, took a fork in the road. My new way of being began to unfold. I became imbued with a desire to learn more and understand a bigger picture. But how to proceed?

I chose Polarity training for two reasons. There was the connection of my friend, Vanessa, who had graduated from the school, which was just a few towns away. The other component was the structure. In the description of the program, it was apparent that the format of the training, not unlike nursing school, would be comfortable and conducive to my learning something unconventional. If I was going to learn to use crystals and manipulate energetic auras, I reasoned it was best to have something familiar in that equation. Another unanticipated benefit was an emphasis on practitioner self-care.

The training is on my resume. If it comes up in the course of an interview, I describe it as "an alternative or complementary healing modality concerned with the human energetic system." Unbeknownst to most, we all have one...

Polarity therapy uses hands-on, massage-like techniques combined with practiced movements that, in combination with the practitioner's mental focus and intention—a state called "alignment"—serve to repair and restore energetic balance and flow to an optimal state. The basis of the theory is that there is a universal flow of subtle energy, not yet understood by conventional science. This energy emanates from a "source," and moves in a circuit-like fashion through the universe in a pattern resembling a torus, or a three-dimensional revolving circle. Think of a doughnut, but with the source at a small doughnut hole, the energy moving around the doughnut and back to the source/doughnut hole...

As this energy flows in its universal circuit, we physical beings are part of that circuit. We have an energetic anatomy with a circulation of that energy. The theory holds that problems with this energetic anatomy—blockages, wounds and other disruptions, etc.—are the basis of physical disease and injury. It's in keeping with the Hermetic principle, "as above, so below." This is similar to the energy endorsed by acupuncture, known as chi. There are innumerable healing methods and disciplines, both ancient and modern, that center on this fundamental creative force of the universe.

That this energy exists is beyond dispute. While its universal nature is both a theory and belief system, the fact that some aspect of it resides within our bodies is evidenced by centuries of Eastern medical and spiritual knowledge. The system of energy centers referred to as chakras act as relay stations, each interfacing the flow of energy with an aspect of our physical selves. While not visible with the naked eye, each seems to correspond with a network, or plexus, of nerves. Because the function of nerves is the conduction of electrical signals, energy, the idea that they serve as antennae for subtle energy is quite viable. I'm sure the textbooks will catch up eventually, but for now the Apollo astronaut principle works fine.

Now, if I could be trained to work with this energy and do healing this way, anyone can. Like athletics or music, however, some people seem to have a greater natural ability. It's like anything; it takes practice. There is a small percentage of people, Vanessa is an example, who have a latent gift and tremendous aptitude for this work. As evidenced by the fact that she was able to influence my physical body using this energy by literally moving me that day in the park, she has taken this to a significant level. Her teacher, a woman from California, had a natural ability to actually see these energies. To her, the world appeared much differently than it does to most people. In addition to the physical reality that we see with our five senses, she experienced a whole other world of energy that made her life complicated, to say the least, until she was able to understand what was happening. She thought she was crazy.

The greatest gift of the training was an upgrade in my ability to sense things. Through practice, I developed the ability to do the "diagnostic" portion of the healing, sensing what energetic issues or problems a person is having. This is taught initially by having the student learn to dowse with a pendulum. Consider dowsing for a moment. It is commonly known as an ancient art of *divining* the location of water or minerals using some "unknown energy." As utilized in Polarity therapy, a small pendulum responds to the practitioner *bodily* knowing before the practitioner is *mindfully* able to intuit something. The novice practitioner asks a specific question, and the pendulum literally swings with one orientation for "yes," and another orientation for a "no" answer. This can be learned in a single day. As a demonstration of this energy/bodily interface, once practitioners have spent a little time with the pendulum, they can hold the pendulum over their other hand with the palm facing up. By simply relaxing and allowing the pendulum whatever motion it will, the pendulum will move in a counterclockwise motion. When the practitioner turns their hand over with the pendulum over the back of their hand, the pendulum will bobble a bit, and then assume a clockwise motion. This is quite amazing the first time it's tried, but it works for ANYONE.

It's not quite as amazing as a woman pulling you off balance without touching you, but it is profound. The point is, this is real.

I practiced with the pendulum, then a dowsing rod. The dowsing rod was a personal modification to the Polarity training that I learned from Vanessa's teacher in a workshop I took concurrently with Polarity studies. I was determined, and my persistence paid off as I was able to begin to trust my intuition. I would sense the answer to a Polarity diagnostic issue or question, and then check by dowsing afterward. Doing this until I grew confident in my ability, I had practiced and developed the natural intuition that we all possess.

The Polarity training was merely one avenue toward greater understanding of the concepts of energy, and the ideas of the third world. While it brought me to a greater and different understanding of reality than I knew previously, it was also incremental. Polarity is a way of healing, and because I defined myself as one who pursued a livelihood in healthcare, it wasn't a huge stretch to connect the two. In the big picture, it was the baby step I needed to begin to move out of my first-world existence.

Staying within the healing model, I investigated other styles, or techniques. They are all based on the same fundamental principle. There is an intelligent, creative force at work at all levels of reality. Also common to the healing techniques is the element of some type of trappings, or paraphernalia. They all had specified details in their approaches that had to be observed for them to work right. I balked at this notion. Even back in Polarity school, I felt some intuitive reservation about the fact that we wore white, no belts, wallets, or metal. As I encountered more of the related "New Age" community, it seemed that everybody had their own approach, often idiosyncratic. Most of these approaches seem to have specific guidelines, totems, trinkets, moves, rituals, incantations, crystals, music, incense, and books you had to have used, experienced, or read, if you wanted the energy to work right. And most of it reeked of human ego. I realized finally, it's all bullshit. THE ENERGY DOESN'T CARE.

This universal energy is absolutely neutral. I don't have to please it, and I don't have to worry about displeasing it. I don't have to wear the right clothes, say the right things, have the right crystals, etc. It's simple. There is the energy, and there is my consciousness. What does help is understanding some basic principles about how my consciousness and this energy interact.

By this point, I realized I was on a journey that was taking me way outside conventional recovery, yet at the same time seemed to be reinforcing and strengthening my recovery. I began to step outside the healing model in my inquiries and researching. This involved a lot of reading. I devoted time and effort to some diverse areas of study, including revisionist history, religion, the occult, and even that area broadly categorized as conspiracy theory in addition to biology, physics, and the applications of the energy field in science.

It became apparent that the whole idea of a supernatural world, where unexplainable magical things occur, is not viable. That science doesn't fully explain (yet) the things that have previously been attributed to acts of God does not mean there is no scientific explanation. Many explanations are out there, as is proof. That these ideas are not widely known or accepted makes them no less viable. Rejecting the idea of a supernatural world is not so much materialistic; rather, it is embracing a holistic perspective.

Another thing became apparent: there is a big picture. In this big picture, people tend to focus on their primary area of expertise at the expense of seeing the big picture. Sometimes we need to step back to see the whole puzzle to best understand what our particular piece of that puzzle is about, and where that piece fits in. My objective was and remains a better recovery for myself and others. Keeping that objective clearly in mind, I began to sample from the diverse buffet of knowledge that collectively entails the ideal of enlightenment. Always abstracting every fact and idea as it might pertain to recovery, a bigger picture began to crystallize. The case for the third world began to accumulate some major exhibits of evidence beyond my two personal experiences.

While I was working my way through nursing school and putting in time as an operating room nurse, world and national events were providing documentary scientific evidence of this third world. Long before I would become interested in such things, some interesting research was being carried out by scientists based in New Jersey.

There are some days when things happen that we remember for the rest of our lives. We remember where we were and what we were doing when we first heard about something that becomes part of history. For example, I remember the day the Apollo astronauts landed on the Moon—where I was and with whom, etc. Three other events I remember in similar fashion are the day the O. J. Simpson criminal trial verdict came back, the day of Princess Diana's funeral, and the biggie—I remember where I was, what I was doing, and whom I was with a few minutes past 9 AM EST on September 11, 2001. This is not uncommon.

As with the Apollo landing in 1969, all these events had a significant factor in common, which linked them to the immediate awareness of large numbers of people. They were all televised and held the collective attention of many around the world. People everywhere watched Neil Armstrong walk on the Moon. I happened to be in a Chinese restaurant at lunchtime when the O. J. Simpson verdict came in. Everyone in the place was glued to the television in the lounge when the verdict was announced. Television carried live coverage of Diana's funeral from London; all the networks interrupted their schedules for coverage. And, of course, the image of the Twin Towers, still standing with smoke billowing from those upper floors before they collapsed, is indelibly etched in my and everyone else's mind. These events were witnessed on a mass scale simultaneously through televised media.

The latter three events, all having occurred in the last two decades, became significant not only in history, but significant as part of an ongoing scientific research study.

In the late seventies, a small dedicated group of scientists at Princeton University started a long-running project to investigate the effect of consciousness on objects in the physical world. The research began humbly and cautiously; in the serious world of academic research, such things were branded and dismissed as parapsychology, or fringe science. By using rigorous scientific research standards and approaching the proposition from an engineering perspective, the Princeton Engineering Anomalies Research group (PEAR) slowly established itself as a credible entity.

One of PEAR's principle research tools is a device known as a Random Event Generator (REG). The REG is essentially an electronic coin toss. It uses an electronic white-noise generator, or similar means, to provide a continuous supply of random "ons" or "offs," that is, heads or tails. Over time, this electronic coin tossing will provide results of 50 percent on, 50 percent off, the random outcome. The machine had originated as an electronic alternative to the extrasensory perception (ESP) cards used in early parapsychology research, the famous circle, square, triangle, or wavy lines. Throughout the years, the device was modified and updated into a reliable, state-of-the-art research tool. Great pains have been taken that the device was completely insulated from all manner of environmental, mechanical, or other conventional influences, such as electromagnetism, temperature changes, or aging of the device itself. The REG is a reliable indicator of The Field effect of a subject's consciousness on a physical object.

The PEAR group utilized the REG in its research studies by having test subjects attempt to influence the random 50/50 outcome with their thoughts. In structured protocols, it was found that most people could cause the REG to deviate between 1 percent and 2 percent. While it doesn't sound like much, it is statistically extraordinary. This alone is compelling evidence for consciousness influencing the physical environment. PEAR began to design new and more creative experiments.

These new experiments were intended to assess the effect of the mass consciousness on the REG. PEAR scientists began by placing them at concerts, sporting events, and celebrations, such as New Year's Eve. Ultimately, they set up REGs remotely, linked to software and central computer servers, for ongoing monitoring in what has come to be known as the Global Consciousness Project (GCP). The intention of this effort is to monitor the effect of group consciousness events in The Field. This has set the stage for some fascinating and tangible observations as historic events have unfolded.

As the project was in the formative stages during the early nineties, the mass attention and interest in the O. J. Simpson trial presented a unique opportunity. The effect of the collective focus of many people on a single event was precisely the type of consciousness energy that the study sought to measure. It didn't seem to matter that there was no deliberate intention to alter the REG devices (the energy doesn't care). Likewise, the locations of the devices weren't significant (non-locality). As circumstances unfolded with the trial, the jury returned late in the day with its verdict. Hence, the delivery of that verdict was scheduled for the start of the proceedings the following morning. Talk about a cliffhanger. Millions were able to know about it and tune in on television, numbers of people on the order of Super Bowl viewership.

REGs at four locations around the country all had significant spikes in activity simultaneously. Not only did these data deviations occur simultaneously regardless of location, but their timing was significant with specific events in the trial proceedings. There was a spike at the beginning of the broadcast, the beginning of the actual proceedings, and… there was a significant spike at the exact time the verdict was read.

Several years later, the death of the Princess of Wales, Lady Diana, was a tragedy that transcended the borders of Great Britain. The world had witnessed her "fairytale" wedding to Prince Charles years before, and she was never far from the public eye. Her vigorous activity for benevolent causes earned great respect in her lifetime and much sympathy in her passing.

By the late nineties, the GCP was fully established. A network of 40 REGs was established, maintained, and networked to Princeton, though now a separate entity from PEAR. During Diana's globally televised funeral ceremony, the REG network tracked a deviation that was outside random chance by 100 to 1. One week prior, Mother Teresa's funeral had not influenced the REGs at all. While the spiritual leader had succumbed after a long, steady decline in health, the princess had been taken abruptly and tragically in the prime of her life. Was the intense emotion of collective sadness a factor in the mass consciousness Field effect?

The GCP REG network was up and running a few years later on September 11, 2001, when the question regarding intense emotion might have been answered. If there is a quantum-field function of collective consciousness that is the result of coherently focused attention, intense emotion might seem to amplify this if the GCP data are any indicator. At the height of the September 11 event, the REGs indicated a deviation from random chance of 1,000 to 1.

Millions of people devoting their attention in a common direction seem to be powerful enough to show effects in the physical world. How does this happen? Remember, REGs were specifically designed for the purpose of measuring this Field fluctuation, and have been modified, tweaked, and basically 'idiot-proofed' to account for every other conceivable influence. Finally, the simplest answer is that there is a quantum field-based effect influencing these devices, compelling evidence for this being a function of the energy field. So then, along with defying space, what about time? Every bit as profound as the mere fact of this effect is that the September 11 REG event measurements began a full two hours prior to the first plane crash. The outpouring of grief and shock measured as subtle energy in the physical world was somehow starting before masses of people had any reason to actually experience negative emotion. The GCP raises some compelling evidence for the effect of consciousness affecting physical reality in ways that seem to defy our understanding of how things work.

Taking a momentary timeout, let's step back and remember the context of what we're talking about. The world is not what we thought it was. The idea that we need to come to terms with is that there is more to reality than what we were taught and what we have believed. Einstein used the word spooky, which conjures all manner of stuff labeled under the broad categorization "hooey," but it's not. The same way we once thought disease happened randomly, or worse, as a result of evil spirits, we eventually learned about microorganisms as a cause of illness. We've been dismissing things as supernatural, or putting them in the second-world box as miracles. There is no supernatural; nothing is without a rational explanation, whether we can yet understand it or not. A miracle is an extraordinary thing that is not explainable in the context of a culture's present understanding.

A miracle is defined as "an effect or extraordinary event in the physical world that surpasses all known human or natural powers and is ascribed to a supernatural cause." There are two important elements here. First, that it surpasses what we know. Second, and as a result of the first element, it is attributed to the "supernatural" or divine. Does surpassing what is known not mean that something is outside the commonly accepted knowledge and understanding of the current timeframe?

For example, say it is 100 years ago. We are shown a bizarre picture frame-like device on a little pedestal which sits on a tabletop or desk. It is connected by wire to a box with lights and a typewriter that is flat. Not only does this "picture frame" have a picture, but it changes in response to messages typed on the flat typewriter. The pictures can even move like those new-fangled moving-picture shows, but these have sounds and amazing lifelike color! But there's more. We can send a letter that arrives instantly anywhere in the world, or have a conversation with someone anywhere while we see them speaking to us. The "miraculous" picture frame can even look at and forecast tomorrow's and next week's weather.

The everyday things we can do with a computer would have been viewed as miracles 100 years ago (or 80 years ago at the time of AA's founding). In the distant and even more recent past, something that defied understanding based on the knowledge of the time was described as miraculous.

Let's look at two examples from history. The Wright Brothers were told that human flight was impossible. Suppose they gave up; what would the world be like without air travel? And would we have ever landed on the Moon? As recently as 10 years prior to *Apollo 11,* there was much scientific opinion that a Moon landing was not possible. Science and prevailing general knowledge changed with new scientific understanding and discoveries.

Now take a look at your cell phone. Even before smart phones, that cell phone almost everyone has contains more computing power than was onboard that Apollo spacecraft! That's how quickly things change. So the question we must come to terms with is the following: Are the matters of the spirit unexplainable, or just not explainable in terms of our everyday understanding of our physical world?

This is where the AA old-timers start to have an allergic reaction. They get hives. They stick their fingers in their ears and loudly hum, "Lalalala." Or they ask, "Can't we simply take this on faith?" We could, but we would continue to get what we always got. For many, this means living life in a constant state of fearing the next drink, waking each day with untreated alcoholism.

The answers are starting to come, if we are willing to ask the right questions. Knowing the answers to those questions makes a difference. Knowing in a general way how something works gives us better results. Understanding why and how the spiritual part of recovery works, and also why it is so crucial, allows it to work better because we start to attach meaning. Whether faithful or skeptical by nature, understanding as best we can how this amazing third world works on our behalf can make an amazing difference— the difference between a tenuous, fearful existence only one drink away from disaster and a happy, joyous freedom that too few experience at present.

Like those Apollo astronauts, even though we can't build it, we want to have a working understanding necessary to fly this contraption we call recovery. While there will always be questions that defy any definitive answer, we can begin to form our own perceptions and ideas about these things. What we perceive is our reality, so we can, at the very least, begin to attach meaning to the issues of recovery and move forward.

CHAPTER 16
More Evidence

Cleve Backster spent many years in the service of the Central Intelligence Agency (CIA). He came to be acknowledged as one of the top authorities on the science of polygraphy, commonly referred to as lie-detector testing. A lie-detector test is a systematic measurement of several physiologic responses while a subject answers a series of questions. These basic physiological processes come under measurable stress if someone is intentionally lying, and the stress responses can be reliably interpreted as lie detection. After becoming a top authority and instructor in the use of the polygraph machine, Backster left the CIA to become a private consultant.

Backster was at work late one night. Likely a bit punchy in the wee hours, he was struck with the impulse to attach part of a polygraph machine to a leaf of the plant his secretary had given him to brighten up the office. The galvanometer, one component of a lie detector, is an electrode that measures subtle electricity of living organisms. The galvanometer measures the electricity, and then it's expressed as one of the squiggly lines on the polygraph readout. More electricity equals more squiggles. He watched as the plant told no lies, based on the flat line on the readout. Bored, he went to another room to get some coffee.

While in the other room, he realized that the lie-detector test was based on asking questions that caused a stress reaction in the subject. He would have to stress the plant somehow. He returned to his office and found a book of matches. His idea was to burn a leaf of the plant to get a reaction. As he was about to strike a match, he noticed the polygraph readout. The plant was having a wild reaction. Baffled that the plant was reacting before there was any physical cause, he took a look at the readout prior to that moment. On the graph paper, he saw another significant reaction a minute or so before and realized that it corresponded to the moment he had thought of using a match on the plant.

He was astounded. It was as if the plant was aware of the threat the instant it was no more than a thought in a human's mind. What started as a momentary late-night diversion for a weary Backster, took on a life of its own. He went on to study this extensively. Eventually, he set up a proper laboratory for this work and made some astounding discoveries. He repeated his experiments. Unfortunately, it's likely that some plants were harmed in the course of the work, which came to be known as the Backster Effect. Plants, without benefit of five senses, apparently have amazing awareness of the environment. Among other things Backster discovered, he learned that plants show measurable reaction to: threats in their environment, actual physical harm or damage to the plant, and… threats or actual harm to other organisms, whether plant or animal. That's right; one plant seems to know when something is happening to another plant. This concept literally extends to the remote and microscopic. A plant reacts in this way when boiling water is poured down a sink drain, killing bacteria living in the drain!

So, how do plants accomplish this?

What plants have is a connection to the quantum field at the most fundamental level. They are living things, but have no consciousness, at least as we understand it. If a plant can "sense" my intention toward it, whether it is to water it or prune extra branches, there is obviously something connecting my consciousness and the plant. The fact is that the plant will sense my intention toward it as the thought forms in my mind and it also senses when I come toward it with water or clippers. It senses my coming toward it just as well as it senses the actual watering or clipping.

This is so simple, yet so profound. We are obviously connected somehow. Is this supernatural? No. Does this make perfect sense in the nonlocal quantum field? Yes. And if plants are connected to conscious beings in The Field, it would stand to reason that conscious beings are connected to other conscious beings. They are.

Japanese scientists studying monkeys on remote Koshima Island observed an interesting behavior. During the course of their study, they noticed the monkeys began washing the dirt off sweet potatoes. This was a new behavior for the monkeys in response to the scientists leaving the sweet potatoes on the beach, and it became established. Eventually, all the monkeys on that particular island were washing their dirty root vegetables before eating them. The researchers documented this and continued their work. Later, the scientists collected and pooled data with information from other studies of the same monkeys at different locations.

The other monkeys had begun washing their dirty food in the same timeframe that the first monkeys had. The same new behavior was initiated at the same time, but with no communication or direct observation. These monkeys were not on the Internet with one another emailing advice about cleaning their food. It happened spontaneously.

This became known as the Hundredth Monkey Phenomenon. It is believed to be a quantum field effect of mass consciousness. In other words, once enough monkeys were doing this, it became part of a monkey collective consciousness. The idea then became easier for other monkeys to think of themselves.

What was considered far-fetched, fantastic, impossible, and implausible is no longer written in stone. From my personal experiences, I learned that the unexpected happens.

To unify the three worlds of my existence, I needed to understand a little more about the "me" that inhabits these worlds. Just as important as my concept of something greater than me is my concept of "me." Before there can be a relationship between me and a power greater than me, it's helpful to come to some understanding of my own consciousness. If I'm going to change my way of being, it's even more essential.

What is consciousness? Great thinkers have wrestled with the understanding of consciousness and debated its nature for centuries. To me, it is all the awareness of all of me. For that to be true, "my thoughts" and "me," while inseparably linked, nevertheless remain separate. What I think is not necessarily me. There is a voice coming from somewhere inside my head that is telling me what words to put on this page. The voice seems to be the result of my efforts to think creatively, coherently, and constructively. There is intention behind it; that intention is to communicate ideas and experiences that have worked in my life, so that the reader can share the information and benefit. So, there is the voice, a motivation to do something, and a process at work—all aspects of "me." My consciousness is like the medium that those aspects of me arise from. Those aspects, that "me" stuff, are made real by my consciousness as they become observed. I observe these words and ideas into existence.

Biologically speaking, we are amazing machines of flesh and blood. We are, all of us, uniquely crafted, engineered, and executed marvels of creation. Eons in the making, we are so incredibly complex that our understanding of our physical selves is but rudimentary. As evidenced by the mind/body quandary that the notion of consciousness raises, we fairly exemplify that Apollo astronaut principle I spoke of earlier. We are "being" without entirely understanding how being works. On a simple level of survival, all we have to do is breathe, eat, drink (water), shelter and protect our physical bodies, and reproduce. That's it. The flesh and blood machines that are human beings can get by with that. Yet somehow, none of that would happen without consciousness.

It is debated whether consciousness is a random result of our brains' physiology, or something else. In strictly Newtonian terms, the materialist perspective, everything *should* be explained as a function of chemical reactions that are simply part of how our bodies work, so it is perplexing that consciousness can't be accounted for that way. The mind, thoughts, and memory are synonymous functions of consciousness. Try as they might, scientists are unable to locate the mind in the brain. The source of thoughts, emotions, and memory is not understood. It's like the ghost in the machine. Where does that voice come from?

Author Michael Talbot's wonderful *The Holographic Universe* discusses famous experiments in which neuroscientists tried to prove the theory that specific memories were located in specific parts of the brain. In the 1930s, neurosurgeon Wilder Penfield performed operations on epileptics under local anesthesia. The patients were awake! The brain itself has no pain sensation; the scalp and adjacent tissues were anesthetized locally, as is done for dental surgery. Dr. Penfield talked to the conscious patients as he stimulated specific areas of the brain. Stimulating a specific area could elicit vivid memories of childhood, entire conversations or other events. Penfield concluded that memories are somehow stored in specific parts of the brain. This later proved to be unreliably repeatable, and only with epileptics. However, the idea of memories stored in the brain somehow stuck in the mainstream.

In behaviorist Karl Lashley's experiments with maze-trained lab rats, different parts of the rats' brains were surgically removed systematically. When the rats recovered, they still negotiated the mazes as if nothing had happened. Their memories were intact. No matter what part of the brain was removed, the rats could still remember how to run through the maze. This contradicted Penfield's work and raised the question of where memories, and other aspects of consciousness, are located.

Lashley's assistant, neurosurgeon Karl Pribram, was the first to postulate that the brain functions holographically. As with three-dimensional holograms generated from interference patterns, there is a tendency for all the information to be stored everywhere.

Another researcher, seeking a more definitive answer (or possibly frustrated and wondering if the memories were shuffling around inside the little rat brains), went back to Penfield's line of inquiry. This time experimenting with salamanders instead of rats, Indiana University biologist Paul Pietsch sliced, diced, and otherwise basically ground up the little salamander brains and replaced them. Exactly like the rats, and once recovered, the salamanders appeared completely normal as evidenced by feeding behavior and other criteria.

Hence, it would appear memories are not stored in specific parts of our brains.

So then, where is the mind in the brain? I like to think we are like computers in some ways. The body is the hardware; the brain is the central processing unit, or CPU. The mind is the software. Memories are like stored files, and like computers, perhaps we have more storage options than we might think at first. In recent years, the concept of remote data storage, "clouds," has grown popular. We can backup our systems and store libraries of files, music, video or pictures, all accessed through the Internet. The information is *out there*; we access it when we need it. Like computers, the aspects known as our minds and consciousness are functioning on the Internet of the quantum field. Theoretically then, our consciousness would be subject to entanglement, nonlocality, and the quantum concept of time.

Actually, our minds as nonlocal things are more than just a theory. Our consciousness is not confined to the space within our heads. But how could such a thing be proven?

How is anything proven? Along with the establishment of scientific materialism, an approach for testing and integrating new knowledge was created. Commonly referred to as the scientific method, it is the widely used format by which a hypothesis or theory, an idea basically, might be proven and generally accepted. Boiled down to its fundamentals, it has eight basic components. A question (1) leads to a hypothesis (2), and some type of prediction (3) is made. The idea is tested (4), and the test is analyzed (5). The results of the test must be repeatable (6), and are then subject to peer review (7). To facilitate steps 6 and 7, data must be published (8).

The first stage is the idea itself, consisting of an initial question, related data, and observations. The idea that consciousness is non-local, as evidenced by demonstrations of abilities outside the five-sensory norm by certain gifted individuals, was a starting point. The questions this raised were ignored for the most part by the mainstream of science, shunned as the most certain way to shoot an academic career in the foot. A couple of unique and courageous individuals were able to pursue this line of inquiry in the 1970s as a result of the Cold War.

Working out of Stanford Research Institute, Harold "Hal" Puthoff and Russell Targ were a couple of scientific outliers. Both were quite passionate about the possibilities presented by the new quantum physics. They saw an opportunity to further understanding of human consciousness potential and seized it. Amid the geopolitical tensions of the day with thousands of missile warheads pointed every which way, and a general attitude of global "us and them," the US Department of Defense was growing wary of the possibility of the Soviet Union developing the capability of spying psychically. The paranormal was more accepted in the former USSR. Whether it was rooted in paranoia or the reality that the other side viewed psychic phenomena more seriously, the US government was concerned enough to become somewhat open-minded. Puthoff and Targ seized the moment.

Enlisting a couple of naturally gifted psychics, Puthoff and Targ applied the scientific method to nonlocal consciousness. Taking the initial question, making observations, and forming a theory, they established a set of protocols. Their psychics were hardly Vegas stage acts. Ingo Swann, a professional artist, had already been the subject of scientific investigation, and was dedicated to the advancement of this cause. He would go on to publish numerous books on the subject. Pat Price was a recently retired police detective who had routinely incorporated his intuitive gift into his work with amazing results. The scientists relied on "the talent" to help them establish a rigorous and objective methodology for what came to be known as Remote Viewing.

"Remote viewing is an ability we all have to a greater or lesser degree, that lets us describe and experience activities or events blocked from ordinary perception by distance or time," said Targ. At Swann's suggestion, sites for viewing experiments were given only as mapped coordinates, longitude and latitude. Experiments were done with participants in pairs, a viewer and a monitor. Through experience, other elements of the work were refined and set up as protocols.

In 1973, Puthoff and Targ had an opportunity to demonstrate Remote Viewing for the CIA. A CIA officer gave them some map coordinates. Swann and Price were to describe the details of the location. They did so incorrectly, but the results were still most unexpected. Both men described, in great detail, some type of military installation. The actual coordinates had been for the CIA officer's vacation cabin somewhere in Virginia. The experienced psychics, focusing on some sort of intelligence related target, had both correctly described something near the given coordinates. Within a mile of the cabin was a secret National Security Agency (NSA) listening post installation. The remote viewers had provided the information that was wanted, not the information that was asked for. The NSA was furious that its secret base had been outed, but the Stanford researchers had made a strong case for Remote Viewing.

The government-funded Remote Viewing research was a top-secret defense project for more than 20 years. After the project was closed in the nineties, the material was declassified, and the researchers could finally discuss it. Much additional information was obtained through the Freedom of Information Act. In keeping with the scientific method, the hypothesis of our consciousness demonstrating nonlocal abilities has been tested, verified, published/reviewed, and has been repeated. All the criteria necessary for a theory to become a scientific fact have been met.

The evidence would seem to support that the mind is not within the brain, but rather the brain exists within the mind.

If the Newtonian, materialist version of consciousness as an interesting byproduct of neurochemical function is not a definitive answer, that leaves the possibility that we are something more. If consciousness is not the result of random or ordered electrical charges bouncing around our brains, perhaps it comes from something more lasting. If billions of people have believed for centuries that we are, at depth, some kind of eternal spirit or soul, and 100 years of neurology can't prove otherwise, it's certainly worth entertaining.

The possibility that we are eternal consciousness, having transient human experiences, is reinforced by the phenomenon of the near-death experience. This is now a well-known contemporary phenomenon. People who are dead, for all intents and purposes, are then resuscitated. As a result of drowning, accidental electrocution, cardiac arrest, etc., the respiratory, brain, and heart functions might be completely negative. These people are clinically dead. The flesh and blood machine is in the off position. They are maintained on life support (oxygen to the tissues), and their hearts restarted by defibrillation and medication (think electrical jumpstart—CLEAR)! After being revived, these people are often able to describe experiences and imagery that has some consistent themes.

People commonly report the sensation of floating above themselves and looking down at the room where the medical personnel are working on them. Also common is the sensation of moving toward a bright light and often being greeted by deceased relatives and loved ones who act as guides. The problem with dismissing this as some byproduct of decreased oxygen to the brain as it shuts down is that it's been scientifically studied, with uncanny results. In one study of the phenomenon, objects were placed in parts of the room that could only be seen from near the ceiling. These objects were successfully identified by people after they were brought back to life. People have been able to describe details of the resuscitative procedures underway, instruments and equipment being used, and details of conversations, even including a nurse flirting with a doctor in the hallway. The patient accurately described the color of the tie the doctor had on. One patient correctly located his own missing dentures that had been hastily put on the code cart and forgotten in the fracas to save his life.

Another major argument for the concept of an eternal aspect to consciousness is the compelling work of Dr. Brian Weiss, mentioned previously, and others working in the field of past-life regression therapy.

Weiss was a conventional psychiatrist, college professor, and academic department head with a busy practice in the accepted mainstream model of psychiatry. A young woman working in his department was suddenly afflicted with what appeared to be a phobic (unfounded or unknown fear) disorder. He treated her with regression hypnotherapy. As he regressed the woman back in her life, all the way to early childhood in search of the cause of her phobia, she was suddenly and inexplicably back in adulthood. On further assessment, it was realized that she had actually regressed past her birth into a previous life. The skeptical Weiss, who was the epitome of the Western approach practitioner, was in disbelief. It went against everything he believed and stood for. In the true spirit of scientific investigation, however, he continued his exploration of this phenomenon.

What Weiss learned was precisely what spiritual teachers currently believe and Eastern religions have known for centuries. We come into lives of our choosing in the interest of spiritual advancement. In his book, *Many Lives, Many Masters,* Weiss states a persuasive case based on years of documented investigation, complete with verifiable evidence. During regression, people have been able to give verifiable details of physical objects, buildings, and locations in remote parts of the world that they could have no actual present-day knowledge of. The work was so compelling that Weiss devoted himself to it, leaving his work in academia to investigate the past-life phenomenon. After all, coming to understand the fact that we are all in a type of "soul kindergarten" is one of those reality and life-changing experiences.

Human beings are unique among all other creatures in one important part of consciousness. We have something called metacognition, or knowing about knowing. This is simultaneously the blessing and curse of humankind. We have thoughts about our feelings and feelings about our thoughts; this gives us a tremendous ability to adapt and survive, while also being the source of most human anxiety. This quality of consciousness is also a part of our alcoholism and addictions. There is a constant running assessment of our state. We are all about how we are feeling at any given moment.

One of history's greatest philosophers, René Descartes, summed up the duality of consciousness—the "I" and the thoughts "I" observe—with his famous quote, "I think, therefore I am."

This brief description of some fascinating ideas and the events that brought them about is testimony to the amazing potential human beings hold. The little-known, as yet little-understood, abilities we mere mortals possess could be tremendous vehicles for changing our lives. In reality, human beings are amazingly powerful. In view of our natural connection to the quantum field, the entire universe, and therefore one another, the isolation we experience is self-imposed. The powerlessness we become so conditioned to is more in the nature of an unconscious personal decision. We see what we believe, not the other way around.

CHAPTER 17
Our Bodies

In nursing school, I learned much more about the human body than I wanted to know. Ten years or so earlier, I had taken a more vocational anatomy course on my way to becoming a surgical technologist. Then I observed the amazing human body on a daily basis while assisting surgeons in all types of procedures. By the time I walked into the classroom for that comprehensive college level anatomy and physiology course, I had literally spent tens of thousands of hours experiencing the human body in action. I had seen the tireless, almost unstoppable beating of the human heart. The disassembly and reconstruction of knee joints and hip joints, the eerie and automatic peristalsis (contracting movements) of the digestive tract, and the inner workings of the eye were all routine to me, even before they were the topics of lectures. After helping to repair defective aortas (the pipe-sized main artery branching off the heart), hearing them described in the classroom seemed a little stale. However, my practical understanding made the new injection of technical knowledge all the more potent.

While the context of an education in nursing has many biases, I cannot understate the value. I knew this even in the midst of my nearly overwhelming training. Of necessity, the education highlights disease and problems. Sadly, the majority of our time spent in the presence of doctors, nurses, and other health professionals happens as we are confronting a health dilemma. I realized that if everyone knew the kinds of things nurses are taught, what an amazing capacity people would have to maintain their bodies and health. Nursing training was a veritable comprehensive overview, heavy emphasis on troubleshooting, on the correct use and optimal performance of the human body. If there was an owner's manual for human beings, a smart nurse would be a walking version of it.

One of the first things nurses are taught is a concept known as a wellness, or health continuum. A continuum is a scale that ranges between two extremes, in this case between good health at one end and disease at the other end. A person can be thought of as constantly moving between the two ends of this continuum, hopefully spending the majority of time at or near the health end. When we feel well, we are at that health end of the scale. If we contract a minor illness, such as a cold, and our symptoms and condition worsen, we move along the continuum toward the disease end. On that day or two during the illness, when we are just down for the count and feeling completely miserable, we are at the disease end of the continuum. As our immune response rallies to defeat the disease process, we slowly move back toward the health or wellness end.

To be healthy, our bodies constantly work to maintain a balance of all systems and processes, known as homeostasis. There is a complex interrelationship, a constant give-and-take, relentlessly working to maintain equilibrium within the human organism. Hundreds of thousands of chemical reactions take place every second throughout the body. When viewed simply as a flesh-and-blood machine, we are incredibly complex.

Every hour of every day the heart pumps the equivalent of gallons of blood through miles of blood vessels. That heart pumps over 100,000 times per day, about 40 million times a year, more than three trillion times in an average lifetime. Rather impressive.

The human body has structures and systems in place that are comparable to a thoughtfully designed modern building. There is a power plant with generators and fuel processing. There is temperature regulation and an all-important electrical system with a central controller that monitors and runs all the other systems, including ventilation, plumbing, security, maintenance, and repair. Everything has been taken into account, and, unimpeded, the body runs like clockwork. In fact, clocks run more like bodies than vice versa.

So, what could possibly go wrong? The answer is anything and everything.

Disease is an abnormal condition of the body. It can originate from an external source or within the body itself. The result of disease is a loss of homeostasis. Congenital disease is present, though not necessarily actively harmful, at birth. From a more holistic standpoint, all disease can be traced directly or indirectly to two root causes: toxicity and/or deficiency. Sound too simple? Pick a disease. The common cold? The causes are exposure to a pathogen, in this case a virus, the presence of which is toxic. The virus challenges the immune system, which might not be up to par due to deficiency of necessary nutrients and adequate rest for repair. The results are cold symptoms. Cancer? Simplistically, it could start with exposure to carcinogens, a toxin. In the presence of a sugar-rich, low-pH environment (toxic), genetic expression of cells that grow abnormally takes place, unchecked by an absence of cancer-killing cells due to their down-regulation from lack of sufficient quantities and combinations of basic nutrients, vitamins, and minerals (deficiency). Again, quite simplistic, but you can see how disease can be traced from these two root causes.

There are some specific events in the health continuum as we move from health to disease, and there are some conditions that have to be met for us to get sick. First, we must be exposed to a causative agent, or pathogen. Let's use the example of a cold virus. Next, that virus needs a way to get to us, referred to as a mode of transmission. Look no further than the knob on the door. It's a microorganism convention. The last element on the pathogen side of the equation is a way in, or point of entry. After touching the contaminated doorknob, we scratch our nose as we unconsciously do throughout the day, and voilà! That virus is now in our nose where the environment is warm and moist and wonderfully hospitable for the tiny virus. It's hit the virus lottery! That virus has packed a lunch and moves in to set up shop.

The next important factor will be whether that virus overwhelms our defenses. It has already breached the first defense, our skin, which acts as a barrier. The virus has exploited a loophole in our defenses by remaining on the outside of the skin, our hands, until it was able to get to a natural opening, the entrance of our respiratory system. Finally, the degree to which that virus is able to multiply depends on the status of our immune system.

In the continuum, all that activity led up to actual exposure. We are now incubating the virus, which is fighting dirty. It is cleverly commandeering the reproductive machinery of the cells it invades, retraining it to reproduce more viruses. We are now in a 48-hour or so period where we don't yet feel sick, but that cold virus is multiplying. Slowly, we begin to develop symptoms, and finally reach the point where we have to admit to ourselves we are sick. This is a major event on the health continuum because we might or might not take action that will affect how far we move toward the disease end of the scale. Suppose we decide to call out from work, stay home, and rest. We eat well, replenishing and bolstering depleted stores of certain vitamins, minerals, and other nutrients that support our immune system, and also providing enough calories to fuel the energy needs of a metabolism that is working to restore homeostasis. Our immune system, like a well-supported army, takes the fight to the virus, and after a fierce battle is waged for a day or so, begins to turn the tide. Our symptoms—fever, sore throat, nasal congestion, cough, and general malaise—have been the result of the immune system response to the virus more than the virus. War is hell.

Incidentally, we are contagious for much of those 48 hours before we even know we are sick.

So, we move from wellness toward the illness end of the continuum. The important events are initial exposure with transmission and points of entry, the incubation period, our becoming aware of the illness, and the immune response and (hopeful) resolution of the illness. Should the illness overwhelm all defenses, we will continue to move away from wellness toward illness, the severity increasing, until we reach "the end" of the continuum, which is death.

From the dark recesses of my recollection of nursing theory is one more useful concept. The best way to manage disease is to prevent it in the first place. In fact, by placing the emphasis on disease, we have the cart before the horse anyway. What do we want? Good health. Ideally, promoting health reduces or even negates the need to manage disease. In healthcare, the concept of "prevention" is a great idea. Unfortunately, it remains more ideal than reality.

In medicine, we think of and approach healthcare in three stages of prevention. The primary-prevention approach consists of routine physicals, vaccinations, and the encouragement of optimal lifestyles with modification where necessary. The objective is quite literally the prevention, or absence, of disease. Primary prevention is that other side of the disease coin; it is more a practice of health maintenance as opposed to illness prevention. Primary prevention is proactive.

Secondary prevention is characterized by the diagnosis and treatment of existing illness in a timely manner. Early detection of symptoms generally makes for better management. Because disease is already present, emphasis now shifts to preventing or reducing severity, complications, and morbidity.

Tertiary prevention seeks to reduce negative impact of existing disease processes by restoring function and reducing complications. The emphasis has now shifted to damage control, and tertiary prevention is by nature reactive.

Now, let's apply these ideas to alcoholism. Or more practically and accurately, let's apply alcohol to what we know and understand about our bodies. I briefly discussed alcohol withdrawal in the context of my story, but we need to back up and look at the basic effects that alcohol has on our bodies.

Alcohol is a chemical molecule. It's an arrangement of atoms, some configuration of carbon, hydrogen, and oxygen, which comprise a broad category of substances we refer to as alcohol. Alcohol easily crosses the blood-brain barrier, which is a circulatory protective measure, the brain's way of keeping out the riffraff.

Alcohol's effect on the brain is to inhibit communication among different parts of the brain by impeding the efficiency and generally slowing down the action of important brain chemicals called neurotransmitters. The degree to which this happens depends on the quantity of alcohol consumed. Whether the perceived external effect is mild euphoria or "falling-down drunkenness," the action taking place is a chemical impairment on a microscopic physiological level. The normal function of the brain is being messed up.

At the risk of stating the obvious... overuse of alcohol, consuming too much in a single instance, initially results in intoxication. Mild mental incoherence and loss of physical coordination are the first signs. As more alcohol is consumed, incoherence progresses to confusion, loss of coordination worsens to the inability to maintain balance. The ability to stand and walk is forfeited. The level of consciousness declines, until consciousness is lost. The intoxicated individual might initially be rousable, then unrousable. Respiratory function will become depressed. Possible complications include vomiting, dehydration, and hypothermia. Thankfully, this is as far as the majority of alcohol overdose goes.

The problem is that there are variables involved in the consumption of alcohol and the timeframe in which ill effects come about. The concentration of alcohol in beverages, speed at which the beverages are consumed, stomach contents, individual metabolism, and the speed at which a person's system breaks down the alcohol, all influence the rate at which someone becomes intoxicated. Hence the tendency for overdrinking. Of course, the attendant impairment of judgment is another major factor.

As intoxication becomes more intense, complications progress to loss of gag reflex, choking, aspiration (inhaling vomit), and poor oxygenation from respiratory depression leading to respiratory arrest, seizures, and death.

Incidentally, because one of the root causes of disease is toxicity, and drinking alcohol (a toxin) results in an abnormal condition of the body and loss of homeostasis, drinking alcohol makes us ill in the most literal sense. All of which is obvious to any seasoned drinker, but bears mentioning. It's much different in technical terms than as common knowledge.

Repeated overuse of alcohol eventually results in the body's decreased capacity for restoring order to the body's systems, homeostasis. The liver, where the alcohol is broken down, or detoxified, becomes less efficient. Recovery time lengthens, hangovers become worse. A ripple effect is set in motion; the physical and psychological effects are compounded. As alcohol dependence is established, a downward cycle of poor lifestyle choices might result in a range of physical problems and complaints.

Nutrition is one of the first things to suffer. Appetite suffers as the emphasis shifts to a liquid diet, and the quality and quantity of food consumption declines. Paradoxically, the body burns more rapidly through vitamins and minerals, especially the water-soluble B vitamins, as their intake lessens. Acid stomach, nausea with or without vomiting, cramps, and diarrhea are common. Hypersensitive (overly sensitive) gag reflex makes brushing teeth uncomfortable, and oral hygiene tends to suffer. The ripple effects of poor nutrition are decreased energy level and decreased or compromised immunity.

Psychologically, the altered nutritional status causes greater risk of depression. Lack of available nutrients, especially amino acids (building blocks of protein) necessary for production of those all-important neurotransmitters, can negatively impact mood. Deficiency of vitamin D has been linked to depression, and, of course, alcohol is a depressant itself.

Over time, blood pressure, circulation, and the heart itself might suffer. Changes in the liver might lead to a condition known as cirrhosis, or scarring, of the liver, preventing it from functioning properly in its many other functions aside from detoxifying alcohol.

Tremors, loss of coordination, and decreased reflexes occur as the central nervous system declines. Eventually concentration and memory become impaired, progressing to an Alzheimer's-like condition, known as Wernicke-Korsakoff syndrome, a direct result of lack of B vitamin thiamin on the brain. Mental disturbance/confusion, drowsiness, and paralysis of eye movements, and a staggering gait are the irreversible symptoms. This is also called "wet brain."

Regardless of whether people drink a single glass of wine in their entire lifetime, or make a decades-long career of drowning their body in a noxious sea of alcohol, the body's response is the same. It's only a matter of degree. The response is identical to the body's response to a simple cold virus or deadly disease. The body works tirelessly, or as best it can, to restore itself to health.

Our physical bodies are organisms. They are a collection of systems, such as the nervous system, cardiovascular system, respiratory system, digestive system, etc. In turn, each system is made up of organs, which are made up of types of bodily material called tissues. Tissues are composed of specialized cells. Cells are made of chemicals, which are combinations of molecules, or groups of atoms. The basic components of atoms are protons, neutrons, and electrons, in addition to numerous other subatomic particles. Everything in this hierarchy serves a specific purpose in our bodies.

Growth of the body takes place at the cellular level. Most cells reproduce by dividing themselves, while others, such as blood or bone cells, develop from different cells before ultimately achieving their final forms. Within cells are a variety of structures dedicated to maintenance and reproduction. The deoxyribonucleic acid (DNA) molecules and segments of DNA, known as genes, are contained inside cells. The average human body has 50 to 60 trillion cells. Because every cell is dedicated to the goal of survival, and therefore maintaining the well-being of my body, it's kind of like having my own country, the United Cells of Keith.

Genetics is the science that studies the role of genes in determining the body's physical traits. This area of biological study has exploded in recent years. The Human Genome Project has successfully mapped human DNA. The result of that map is an avalanche of data that the world's best minds are working to interpret in an effort to better understand how DNA and genes code for the body's physical traits. Knowing which gene codes for blue eyes still doesn't explain how that causes blue pigment to form in the iris of the eye, for example. Many questions remain.

Charles Darwin came from a wealthy family and was that child who could not figure out what he wanted to do, to his father's distress (hmm, did I have *Darwin issues*?). After dropping out of medical school, he earned a bachelor's degree with the intention of studying theology. He then became interested in subjects such as entomology, zoology, and botany. Darwin went on an almost five-year sea voyage on the HMS *Beagle*, whose (five-year) mission was to (boldly) map coastlines in the western hemisphere. Darwin's father reluctantly funded Charles' participation on the voyage. Charles' purpose was to gain experience as a naturalist, observing, collecting specimens, and writing notes. He developed ideas on species and their creation, through seeing the incredible diversity, notably in the Galapagos Islands. He went on to write the famous *On the Origin of Species*. While others had similar ideas, Darwin's name is synonymous with the theory of evolution—that organisms evolve when an inherited trait becomes more common or less common over time. Integral to this theory was the notion of "survival of the fittest," the idea that competition is the natural order, and that the strongest survive, while the weak perish.

Darwin's work was at first controversial, but gradually took hold. Long before DNA was found to be an actual genetic code, Darwin's theories were accepted. Almost a century after Darwin's voyage, a couple of molecular biologists, James Watson and Francis Crick, were the first to describe the actual structure of DNA.

From Darwin noticing that species evolve over time to the central dogma of Watson and Crick, the result has been that we believe in genetics. During the years and decades, the central dogma has been accepted, but not proven. We believe that we are the products of our genetic code, and that much of our lives—from our physical characteristics and health, to our personalities and the way our lives unfold—are dictated by our genetics. This is WRONG!

One of the first people to question this was a microbiologist, Dr. Bruce Lipton. He cloned stem cells and observed that they differentiated based on their culture medium, or environment. Stem cells are the blank check of cells and eventually will evolve into specialized, or differentiated, cells corresponding to their location. This was thought to be based on genetic programming. The stem cells that Lipton created were not genetically programmed to become specialized, but they did. It was the environment that caused the stem cells to differentiate, not genetics.

We are made of cells. Doesn't the environment play some role, along with genetics, in how we grow, develop, and most importantly, change? That's where I'm going with this concept. Our environment literally changes the way our genetics are expressed. Our cells, the basic units of our bodies, and the unsung workhorses that make our existence possible, respond to stimuli that are both chemical and energetic (vibration). This causes the production of proteins that actually change the DNA. That's right! Receptors on the outer membrane of the cell send signals into the cell, which directly affect what parts of genes reproduce themselves. Just as important, those signals tell genes to produce the proteins that control all the functions of our bodies. It's the environment that controls what goes on in our cells, our bodies, and therefore our lives.

Therein lays the key. In knowing how the mechanical effect of environment on our bodies works, we can intentionally use this information. We can better control and change our bodies. We can improve our health, immunity, and overall wellness. But more importantly, we can literally change ourselves into a different person.

Finally, there is our everyday way of thinking and believing about our bodies. Like our addiction, our way of being from the bodily perspective grows and takes on a life of its own. It is one of the great challenges of recovery to develop a new relationship with our bodies.

I remember when I was younger; I seemed to have a much lower tolerance for life's minor aches, pains, and discomforts. Mosquito bites used to drive me insane. And of course, there was a whole host of minor bodily issues that went along with my drinking and partying lifestyle. My stomach was always in knots. I always had cramps, frequent headaches; and I always seemed to be focused on these things. I was extremely in touch with whatever was going on with my body; I was all about how I felt, my current state. This preoccupation with how one is feeling physically is a hallmark of alcoholism, and addiction in a broader sense. It's an outgrowth of the fact that our way of being has become about controlling our state. Chemical control of our state of mind, which is inseparable from our bodily state, is the focus of our daily routine. The top priority, whether conscious or not, is to achieve altered consciousness; the sun rises and sets on it. Hence, our bodies become alternately and paradoxically first ignored, then the focus of our attention.

The consequences of alcohol and drug use were the last thing on our minds when we drank or used. No penalty seemed real in the face of the need to drink or use, at least not real enough to stop us. The physical cost of a binge would be paid later on credit, and our bodies would have to pick up the tab. The desire to get drunk or high literally altered our thinking, and short-term relief always looked preferable to long-term conditions and possible outcomes.

Then, after the binge, when we came back to something approaching reality, our misery was compounded. Usually too much to face, a sense of guilt was the emotional price, but was quickly set aside to focus on the immediate concerns of bodily discomfort. My head! My stomach! As the pendulum swung back, the irony of the situation was, of course, lost on us. Stuffed away with the guilt was any sense of responsibility, or that the consequences now upon us were directly of our making. Whether a temporary byproduct of overindulgence or the aggravation of chronic and life-threatening, drinking-related illnesses, such as liver cirrhosis or esophageal varices, we obsessed over our bodies in the moment at the expense of the bigger picture.

Part of that bigger picture is some conditioning that we all experience to varying degrees. Society tells us, in a thousand subtle and unsubtle ways, that we need not suffer. We are trained to believe that we need not tolerate the slightest discomfort, distress, pain, or annoyance. In this miraculous modern age, why should we? After all, we are entitled to better living through chemistry. The glossy, full-page magazine ads told us to ask our doctor about new (fill in the blank). There should be no bodily problem that we cannot address. The miracle of modern healthcare's approach of symptom management can make us as good as new—or so we are led to believe. This widespread programming only serves to reinforce a state of mind and body that epitomizes the term "psychosomatic." Directly or indirectly, our bodily problems stem from our mind, as evidenced by the preoccupation with them experienced by the alcoholic and addict.

This quick-fix, biochemical control of our physical state is little different than the approach we took with altering our mood and consciousness chemically.

As a byproduct of my recovery, I resolved my preoccupation with my bodily comfort level. My physical discomforts are infrequent nowadays, not the more or less daily event that they were during my drinking years. Also, my attitude toward my body has changed profoundly. I am in awe of this gift I was given to manage for my time here on earth, as well as the miraculous way it functions. And, as with most other things, the more I understand about it, the better it works, and the more I appreciate it.

In conclusion, our bodies will always forgive us for our alcoholic transgressions against them as long as they are able. When we give them a chance, they will heal themselves. In fact, it's almost impossible to stop the body from healing itself. The heart beats, we breathe in and out, and thousands of processes and chemical reactions go on every second. We don't do that. The life force that keeps all those amazing things in our bodies going on is something else, something beyond our current understanding. The point where the physical realm ends and something else begins is the next important concept in the progression toward changing our way of being.

CHAPTER 18

Our Spirit

Whether we know it or not, we are searching for something greater. We are constantly striving to get beyond ourselves. Those random moments stick in our minds when we accidentally experience a stronger connection to that something greater. Unconsciously, or even consciously, we wish to experience them more often; we wish that every day was full of those moments. As the five-sense, cause-and-effect first world reality pulls us away from the momentary distraction of dwelling on the feeling of lightness and of heightened connection, we are drawn back to the dense and heavy feeling of our lives. The connection fades.

But what if we could maintain that feeling, that state of being connected? The secret lies in the awareness that the connection is always there. It's our awareness that flickers in and out. And the more time that awareness spends "flickered" out, the greater our feeling of disconnection.

Earlier, I talked about an experience I had on my fifth day of sobriety. Something happened that was so unusual, so unexpected, and so profound that it completely took over my attention. This was a minor example of the kinds of things that have been happening to people for centuries. Mystical experiences have been described by people all through history. Common to mystical or spiritual experiences are the elements that they are personal, extraordinary, and involve connection to some greater or higher power. They occur both within and outside religious context.

My spiritual experience propelled me forward in my recovery. First, it initiated the psychic shift we often hear described in the old-school, Big Book AA parlance. Following the shift, I found a new belief system in its wake, the result of being open-minded. Finally, I realized that I had been transformed. I had attained a new way of being, and somehow become a different person from the man who could not go a day without a drink.

This was development in a spiritual sense. Essential to each of these phases was living in a context of a deeper meaning than the superficial, materialistic, cause-and-effect reality of everyday life. Everything was happening against the backdrop of something greater working in my life. There was a gentle hand loosely observing events as they unfolded, like a spotter in the gym—ever ready to reach in should the need arise. Like that spotter in the gym, there to protect me from harm, faith enabled me to stretch the boundaries of my comfort zone to newer and greater limits. I didn't know exactly what, but I knew there was more… just more.

My thought processes, my attitudes, and my beliefs about me and drinking needed to undergo a major change. I needed to move alcohol out of the center of my thinking. I needed to believe in my own ability, first to not drink, and later to stay sober under all circumstances. The lingering doubts, tendency to rationalize, and incessant worry and obsessing needed to be replaced. I needed a certainty that my path in life was as it should be; the pursuit of recovery was the right thing for me to do. I had to adjust and modify my thinking to move beyond the fallibility that had characterized my drinking. I needed a reliable clarity, free of my own shortsightedness, so that I could know the difference among wants, needs, and plain stupidity. I needed a new operating system for my mind.

As I began my journey into the realm of the spirit, I encountered some obstacles and issues, which I think are common to many of us. How do I connect with spirit? How do I find a comfort level with my own conception of spirit versus a more conventional conception? And while I didn't know what I was experiencing at the time, there are some uncomfortable feelings that result from moving toward a spiritual way of being and letting go of old ways. How do I withstand emotional discomfort?

Like my spiritual experience, my spirituality is unique and personal. That it seemed the result of an extraordinary experience is only my personal circumstance; the experience was not necessary to become spiritual. However, all I did to initiate my profound, semi-mystical experience was to invite it and pay a little more attention than usual. By getting on my knees and asking for a sign of some God, higher power, or spirit, I opened the door. These spiritual goings-on are happening around us constantly. While there is no way to anticipate the unexpected, it is possible to move toward a state of open-mindedness where I'm more likely to notice. There are four stages to attain this spiritual state of mind:

1. I believe in a spiritual process all around me, and I am part of it.
2. I will expect this spiritual process to come into my awareness in surprising, unanticipated ways.
3. I will trust this spiritual process and the messages it conveys.
4. I will act on the messages and information that come to me through this spiritual process.

I believe that my inviting a power greater than myself to give me a sign was paramount, and, that by doing so, I initiated the extraordinary experience that I had on my fifth day of sobriety. In return for my initiative, I received an answer to a prayer. I moved into that first stage, belief. This enabled me to take my first fledgling steps toward spirituality. As the Eleventh Step says, I began to open "a channel."

As I moved through successive stages of spirituality, challenges arose. Just beneath the surface, there was a battle going on within me. In accepting and moving toward a spiritual basis for living, I was in a huge transition. Not only was I embracing a new way of being, I was releasing an old way of being. The previous Keith did not go quietly. Letting go of my alcoholic, spiritually bankrupt ways was painful, and I didn't even understand why. In the releasing of them, the calling up of all the bad decisions, bad endings, and regret of roads both taken and not taken was an emotional minefield that I unknowingly ran through helter-skelter. The isolation, self-doubt, and depressive feelings tested my developing faith.

What I hung on to, and what sustained me was the idea that all the things which felt wrong as I looked back were really still in a state of play. The ending was not yet written. Moving forward, if I could apply some lesson or insight from all those past debacles to some future situation, then there were no mistakes or wasted time. There were only lessons in a life that was richer for having learned them. As my faith began to gain traction, a central question became more pressing. What exactly do I believe in?

The byproduct of new-found attitudes and a more positive outlook, I began to process, sort, and integrate all the different ideas and information that seemed to literally flood into my awareness. These ideas about the nature of life as a being of flesh and blood, and also as a spiritual being started to gain some clarity. Out of all the possibilities, perspectives, and approaches to spirituality, the ones that suited and resonated began to settle in, take hold, and configure themselves into something cohesive. It started to make sense. My belief system began to take shape.

As I moved toward a unique personal perspective, there was a price to be paid. The path of least resistance was the more conventional, pedestrian perspective on spirit. God with the capital "G," liberal use of the pronoun "He," and frequent reference to "his will" seemed to be the mainstream way. This was not the path I chose. As I began to float my more original ideas and began asking questions at meetings, I encountered a fair amount of negative reinforcement. That nail that sticks up is always the one that gets hammered down. We can anticipate resistance. If we persist, we will break through the barriers and enter a zone of quiet confidence and serenity with our own spiritual perspective. It is all the more sweet because we come by it honestly. We need not wait for permission to believe what we believe; we give ourselves permission.

The things that came into my awareness through actual experience naturally felt more real. The power of the so-called coincidence was just not to be ignored. Hearing and seeing the same thing come up repeatedly tends to reinforce the notion. The conviction that we are spiritual beings having transient human experiences crystallized. This became the hub of a belief system that left room to embrace and accept the more rigid religious, agnostic, and atheistic perspectives. There was room for these in my way of thinking, though there was not room for my ideas in finite, inflexible, religious dogma. I was okay with that.

Next came those larger questions. Having arrived at the idea that I was something along the lines of eternal consciousness, a spirit or a soul, and that there is more to all of us than animated collections of component compounds, I couldn't stop there. It was a domino effect. Answering the question of what I am (in that larger sense) only raised more questions. Where do we come from, and where do we go? What is the real meaning of being a human being? And finally, but more immediately, what is my purpose in life?

This was more than a simple questioning of what did I want to be when I grew up. This was the existential question of "What am I doing in the world?" Again, this opens the Pandora's box of those deeper fears. I had to look at my journey to that point. I had played music and gotten drunk. Both were propositions in self-indulgence for the most part. Aside from giving a few people an excuse to dance or snap their fingers, I couldn't find too much about 20 years of playing the drums that had been for any greater good. I had existed in a culture of enclosed little band units, otherwise known as breeding grounds for narcissism and over-inflated egos. It was an exercise in self-absorption. Entities that existed primarily for their own advancement, popular music bands aren't exactly curing cancer.

But wait! I had a day job where I did literally help to cure cancer. I can claim no particular wisdom or insight for getting myself into my position as a surgical technologist. Other than a means to pay the bills and buy drumsticks until I was famous, my day job was just something that came about. Now I began to view it in a different light. Perhaps I was warming to the idea of being more part of the establishment and less of a rebel. In a larger sense, I began to view my participation in healthcare as something more than a weekly paycheck. Was I not making a contribution to the health and well-being of my fellow man? And furthermore, was I perhaps capable of challenging myself to make a more substantial contribution? After about eight years working as a surgical tech, seven years at the same job, I had more or less mastered my direct responsibilities. I was observing and absorbing more of the bigger picture going on around me.

At this point, the universe sent me a couple of messages. The first came in the form of a familiar face in the pre-op holding area one afternoon. I was returning from lunch, and my afternoon assignment was to assist a thoracic surgeon with a minor procedure. To me it was minor, but to the woman waiting for her diagnostic operation, it was no trivial event. Her name was Lucy, and I knew her from AA meetings. She was our next patient and would be having a two-part procedure to diagnose the possible presence and extent of cancer in her lungs and airway. She was a nervous wreck.

It was completely by happenstance that I even noticed her. Returning from lunch break, I decided to stop at the desk. I randomly looked over in the holding area and saw her and went to say hello. She was visibly relieved to see a familiar face at that fearful, lonely moment. I was amazed and a little overwhelmed at the tremendous comfort she took from my presence. As my role in procedures was concerned with the instruments and equipment, I did not typically have direct patient contact. Most of the time I was already in the operating room, scrubbed up in a surgical gown, preparing the sterile surgical setup at the time the patients were wheeled in. I told Lucy I would be present during her operation, that I would go check on my responsibilities, and return if I was able.

As usual, the surgeon was running late. I set up my tables, "broke scrub," and returned to keep Lucy company. She seemed deeply grateful that I would be there, and though this was not my familiar role, I somehow did and said the right things. I was able to comfort her during a time of extraordinary apprehension and stress. This was completely new and profound to me.

Lucy came through the procedure just fine, but the news was bad. She had terminal cancer. In the days that followed, her brother and sister-in-law, whom I also knew, made me aware how much my talking to her had meant. In the weeks and months until her death, we shared an amazing bond. The paradox of it is that those few moments of comfort I gave Lucy changed the course of my life.

The experience with Lucy in the first year of my recovery had started me thinking. I had no idea that I could speak with someone and help them. As I was learning about myself, that larger question, "What was I doing in the world?" kept popping up.

A few months into my second year of sobriety, the universe sent me the second message. I touched on this chronologically in an earlier section, but the synchronistic element bears further accounting. This message came in the form of advice from an objective observer. Lou, a nurse anesthetist was working in our operating room. He was a "temp," just passing through for a few weeks or months. Now, anesthesia is a paramount function in any surgical procedure. A large proportion of our surgery was done under general anesthesia. The anesthesiologist and nurse anesthetist put the patient to sleep. The anesthesiologist leaves the room, and the anesthetist monitors the sleeping patient. They basically observe. Occasionally making adjustments or putting medication through the intravenous line, the nurse anesthetist essentially spends the day watching sleeping people. Often without much else to do, they also watch the people doing the surgery.

After a few days with us, taking things in and assessing the dynamics, personalities and general goings-on, Lou pulled me aside. In the well-meaning, fatherly way a man my age now (50ish) would give unsolicited advice to a man my age then (30ish), he said, "I've been watching you. You could do this (surgical tech) job in your sleep. Why don't you get off your ass and go to nursing school?"

The timing could not have been any better for me to hear something like that. I was asking myself the larger questions to the point of starting to feel adrift. I pondered Lou's question and talked to him and others. In a matter of weeks, I was enrolled in a college anatomy course and on my way toward nursing school. This chain of coincidences traced itself back to my experience with Lucy when I was just a few months sober. I used the expression that the universe sent me messages because these occurrences showed me things that made me first think, then act toward making changes in my life. I believe such things are expressions of spirituality at work and an example of direct communication from whatever creative and loving intelligence underlies our existence. They are also examples of interactions with the consciousness, spirit, or souls of others who serve some purpose of helping me on my journey. To the extent that my mind was open, I received guidance and direction toward realizing what I now believe to be my purpose in life. It's also an example of trusting that guidance and acting on it. The larger questions persisted, but I was at least moving toward a life's purpose much more in tune with a spiritual basis for living.

So then, what is God? Everyone has an idea. No one knows.

There is a human tendency to see human faces in all kinds of places. We saw a human profile in the rocks of a mountainside in New Hampshire, the Old Man of the Mountain (until the elements finally gave him a nose job)! We see faces in cloud formations. The face of the Virgin Mary has been seen in a tortilla in Guadalajara, which was later sold on eBay. We also like to assign human attributes, characteristics, even emotions to our pets. Some people name their cars and give them a gender. Essentially, we have a tendency to make things appear like us in our minds. This has also happened with God. My first concept was that bearded Charlton Heston/Moses image.

For me, the idea of God is no longer that finite and not remotely humanlike. In the early years of my recovery, it evolved into and has remained the ultimate, underlying force of nature, and also broadly categorical. Universal creative intelligence works fine; it is descriptive, not definitive. A fatherly, Charlton Heston-like man sitting on a throne in the clouds, overseeing the day-to-day operations of the universe, can easily fall under the umbrella of universal creative intelligence. For me, the beauty of that is that it fits into a larger picture that makes sense in the world as I understand it.

Going back to the idea of a third world that encompasses everything else, what better concept for the realm of a universal creative intelligence! The foundation of everything in the universe, from the everyday, material reality through all the belief systems and everything we've called the supernatural, this field or matrix is the medium and probably the substance of the idea of God. It is the force that follows the blueprints of our DNA, telling our bodies what shape to grow in and hold. It is the stage on which the amazingly intricate choreography of our eternal spirits dance; our spirits intermingle and influence one another's paths like the intersections of the ripples from a large handful of tiny pebbles thrown onto still waters. In the version of the world that tells us we are waves of energy at the most fundamental level, entangled with everything regardless of space and time, the idea of constant connection, indeed actually being an aspect of the divine makes perfect sense. We are like individual branches of the same tree.

My ideas about my relationship with God also underwent an evolution. The religious notion holds that God is all-powerful. Omnipotent is a word often associated with the almighty deity of the major religions. Because the original idea of AA's higher power came from that, the program conditions us to the idea that, "there is one who is all-powerful." Implicit in this seems to be the notion that we are insignificant. God is everything, we are nothing. My will must ally with the will of God, or I might as well forget it.

Instead, I've adopted a different concept of this. After all, the God of my understanding, while the ultimate force of nature, is the all-encompassing matrix of energy of which I am part. If this scientifically verified energy matrix connects everything, I am always connected to God, the way even the most distant twig branch is connected to the main trunk of the tree. This understanding supports a more collaborative relationship. After all, I am a consciousness who observes my reality, good or bad, into being. In a relatively neutral universe where my experience of reality is the product of infinite possibilities, my consciousness could manifest either heaven or hell. It supports the concept that I am an architect of sorts; God is the ultimate contractor. I can design the life of my dreams or nightmares. God will build either one. The relationship is one of cocreation, and the choice of outcomes rests with me.

So, what if the universe is a kind of grand cosmic copy machine? What we send out, good or bad, comes back a hundredfold, even a thousandfold. And doesn't every copy machine come with instructions for proper use? If I want my copies, or my life, to come out a certain way, it would be worthwhile for me to understand a few simple principles. As will be discussed in Part IV, the universe, while more vast than we could ever begin to comprehend, might not be as complicated as we've been led to believe.

Why does this notion of spirit work for me? Because it is the philosophical equivalent of physics' Holy Grail, the unified field theory. This idea of spirit, universal intelligence or God, is well on its way to that point down the road where religion, science, philosophy, and every other worldview, way, discipline, or mindset will eventually meet and come to agreement. This works for me because if God can be described as an all-encompassing field of energy underlying all existence, then there is a primary spiritual truth—that *separateness is an illusion. Everything is connected at a fundamental level.*

And so, if separateness is only our perception of that connection to something greater fading, we can remind ourselves that we have more than a mere connection. We ourselves are aspects of a universal creative intelligence, higher power, or God. We are splinters of the divine, connected by unbreakable threads back to the source. Our consciousness knows this. The challenge for us during these transient human experiences is to bring that knowledge through to our earthly awareness. When we do this, earthly human dalliances, such as alcoholism, begin to pale. Part of our purpose is to transcend them.

Once I was a man who could not go a day without a drink. Now I never, NEVER think about or want to drink. Of myself, I did not do that. It was that aspect of me that connects to something greater, indeed, it was something greater than me that made that recovery possible.

CHAPTER 19

Our Recovery

From the first inkling that we have a problem to the transformed life of our dreams, we are in the process of recovery. It's another version of the wellness, or health continuum discussed earlier; we move along a scale from being diseased to being recovered.

Once we enter recovery to a certain point, it is difficult to turn back. Recovery has a way of hooking us; learning the truth about ourselves makes it impossible to free ourselves and move back to our previous existence. Make no mistake, the disease will pull us back, but at some level this will feel utterly wrong. Once we know something about our way of being, we become responsible for that knowledge. The fact is that we can never be the same. We will experience a vague sensation of unease that will increasingly demand we address it. That sense of unease will eventually fester until it requires a significant expenditure of effort. It won't go away. In reality, the fear of the thing is worse than the thing, but it is still a courageous act to turn and face ourselves. The alternative is to throw more drugs and alcohol at the issue, but that can only go on so long.

Recovery is about power, personal power, and relationship with power structure, not just power over alcohol. Behind many addictions is some type of psychic wound that takes our power away. People, places, and things have power over us largely because we allow it. The result is often coexisting issues, such as depression, sadness, and lack of energy or motivation. These problems often form the basis for excuses. The real recovery process is about resolving these things and other issues of power.

The Twelve Steps are brilliantly cohesive. Methodical, orderly, and sequentially logical, both the substance and subtext of their suggested program are inspired. As a simple roadmap, they act as a literal repair manual for the addiction-shattered life. By first looking within, and simultaneously establishing a new relationship with power, if we continue to follow these suggestions our lives will surely transform. On a deeper level, they address the need to heal the mind, body, and spirit, and in this more substantial process, potential is limited only by the degree to which we are able to manage our own fear.

My recovery started out conventionally. I got sober in the standard, Twelve-Step, Alcoholics Anonymous way. After only minor reverberations of questions and doubts in my early years, I went partially renegade. While never abandoning the Twelve-Step model, I began to bring in other elements, in addition to looking at the standard approach in a more abstract way. I would encourage anyone starting out in recovery from alcoholism or addictions to learn the fundamentals of Twelve-Step recovery, go to meetings, get a sponsor, and work the steps.

The Twelve Steps of Alcoholics Anonymous begin with the admission of powerlessness. It is stated as powerlessness over alcohol, but the qualification of a life unmanageable implies more. The theme of power and powerlessness keeps coming back.

In my case, I was powerless over events of my earlier life. I'd been powerless over my mother's alcoholism, and I'd been in a power struggle with my father in which I'd been emotionally damaged. As a result of those two issues, I was hobbled in my relationship with the external power structure. Could it have been any more ironic that I found myself in an environment based on a matriarchal authority structure (the nursing world), and in a specialty area that surrounded me with father figures (surgeons)? My mother's parental failings resulted in my subconsciously sitting in judgment over the competence of any woman I worked with, particularly those to which I was subordinate. And judging them less than competent, the only resolution of my powerlessness over that was bad behavior and/or drinking. It was a power struggle every moment.

My conflict with my father had been primarily around my desire to pursue music as some vague career choice and my drinking secondarily. My father's inability or refusal to validate my considerable musical ability was painful to me, but did not deter me. The party-animal lifestyle enmeshed in my music and everyday existence only served to further alienate him. Our conflict escalated to his rejection of me after I graduated, and again several years later when he redrafted the divorce agreement to exclude any wording of obligation for college support. My choice of "day job" was me proving to myself, and my father in absentia, that I was capable of undertaking a kind of respectable existence. I wanted his approval. Conforming to the power structure of operating-room hierarchy was my subconscious demonstration (to myself) that I was good enough for my father.

So, if someone asked me why I drank, the honest answer would've been something like, "Well, if you lived your life unconsciously compensating for self-perceived failures in past parental power struggles, life disappointments, and the associated feelings of personal inadequacy, you'd drink too!"

I drank because I was powerless over much more than alcohol. Surrender, acceptance, and belief are what I learned from the first three steps. In broad strokes, the first three steps began to redefine my relationship with alcohol and everything outside myself. The theme is change, and it starts with something external; alcohol and the chaos it brings is the prime mover. As I progress, I learn that I do not need something outside of me to change what goes on inside me. I need not wait for catastrophe or dire circumstances to motivate me; I can change; first out of desire for freedom, and then to gain enlightenment.

Steps Four and Five direct my attention back to myself. While in the context of my relationships with people, places, and things, the focus stays on me. The inventory is but a beginning in what must become part of my way of being. The ability to look at myself in situations objectively, accurately, and, most of all, fearlessly is a life-long goal. If Step Four is like writing an expository article about me, Step Five is the fact-checking step in the process and serves to ensure that my work has been nonfiction. My honesty is a measure of my courage and desire to be in the process. While I tell my Step Five confessions to another person, it is also testimony before God, and the initial broadcast of my changing my ways.

We are our own harshest critics. I was this way, and it's a habit that is hard to break. As a nurse, it was impressed on me that I must never judge a patient because it influences or harms the therapeutic relationship. If I am my own patient, shouldn't I bring that same nonjudgmental approach to my own treatment? And remember that judgment and objectivity, one of my main goals, cannot coexist. My efforts at self-examination will benefit from every ounce of detachment that I can muster. This is not about shame or contrition; this is about understanding my past actions and what motivated them so that I can change that man. Learning from the experience of the past helps me form a better vision for the future.

In Steps Four and Five, I begin to assume responsibility for my choices, actions, and inactions. Just as important, I come to understand the consequences of those choices, actions, and inactions. However, before becoming willing to accept those consequences, I need to work to ensure that the underlying character defects have been eradicated. Becoming a different man than the one who drank every day is a long-term vision, as opposed to a short-term goal, and a new way of being requires attention to some details. In Step Six, I review my character flaws and their results, again without judgment, but with an intensity that will turn them into mental warning beacons that cannot be missed or ignored in the future.

Step Seven sets a new precedent. In asking to have something done for me by something greater than myself, I'm entering uncharted waters. In the previous steps, I performed the action. I admitted, I came to believe, I turned my will over... I made inventory, shared that inventory, and then became ready to take this next step of humbly asking God to remove my defects of character. While my asking is still me performing an action, the details of how the outcome is reached are different. This step is a test of the new collaboration between the contractor (God) and the architect (me). I have to believe in the blueprint enough to be willing to go to any lengths. To make the end-product possible, I have to do more to ensure the result than just imagine what it looks like. That's where the humility comes in.

If God and I are teamed up here, I need to be a team player. Nursing taught me this valuable skill. On a team, I need to do whatever needs to be done for the team. On a team, the greater objective comes before the individuals. On a team, good leadership means being a good follower. And in my collaboration with God, I need to do whatever heavy lifting is necessary. I need absolute willingness to mop the figurative floors and clean the proverbial toilets of my recovery. God gives me the opportunities and works out the details, but it's not going to be a supernatural, miraculous instantaneous change. If I want to build a new life, I have to be willing to pitch in and clean up the construction site.

When I ask for my shortcomings to be removed, I can anticipate that the question will be answered with more questions. My humble request for the removal of my difficulties will be met with a response from the universe, as if to say "Do you really want to change? Show me!"

My desire to have my impatience removed will result in situations that test my patience. My desire to stop judging will result in opportunities to judge or choose not to judge. And the biggie, my desire to be free from fear will surely bring circumstances where I must face fear. And so it goes, a continual process. No bolt of lightning, no supernatural transformation. It's just me and the universal creative intelligence, my collaborator, working on a daily basis to change me. And it is work. As with any work, it's not accomplished instantaneously, but rather bit by bit. The first stage of my character defect work must be in remembering that I am committed to this goal. Whenever these opportunities to work through one of these issues arise, I can simply be aware of what's happening, and grateful for that. Then, I can take a breath, and do my best to have patience, put my judgment aside, or face that fear. I can make having this awareness one of my first objectives.

I am now ready for a change in focus. I am now at a pivot point. Up until this juncture, the spotlight of inquiry has shown on me. My history, behaviors, habits, feelings, outlook, and interactions—in brief, my entire old way of being—have been the subject of my inspection. While in the framework of my environment, this has been an exercise in self-examination. The state of my character, though still rough, is starting to resemble a more finished product. As I seek to solidify and further improve my new character, I turn my attention outward.

To make my transformation a reality, it must apply to my relationship with my entire environment. My personal transformation must apply to my relationships with all the people, places, and things of my existence. This is the real purpose of Steps Eight and Nine. Much more than a list of apologies I need to make, my work on Step Eight has to reach down to the substance of my entire history of conflict and strife. To amend something is to change it. Making of amends is putting something right, correcting it. Best performed from a place of strength, not weakness, from conviction rather than uncertainty, and from security that I have truly changed, the preparation for the step to follow is motivated by strong desire to send the universe a memo. That memo says I am not the same person. If this is true, I will send a signal that reinforces this.

As I go forward with Step Nine, I need to be aware that I am sending a signal on a couple of different levels. My words and my actions send a message that will register in the thoughts of the people I approach. If I am truly now operating on a new basis, my energy and intention must also broadcast a new message to their hearts; as I amend the situation, I am establishing a new basis for the relationship.

This new basis will likely fly in the face of an established dynamic. If we have long been the cause of some pain, resentment, or negative emotion in someone's life, they have likely been adapting to that. For their own peace of mind, they have simply accepted and settled into a particular way of viewing us. We are now setting out to modify or even break what has become an emotional agreement. The way of being between us has been a certain way, and we are now sending a message that it's changing. This message might or might not be received or accepted.

The success of Step Nine, and of my transformation for that matter, is contingent on the modification of these emotional agreements. They are the energy and substance of the relationships, and translate directly back to my defects of character. Suppose I need to make amends to someone for dishonesty. In the dynamic of our relationship, there is an underlying pattern, an emotional agreement, which has set the tone for that relationship. That's what it has been about in the past, just certain chemistry with a certain result—my dishonesty. The dynamics of that relationship will likely make it challenging to be honest going forward. Whatever compelled my dishonesty in the past will not miraculously go away because I am raising the bar for my own behavior. The other person will not change simply because I have more honorable intentions than before. The new me will meet with resistance both subtle and obvious, and I need to keep the intensity of my new intention at a top level. It must have more power than my old pattern. Remembering that the amend was more than an apology, I must maintain resolve to remain on that new basis.

Understanding what forces underlie my efforts will help me stay on task, and so will my reviewing the status of these efforts. Understanding how it works will help it work better, and assessing my progress at changing myself keeps me on track toward my vision. What better point in this undertaking than to set something in place to monitor my own progress? Step Ten fulfills this need.

Part of a viable approach to solving any problem is evaluating progress. Whether in science, nursing, or recovery, this makes sense. Scientists publish their findings so that others might verify them. Nurses assess the effectiveness of their interventions. In my recovery, I need to ask myself how I'm doing, and answer that honestly. Moreover, my continued personal inventory in Step Ten will likely raise the need for further changes and corrective actions. As part of this step, I must remain willing to take action.

Here, we need to use that objectivity that was hopefully one of the direct benefits of our previous personal inventory in Step Five. Our improved knowledge and working relationship with our character defects is our principal tool; desire to remain free of those defects is our motivator. Our lives are dynamic, constantly changing, evolving and in motion. We can't stay home where no trouble would find us, nor would we want to. While we are in the process of becoming new and upgraded versions of ourselves, people, places, and things will always be beyond our control. They will always present opportunities to fall back into old ways.

My resolve to transform is important, but I need the practical help that Step Ten affords me. The daily inventory then should be more than a figurative taking of my emotional temperature. It's not enough to know if I have that "emotional hangover"; I have to both know and address whatever caused it. What character defects and old emotional agreements are at work in this situation? How did the previous Keith react in similar situations? How am I reacting now, and how would the man I desire to be not so much react, but rather respond, in the situation?

Importantly, I must step back emotionally. The same previous criteria regarding judgment apply. I must be objective. Because I will be unable to address an emotional disturbance while I am experiencing the same intense emotions, by consciously applying Step Ten to the situation, the mere intention, I am initiating a corrective measure. Simply thinking about the step begins the process of thinking about my thoughts, rather than simply being in (and reacting to) those thoughts.

In addition to being an ongoing measure of progress, and thereby a useful tool, Step Ten has the practical benefit of removing obstacles to intuition. What starts as vague feelings or perceptions will then begin to crystallize into a kind of knowing. This knowing is a dividend, a byproduct of the work we have done up to this point. We have moved from subjective viewpoint toward objectivity. We have become willing and moved toward honesty and open-mindedness to possibility. We have moved from selfishness toward selflessness. And we have sought this enlightenment not for specified outcomes, but for its own sake. So when we have those moments, and that's all they are—blips on the radar, Step Ten serves as the security system that will alert us to breaches and threats to our peace of mind, and hence our recovery.

How does something feel? Disregarding my intellectualization and the pride, insecurity, and associated thoughts of what I (selfishly) want, what feelings am I left with? In my gut, what's going on? "Wrong" just has a feeling about it. I can recognize it, but I have to be aware of its potential and be open to it. And this will not happen as long as my mind is racing with crazy thoughts and is overwhelmed with the heat of the emotion of the moment.

"Right" is also a feeling. It's like the middle of my stomach has a little brain of its own that thinks those thoughts of right and wrong. This is intuition at its most fundamental level.

Intuition is of course a direct channel to that divine creative intelligence that is God. The aspect of our higher self which connects to that is a voice of guidance. The cultivation of the ability to hear this voice is both the objective and direct benefit of developing a spiritual practice. This is addressed in Step Eleven.

Building on Steps Two and Three and those elements of Step Five and Seven, which enlist a power greater than me, I will seek to further develop that relationship. This creative, loving intelligence, this higher power of my personal understanding that I have such vast gratitude for, and so much awe—this underlying force that is all of nature is what gives me the gift of this earthly existence. The word God seems almost trite. When I've said that my relationship with this greater power is one of collaboration, it is with the deepest humility and reverence. I'm filled with wonder and veneration. When I likened the universe to a grand copy machine, it is homage to both the simplicity and complexity that is creation. The basis of this relationship is love; that love is the substance of God, and by extension, because I am fundamentally connected (separation is an illusion), the substance of me. I love my higher power.

In Step Eleven I seek to improve my conscious contact with my higher power. In this case, the context of "conscious" means mindful and aware. I can expand on that to mean improving my consciousness' contact. I am, after all, eternal consciousness in the midst of a human experience. And because that consciousness is already linked to the divine, making contact is about connecting to that part of myself that is God. All the links are already there. Working Step Eleven is therefore about the removal of barriers and obstacles, just as recovery is about the removal of addictions. My alcoholism and all the attendant human drama and character defects can now be viewed as just that, barriers and obstacles to the advancement of my spirit.

This process has brought me through an orderly sequence. By redefining myself and accepting the fact of my alcoholism, then establishing a working basis for a relationship with a solution to that alcoholism, I have set myself on a course of change. Through self-examination, I gain understanding of my way of being. As I share that understanding, the difference between the man I did become and the man I could and should have become turns crystal clear. To meet the objective of moving from that old way of being to a new way of being, or bridging a gap, the focus of the orderly sequence shifts outward. The transition moves from me to me in my world, and then to that world. My new way of being moves from inside of me to outside of me. Through corrective action, my inner state will begin to redefine my outer reality. I will then monitor the ongoing progress of this work, making adjustments as needed, the objective being constant progress in this transformation. Further, I need to look beyond the everyday, cause-and-effect part of my world(s). I need to address and come to terms with life's larger questions in view of my new way of being.

There is something familiar about this sequence. In a symbolic way, the actions I am undertaking correspond to the accepted means by which all things are proven. Step One, by the admission of alcoholism, raises the question (though unspoken), "What am I going to do about it?" Step Two leads to the idea that this can be changed. Step Three predicts how this change can be done. Steps Four through Nine test this idea and prediction. Step Ten is the ongoing evaluation of the test, and the work is repeated daily. On a daily basis, in both our lives and the recovery community, the outcome of our work is under constant review. Steps Eleven and Twelve are figurative publication, broadcasting our new way of being in both our physical and spiritual realities. The process is not entirely unlike the scientific method in which things are proven and questions settled. Just the way an idea moves through the process to ultimately be accepted as a law, my recovery moves through the process and ultimately becomes a transformation.

Step Twelve allows that I have removed barriers and obstacles. I have achieved some measure of transformation. While my goal is a perpetual continuation of this process, moving constantly toward a higher objective, I can acknowledge that I am living on a new basis. I also understand that my new way of being can be self-sustaining if I expend effort on its behalf daily. And finally, I must broadcast my new way of being, to the world in general, and to those like me in specific. The simple reality of the whole AA program, the simple foundation underlying all of my transformation, all of my new way of being, is that idea of one alcoholic helping another.

In any context, a spiritual awakening is a significant, life-altering thing. It can be in the form of an abrupt "lightning bolt-like" event. It can be in the form described by philosopher William James in the second appendix of the Alcoholics Anonymous book, a gradual educational experience. As in my case, it might be the cumulative effect of some combination of the two. The end result is profoundly altered knowledge, experience, and emotion. It is a different and new way of being.

This new way of being gives us a sense of reverence. We respect one another. We respect life in general. We have a really good general idea of our relationship to everything else that is, the entire universe. We know where we stand. Knowing that we are a grain of sand on an infinite beach, we also know that we have our rightful place on the beach with all those other grains of sand. It would be a different beach without our individual grain of sand; we belong there, just as all the other grains belong. And whether we subscribe to a religious perspective, atheist or agnostic point of view, or the quantum model, we have a sense of connection. We are "a part of," no longer "apart from."

Contemporary twenty-first–century life is a far cry from the decades when AA was founded. Though we are the same species of human beings, culture and society are strong influences. We are conditioned in the cause and effect way of the first world I described earlier. The product of every experience, good or bad, we are different and unique individuals in a culture that has come a long way since the 1930s. Information has doubled several times since then. Technology has given us connection, but everything has its price. With one type of connection comes another type of isolation, and with it emotional consequences. The pervasive "better living through chemistry" way of the world has transformed the recovery landscape. Teenagers and twenty-somethings are landing in rehabs in droves, having used every substance on the admission questionnaire for years already. While I came to the end of my 20s and my drinking simultaneously, almost as a product of finally growing up, this polysubstance phenomenon is having another dire consequence. The lasting physical, psychological, and emotional consequences of intensive use of anything and everything mind-altering will destroy a life long before someone can progress to becoming ready to change. Unfortunately, there is no substitute for readiness. After decades of bottoms getting higher, bottoms are on the way down again. The recovery landscape is more challenging than ever.

The balance we seek in our recoveries and our lives becomes more challenging to come by, almost daily.

Part IV
Sustainable Recovery

"The field is the sole governing agency of the particle."
~ Albert Einstein

CHAPTER 20

In Love with Life

Is an amazing recovery an accident? Does it happen randomly? Did I just follow some suggestions and have a good outcome? Did I just go to some meetings, follow a sponsor's suggestions, and become someone who doesn't drink?

I don't think so.

From AA Steps One, Two, and Three, I have learned surrender, belief, and acceptance. I understand that addiction and recovery are both about a balance of power. I am simultaneously powerless over alcohol, while powerful in other ways. My God-given freewill is powerful, and I am responsible for using it constructively. Toward that end, I need a vision for my recovery and also for my life. I need a clear intention for the change I want to experience, in addition to the willingness to go way beyond the beginning of the first three steps. I want to transform into a different man than the one who drank daily.

In my early recovery, I thought about what I wanted. Essentially, I wanted what I have today. In general terms, I desired to be happy and lead a productive life, no longer a slave to drinking and alcohol. Only after I could pinpoint that and understand it could I begin to move toward it. I needed a vision.

What is that vision, and how would I create it? That vision is fundamentally about life's larger questions. To begin to develop it, I needed some understanding and answers to those larger questions. I began to envision a belief system that worked. I began to envision myself initiating and bringing about profound change in my way of being. I saw myself thinking differently and also feeling and acting differently. Where I had formerly been someone who could not go a day without a drink, I wanted to be someone no longer limited by the ball and chain of alcoholism.

At the other extreme, almost daily I see recovering people living in a limited state. They're limited by their own beliefs about what is possible. They do not wake up in the morning with the intention of being limited. Quite the contrary, it's been a lifelong process. They have been essentially told their entire lives, "This is how it is. This is how it's been. This is how it will be." They have been conditioned and they've accepted this, and as a result they have a disease that's only been anesthetized. Living each day in fear of their disease, they're in a self-constructed prison. Their cellmate is a horrible alcoholic monster, merely dozing, and it could awaken and run amok at any moment.

If they even have a vision, it likely doesn't reflect their potential or the infinite possibility that we are all capable of bringing to reality.

We don't need permission to want something more from our recovery. We don't need permission to do something new, different, and better. And it's not a case of either/or... it's not limited to a choice of the old way or a new way. We can take the best of what AA has always done, and we can do more with it. We can understand specifically what about AA worked, why it worked, and we can make it work better...

We can have what's worked the best for the most for the longest, while making it into something so much more. We can be so much more.

When I was a kid, we used to go on field trips in school. Once or twice a year, there would be a trip to the Museum of Science or the New England Aquarium, or something similar in Boston. Announcements would be made, permission slips would be obtained, and the day would finally arrive. I remember always having trouble getting to sleep the night before, while I thought about going on the trip the next day.

In my mind, I would imagine all the details. Based on my experience of past field trips, I would think about the things I might see the next day. Using my imagination, I could make those images of the trip that was yet to come absolutely real in my mind. It was as though I was already experiencing it the night before. Eventually I would tire and fall asleep, only to waken the next morning full of energy and enthusiasm. I got up before the alarm. I got dressed and ready; I even made my bed!

I had successfully experienced the trip I hadn't even taken yet, including all the feelings of excitement, happiness, and gratitude. I didn't know it at the time, but I was in love with life that day. I had used something that Step Eleven refers to as constructive imagination.

What if every day could be like that? And why isn't it?

For one thing, as I grew up, the world reconditioned me from my childhood imaginative state. The world told me that everything was about cause and effect. The world told me that I should forget about Santa Claus, the Tooth Fairy, and the Easter Bunny, and focus more on what I could see, hear, feel, taste, and smell.

For another thing, the world gave me responsibilities and obligations, and it just got complicated in general. The results were fears, insecurities, and anxieties, which served to distract and preoccupy me.

Fundamentally, I can be in one of two general states. My mind, which is constantly thinking about my own thoughts (that 10-cent word, metacognition, that I talked about earlier), is going down one of two roads. The consequences of this are that I'm either in a state of growth or a state of decay. Emotionally, it's one or the other; I can't be in both simultaneously. Feelings such as gratitude or insecurity are mutually exclusive. It comes down to my mind being in a state of creation or a state of survival. Based on which path I'm on at the given moment, my mood, the byproduct of my thoughts and feelings, will be in a positive or negative state.

When I say my mind is headed down one of two roads or paths, what exactly do I mean by consequences? In terms of my mood, there is a fairly direct relationship between what I'm thinking and how I'm feeling. If I have a thought, it begins to create a feeling. For example, if I have an anxious thought, it sends a signal to my body and a chemical is created. The chemical begins to create a feeling consistent with that anxious thought. As I become more aware of that new feeling in my body, it would tend to reinforce the anxious thought. A repetitive cycle has now been created; the reinforced thought sends more signals, which create more chemicals, which create more feelings, which reinforce more thoughts, etc. The result is that the mood becomes stronger.

So I have that one little momentary anxious thought. It can result in a full-blown, mood-changing, sharp turn down Negative Street.

When I'm feeling anxious, I start to worry, and when I worry I start to think selfishly, and when I think selfishly I start to lose patience with others. When I'm impatient, I become judgmental, and when I'm judgmental, I can start to become angry... and so on. Likewise, suppose I have a grateful thought. I'm just thinking and feeling grateful for the good things in my life. It's a short association to thinking about wanting the same good things for others, and when I want good things for others, I am thinking and feeling compassion, and when I'm thinking compassionate thoughts I start to feel empathy. When I am feeling gratitude, compassion, and empathy, I start to feel love for others. Soon I'm having thoughts and feelings of being in love with life.

If I reduce whatever I'm thinking and feeling to its most basic ideas, it's that simple. It's positive or it's negative. Quantum physicist David Bohm described reality as existing in either the implicate or explicate orders; either folding in or unfolding out. Everything is either growing or decaying. It's building up or falling apart. The philosophical physics question of whether the universe is becoming more organized or disorganized tells us that everything, including us, is in one of two basic states.

At the level of my physical body, I can be injured, diseased, breaking down. etc., or I can be in homeostasis (balance of the body's systems), healthy, or growing. Mentally and emotionally, I can be stressed, fearful, unfocused, angry, or sad, or I can feel on my game, be secure and confident, focused and loving. Ever notice how it's difficult to experience both sides of the spectrum at the same time? If I'm full of fear, it's hard to feel loving. If I'm full of gratitude, it's hard to feel insecure. My mood is going to be essentially on either the light side or the dark side.

Getting back to the idea of being in love with life, like the day of the field trip, it's important to realize that I did that. While it started with something outside me, the field trip, I created the positive state of mind. That all happened inside me. I used my experience of other field trips to form my mental pictures; I just took an idea and things I already knew and moved to a positive way of being. The happiness and enthusiasm I felt were absolutely real, and I created them. Even more importantly, everything I experienced happened before I even got on the bus to go on the trip.

Why can't my recovery be one long field trip? Why can't I move beyond all those limitations and obstacles of the cause-and-effect world? I can! But to do that, I need a vision. I need a goal, an objective to work toward. And I need to bear in mind that it isn't likely that the objective, which is an amazing recovery, is going to happen by itself. The more clear I get on what I want, the better the likelihood that it will happen.

Great people seldom did great things by accident. Sometimes their accomplishments exceeded their wildest dreams, but they had dreams and desired outcomes nevertheless. Sometimes it's hard to think in terms of great things for ourselves. After all, recovery stresses humility; we are supposed to keep our egos in check and avoid grandiosity. We have to achieve an absolute level of comfort with the fact of setting a high goal for ourselves and our recoveries. This is where we need to reconcile our ideas with some long-standing AA dogma. The old adages "Keep It Simple" and "One Day at a Time" are examples.

Throughout the years, as I developed and shared the ideas that eventually became the ideas in this book, I met with resistance. People always said, "Keep it simple." What they really meant much of the time was, "Don't make me think about new ideas." New ideas had a tendency to threaten old ideas. If someone's way of being was based on those old ideas, their security was threatened along with their ideas about recovery. If life was simple, would we even be here thinking about this? If my life had been simple and uncomplicated, would I be an alcoholic?

The status quo of Alcoholics Anonymous offers 80-year-old answers to increasingly more complex contemporary questions. I appreciate everything it's done for me, and I love AA. However, the "simple" fact is that I, like many of us, have questions that are outside the AA box. I want the benefit of the newest possible answers. Life is complicated and getting more so each day. I need to accept that complicated problems might not always have simple answers.

As a group, we are people who tend to ask "Why?" When told "No," our response is usually, "Why not?" Deep down, we want to know the reasons for things, and we want to know how things work. More and more, people need to attach meaning to things. I have shared a lot of information in this book, some of it medical and scientific, and some of it is complicated. I have tried to break it down, but some of it is still just hard to understand. The reason it's necessary is because the kinds of things we're talking about work better when we understand how and why they work. Like the astronauts who flew to the Moon, we can't possibly know everything, but as much basic understanding as we are capable of absolutely enhances our ability to change. Understanding fosters belief, belief supports faith, and faith makes recovery possible. For better or worse, it's that simple.

We live our lives subject to an agreement about how time works. As discussed earlier, time is a concept, and in the practical everyday world, it gives us a structure. To varying degrees, it seems to govern our existence. We measure time in cycles of various sizes: seconds, minutes, hours, days, weeks, months, years, etc. When we first get sober, a day without a drink is a really miraculous event. We absolutely need to credit ourselves with a healthy self-respect for going one day without one drink. As we develop coping skills and defenses against that first drink, the obsession eventually abates. We are now in increasingly larger cycles of time without drinking. We stay sober for days, weeks, etc.

As we discover the reality that we must change in order to stay sober, that we can no longer be the same person who drank daily, we view and measure this change in relation to these cycles of time. We do not notice much significant change in shorter cycles of time, as from one day to the next. However, at the end of the first month of recovery, we might reflect on and notice tangible evidence of changes occurring in our lives. The same is true for time cycles of several months, and it becomes more obvious with the longer cycles. The change is there to see.

On the occasion of my fifth anniversary as I sat in front of my home group, I was absolutely struck by the amazing change from my first day of sobriety. I sat there reflecting on how I had felt and what was happening in my life back when I could barely stay sober only through an exhausting act of personal will. The transformation was a byproduct of that longer cycle of time. I had quit drinking, drugs, and smoking cigarettes, earned a degree, become physically healthy and fit, and bought a home. So in addition to the usefulness of measuring the short-term goal of staying sober for one day, the longer-range time cycles are important in a bigger vision of recovery.

I cannot take the concept of keeping it in the day too literally for too long. When I struggle to stay sober, it is everything, but when the time comes to focus on the transformational process, I mustn't limit myself.

There was a marvelous movie called *Groundhog Day*. The main character was a self-absorbed jerk who found himself repeatedly waking up at the same time on the same day in the same place, doomed to repeat history, apparently forever. At the end of every 24-hour cycle, the same thing would start over. The lesson he finally learned was that, while the 24 hours would remain the same, he could be different. He began to change as the result of doing something different each 24 hours. The cumulative effect of his change was the happy ending, where he transcended his old way of being and finally woke up on the next day, a new man.

The point is that I want to experience the same kind of change that the *Groundhog Day* man experienced. I need to focus on the desired outcome and work on changing toward that goal during each 24-hour period. Staying sober for that day is a great short-term goal, but I also need a long-term vision.

I want to emphasize that my moving toward a vision for the future recovery means I am moving away from my alcoholic past. I am making a clear decision to transcend what I believed were my limitations. First, I must be free of any lingering doubts about my alcoholism. My conviction that I must change has to be absolute. If I am in the process of working the steps, I have already begun to let go of some old ideas. Do I struggle with the issue of worthiness? Did I deserve the unfortunate things that came my way in life? Am I supremely sincere in amending every wrong aspect of my reality, or in my desire to do so? As long as I am aware of and want these things, I'm making the necessary beginning. There is always a place I can start. If I don't yet want these things, I can think about them. I can move toward wanting to want them. So, in establishing my vision, I need to spend the necessary time and work toward creating it.

You can keep it as simple as setting the goal or making a vision of creating your vision. You can break it down into the simplest initial steps.

Remember that there is no wrong way to undertake this process. It might be confusing that your individual circumstances don't seem to line up in some orderly progression. Perhaps you are new to recovery and haven't yet worked on the steps. Perhaps you are full of questions about everything from what goes on in AA to how sponsorship works. Perhaps you have been sober for years, but find yourself struggling with the desire to drink. The tremendous fact is that all possible experiences in recovery have the tendency to come together and make sense in a big picture way. It's simple—all it takes is a desire. If you want (or even just want to want) to stop drinking, and if you want to be honest, open-minded, and willing, you're on your way.

The next part is to set your intention. You can make up your mind. It's as simple as deciding that you'll do something. Is it really such a stretch from wanting something to making a decision about it? Absolutely not. Think about that decision, and then make it! And be ready. When you make that decision, make it with power and conviction. Think about making that decision with more energy and force, more intensity, than the emotional attachment to whatever stands in the way. You can make that decision more powerful than self-doubt, feelings of unworthiness, even your own emotional and physical addiction to alcohol or whatever. You can do this! Focus your intention.

As you begin to contemplate your vision, take your time and relax. You are now in the act of creating. If you are inclined, you can ask for guidance. Thoughts and ideas will come. Be patient. You need to go deep. Ask yourself, "What is my heart's desire? What kind of recovery do I want?"

For me, the answers to those questions were basic, yet somewhat ambitious. I wanted a contented, productive way of life. I wanted some level of reckoning with those larger questions about my existence. And I wanted a recovery wherein I could securely expect that I would continue to stay sober if I continued to work that recovery.

Those things are fairly simple, yet a far cry from what felt possible to the fearful, physically sick man that was me on January 9, 1991. The best vision I could muster that day was for my skin to stop crawling and my appetite to return. Remember, we have to move beyond the short-term goal stage before we get serious about our long-term vision.

The creation of the vision for my recovery and my life was the first stage in creating that recovery and life. It was the first stage in consciously and deliberately becoming a different person.

Ultimately, I must become clear on what my vision is. This is important, because if the universe functions like a cosmic copy machine, I need to give it specific instructions. Here is the key: the universe has a tendency to respond to how I feel, not so much what I'm thinking. If the substance of my vision is actually a 200-pound pile of subconscious insecurity, self-doubt, and confusion with a thin whitewash of vague good intention on the outside, what signal am I really sending? What communication is stronger? The positive attitude I'm struggling so hard to think about, or the insecurity and self-doubt I'm experiencing and feeling? Mixed messages won't cut it here!

So, how then can I get my thoughts and feelings on the same page?

Remember when I compared the habit and behaviors of drinking with driving a car? How things become second nature? When we start learning to drive a car, we have to think about every phase and aspect. It's a mechanical process. As we practice and memorize the skills involved with driving, it gets easier. Then finally, after much practice, we get in the car and later arrive somewhere, only to realize we did it completely automatically.

Making my thoughts and feelings consistent also takes practice. How shall I practice this? This is exactly where the basics of the AA program have tremendous benefit. It was impressed on me early in the program that I needed to build a foundation and establish a routine. Once I'm in a routine, the things I'm doing tend to become automatic, and, like driving the car, doing things that will strengthen my recovery start to become second nature.

When I say routine, it's important to remember that this routine is in the interest of laying groundwork on which we will build later, just like a building's foundation. As with the literal building, this foundation is the underpinning that will support future construction. We want to use the positive elements of a routine, stability, and structure, in anticipation of the benefits. A routine will provide a sense of purpose along with confidence. What we must avoid is falling into a rigid mindset in which the routine is at risk for becoming limiting. Keep it loose. Flexibility is both an asset and a virtue.

CHAPTER 21

The Foundation

One of the important elements of a recovery foundation consists of two closely associated parts: groups and meetings. The words are often used interchangeably, and while there is a direct relationship, these are still two different concepts. Quite simply, I think of the group as being like a living entity, while the meeting is an inanimate thing. They are both important, but it is helpful to understand the differences and the relationship.

An AA group is indeed like a living thing. It is dynamic and constantly changes and evolves. It has a personality. It usually has something akin to the intangible qualities of mood. In short, a group has energy about it. Of course, the group is composed of individuals, with unique personalities, moods, and energy. As with any collective of individuals, the cumulative effect results from whatever those individuals bring. The group should serve the needs of its members, and a healthy group is open and welcoming of new members.

While the primary purpose of the group is literally to help those who still suffer, its strength lies in the relationships within it and the sense of community it fosters. The highest interest of the individuals is served by the group's promotion and affirmation of the positive emotions of love, compassion, empathy, and gratitude. Attraction by example and sharing of collective experience and knowledge are the underlying principles. For the individual, the group is a source of strength, guidance, and reassurance.

The meeting is the event that the group experiences. In a strict sense, it is a time and location where the group convenes, but the idea of the group experience gives the meeting more dimensions. The meeting itself has a mood and tone; a meeting can have its own energy. This energy of the meeting, while a direct byproduct of group energy, results from circumstances of the moment. Is there something happening that day? Perhaps a group member is celebrating an anniversary, or maybe it's the anniversary of the group! Possibly the meeting day falls on a holiday, and attendance is high or low. Perhaps there is inclement weather; some of the most energized meetings I've ever observed happened on days when a mere handful of dedicated people fought their way through snowstorms to be there. While the group is more constant, meetings are like snapshots of that group on a particular day.

The meeting is often the catalyst for new experiences and new ideas. Without these things to stir the proverbial pot, nothing and no one would change. If we are willing to tune in and get a sense of how a meeting feels, we can get a fairly clear reading. There are meetings that are run-of-the-mill, and there are meetings that seem powerful and intense.

As a group, we are at our best when called on to support a member or members of the group who might be struggling. We demonstrate our empathy, compassion, and love for those in need. This win-win situation raises the level of focus. All present experience elevated emotions, while the one who is struggling receives needed support. This is where the level of subtle energy present at the meeting can go through the roof. This type of focused consciousness heightens the experience for all concerned, and the unspoken consensus (even sometimes acknowledged) is usually that everyone leaves feeling better than when they arrived. This raises an interesting point. In this Newtonian Model, cause-and-effect world, where mass and energy in should equal mass and energy out, how do people leave feeling better than when they arrived? Where does that come from? Are the folks at the meeting across town leaving feeling worse than when they arrived? NO!

There is something extraordinary going on at some AA meetings. I propose that this is a quantum field effect of focused collective consciousness. This was illustrated earlier in discussion of the Global Consciousness Project's work with measuring Random Event Generators' response to groups' focused attention. Groups of recovering people, in the course of a routine Alcoholics Anonymous meeting, are channeling or converting some type of energy. They are raising the level of subtle energy that people feel and sense. Collectively, emotions are being converted and raised from those negative emotions of survival and shifted toward the positive emotions of creation. What accounts for this? Something else is entering the equation. While everyone has his or her own conception of what a higher power is, this would seem to be access to something greater right at the source. This aspect of AA groups and meetings is truly amazing and serves to support the idea of the universe as a cosmic copy machine. We get back what we send out, and this effect is strengthened and more focused in a group setting.

Does this happen every day at every meeting? Unfortunately, it does not. Therefore, in adding the elements of groups and meetings to our foundation, we should try to have some awareness of a bigger picture. In this way, people who are prone toward negativity in its many forms—complaining, judgment, limitation, or plain old selfishness—will likely feel a resonance with groups that have more members mired in similar negativity. While it might initially feel uncomfortable, a conscious choice is necessary if we are going to raise our personal energy. We need to seek out groups and meetings where the overall experience will benefit and support us.

By establishing a routine, particularly in regards to meeting attendance, we are forming the habits that make up the foundation of sobriety and recovery. By seeking experiences that reinforce our positive thoughts with positive feelings, we are now starting to become more coherent in our way of being. The way we think and the way we feel will come increasingly into agreement.

Another important and traditional element of recovery is sponsorship. The idea of mentoring has been embraced by recovery, and has been an integral part of Alcoholics Anonymous since the day Bill Wilson met Robert Smith. While the lack of any formal orientation process for new members might be viewed as an organizational weakness, sponsorship is the corresponding strength that serves that purpose. Sponsorship could be defined as a mutually beneficial relationship between someone experienced in recovery and someone seeking to gain experience in recovery.

The benefits of sponsorship are several. As mentioned, a sponsor is a walking, talking, instruction book on how to stay sober, how to live life in recovery, and how the program part of Alcoholics Anonymous works. Whenever you start a new job, there's usually some sort of orientation. Think of a sponsor as your living copy of the AA policy and procedures manual.

There are countless types of sponsorship relationships, spanning from the traditional to the nontraditional to the unconventional. The long-established ideal has always been that of a sponsor who possessed a more vast experience in both recovery and life. The dynamic might begin as a teacher-student association, and then evolve as the sponsee gains experience and knowledge. There are varying degrees of formality. I had a sponsor whose ground rules were daily contact for the first 90 days, and also that I read a Big Book chapter daily for the same period.

I have had a sponsor every single day of my recovery. As I write this, I have had the same sponsor for nearly two decades. Decades into my recovery, I find that a bare minimum of weekly contact, preferably face-to-face, works best. I've done the experiment of minimal contact, going as long as two months without even an actual phone conversation. Phone tag did not work well.

The elements of my personal sponsorship relationship, which I consider successful, include, but are not limited to the following: We live in fairly close proximity. We share some life experience—we both played drums professionally and then moved on to pursue other careers. Sobriety and recovery are supremely important to both of us. Though our connection is through recovery, we are familiar with and support each other's outside endeavors. Our recovery and meeting traveling circles overlap somewhat, but are far from identical. Beyond those basics notions, there is a valuable component of knowing each other quite well for a long time. If something is disturbing me, my sponsor knows this from the way I say hello on the phone. As the saying goes, "priceless!" And every time throughout the years that I've thought our relationship was getting stale, some situation arises where his life experience proves invaluable. I count him as both a mentor and one of my best friends, in addition to an important part of my own foundation.

The less traditional approaches include having a sponsor of the opposite gender, more than one sponsor, or a long-distance sponsor. One approach that has never worked in my observation is keeping a sponsor after he dies. When I've been at meetings and heard people say "My sponsor always *used* to say…" the hospice and psych nurse in me knows there's a problem when it goes on for too long.

Why is this relationship mutually beneficial? The sponsored individual (sponsee) is the recipient of numerous and obvious benefits.

What's in it for the sponsor? Actually, there's more in it for the sponsor than the sponsee. The sponsor is challenged to live the concepts and values that he imparts, and the relationship becomes a looking glass reflecting the quality of the sponsor's own recovery. Sponsorship is also a safeguard against the sponsor's program becoming stale; valuable challenges will constantly arise. The sponsor now has a constant reminder of why he or she needed to get sober in the first place.

Entire books could be written about groups, meetings, and sponsorship. These are the basics, the staples of the foundation of recovery. They are the traditional elements, and have been this way for decades. Like the breakfast-cereal advertisements, which claim to be "part" of a nutritious breakfast, they are part of a sustainable recovery, but only a part. By themselves, or even combined, they are no assurance of an enduring, contented recovery. They are no guarantee of sobriety, or a defense against the first drink.

The next part of the foundation to be considered could come under the broad heading of fellowship. AA is a team sport. I've thought it myself, and heard it said many times by others... how wonderful and easy my life would be if I were the only one in it. The reality is that we grow up with, work with, and live with others. The biggest challenge we face in recovery, indeed as members of the human race, is getting along with one another. In recovery, as in life, we are part of a community. In this recovery community lies strength and experience. The community is one of our best resources. Quite simply, there is strength in numbers. Developing relationships—from nodding acquaintance to lasting friendships—strengthens the connection to recovery and the foundation itself.

The term fellowship has several meanings. There is the fellowship that is the organization of AA. There is the idea of fellowship representing AA's unique culture. There is the notion of the fellowship that means friendly, supportive companionship. It's the support piece that seems to be one of AA's chief strengths. Working with others, as it's commonly referred to, is another type of mutually beneficial relationship. Just like sponsorship, this has numerous advantages for everyone involved. One alcoholic helping another is an additional example of an energy exchange in which the final product seems to be greater than the sum of its parts. The net results are usually negative emotions transmuted to positive emotions with unaccounted for energy (higher power?) entering the equation somewhere. Does someone feel better when they receive help? Well, yes! Does someone feel better when they help someone else? Well, yes... it's a little mysterious, but it works. Anyone who's done it will tell you that there is no better feeling than sharing experience with someone who relates to it and benefits.

The well-rounded foundation should also include a knowledge base. The program of Alcoholics Anonymous is a set of concepts and principles along with suggestions for implementing them. The wisdom and experience set forth in the books *Alcoholics Anonymous* and *Twelve Steps and Twelve Traditions* are vast. Studying and learning what Alcoholics Anonymous believes and knows about the disease of alcoholism is prerequisite for lasting sobriety. Remember, we are setting our sights high, so a firm grasp of the concepts put forth in the first section of *Alcoholics Anonymous* and working knowledge of the Twelve Steps of recovery are vital. While some folks in recovery make a career out of studying AA's texts, bear in mind that type of lopsided focus might come at the expense of that well-rounded foundation we are seeking. Remember that our objective is something sustainable. Book smarts should not be at the expense of practical experience; doing is as important as knowing. I want my knowledge base to be that type of working knowledge...

The phenomenon of the "Big Book thumper" is fairly common among the fellowship of Alcoholics Anonymous. The sober individual who relates any topic under discussion back to the fundamental ideas expressed in that first section of *Alcoholics Anonymous* and the Step Book is a familiar icon in most meetings. Phrases such as "The Big Book tells us..." "The founders of the program meant..." or "It says..." along with quotations, chapter citations, or even page numbers are the familiar indicators that somebody has done a lot of reading. Knowledge is valuable, but the knowledge based on practice is more valuable. When I hear Big Book thumpers speak, I listen to hear how they are applying their knowledge. After all, what we endeavor to share is our *experience*, strength, and hope. I don't need someone to tell me what the Big Book says, I have my own copy. If there's something I don't understand, that's what my sponsor is for; after all, I have chosen him for that purpose. Someone else taking it upon themselves to enlighten me feels a little presumptuous. Is there an opinion being expressed that is rooted in practical knowledge that has led to an enlightened perspective, that is, wisdom? Or is someone simply reciting things they haven't personally tested? Who is better qualified to give advice on driving? Someone who still needs to consciously think about every step of the driving process, or someone so experienced they arrive at their destination automatically?

Be wary of the Big Book thumpers. Their philosophy of absolutes is black-and-white, while recovery and life are full of gray areas. This fixed way of being is rooted in the idea of fundamentalism, which gave us such unenlightened things as the Spanish Inquisition and Islamic Jihad. Value the thumpers' knowledge (and their ability for memorization); avoid their limitations. While they'll tell you the Big Book says it is not enough to merely not drink, they might not actually "be" the sermon they preach. The Big Book thumper keeps too many eggs in one single basket.

Listening to the personal experiences of others who have applied the principles of recovery in their own lives has tremendous value. The Big Book and Step Book meeting formats, the texts themselves, and the resources of sponsors and others are our principal means of education in these matters. Learn the basics and continue to study and absorb them.

The working of the steps is a practice that continues throughout recovery. It is a primary pillar of the foundation, the initial catalyst for change. The benefits and underlying principles were discussed earlier; the importance is stressed here. No single suggestion (except for not drinking) in the program of recovery should be encouraged as strongly as working on the steps of recovery.

Last, though certainly not least, is the development of a spiritual practice. The spiritual aspect of the foundation cannot be emphasized enough. The cultivation and nurturing of a personal approach to spiritual observance is paramount. Again, while the depth and breadth of spiritual experience was touched on before, the substance and value is stressed here. The simple reason is that our disease and our diseased way of being resulted from our existence rooted in an everyday, cause-and-effect reality, which I described earlier as the first world. While we can make a beginning through doing practical (though different) things in the context of that first world, ultimately the problems and way of being created in that world cannot be changed in the context of that first-world way of being. A transformation is required. There will come a point where the old way, with all its cause-and-effect human limitations, will fail.

As the same person in the same world with the same way of being, my alcoholism has gone to sleep at best. Unless I can access some greater resource beyond any part of my material environment, I will never know when that sleeping monster might wake up. At best, I will live a limited existence, still dragging the ball and chain of my alcoholism with me everywhere I go. At worst, I will drink again. Unless I can become something greater, that is, bring some greater energy into the equation, I will fall short of the vision of amazing recovery I have set for myself.

So I need to make some kind of beginning. There is always a starting point. That day, decades ago, when I got on my knees in the bathroom, I wanted to believe. Before that, I had wanted to want to believe. Whatever degree of separation, whatever slow stages of movement in the right direction were necessary, as long as I had that desire, that intention of moving in the right direction, I would be okay. Eventually, I got the spiritual angle.

Whatever personal approach we choose, it is essential that we incorporate the dimension of some understanding and relationship with something greater than ourselves.

There is one other indispensable part of the foundation that I will include here, primarily because it is considered an element of spirituality by most. It is actually a necessary piece for developing a true vision for recovery. Though meditation as a practice has been around since antiquity, the founders of the AA program were way ahead of the curve to advocate its use in Step Eleven. The range of benefits is amazing. The approaches are absolutely too numerous to begin to mention them all. As a fundamental skill in recovery, meditation is the principle means of accessing that connection to the divine, that part of us that is one with everything else. The next section is a little detour by way of explanation, discussion, and a practical guide for meditation.

CHAPTER 22

Meditation

I once heard someone speak at a meeting, talking about selecting a sponsor. He said he was deciding between two men he knew. The first man encouraged him to meditate. The second did not. "I can't stop the noise in my head for five seconds," he said, "how am I going to meditate?" He chose sponsor number two.

While attending a Step Eleven meeting that included a group meditation, I observed a newcomer arrive late. After searching out the right entrance to the meeting hall, the bewildered man entered a darkened room with one candle burning in the middle of a table surrounded by 20 silently meditating people. As it turned out, this was the man's first AA meeting.

It's not hard to imagine where the idea that AA is a cult comes from, based on these experiences. The first chap's brain was still scrambled. The second fellow had an unfortunate experience best likened to walking in during the middle of a movie. Had sponsor number one bided his time, scrambled-brain guy would have had exposure to meditation down the line. Of course, I want to think sponsor number two was in fact biding *his* time...

We don't unpack the tool of meditation during the first days of a newcomer's recovery. It stays in the toolbox, at least until someone's stopped vomiting. Along with anxiety-inducing explanations of Steps Five and Nine, it's not among the first bits of information a newcomer needs. To prioritize, not drinking or using and regular attendance at meetings and sponsorship are all ahead of honing meditative skills for the beginner. Basic knowledge of how AA works and a beginning with Steps One through Three are good too. Beyond that, broaching the idea does not need to wait for Step Eleven. In fact, any time after someone expresses a desire to stop drinking, meditation would likely be of benefit. Only if someone is averse to the idea, like the fellow I mentioned above, the concept should be offered sparingly. In most situations, it is only during the window of time in which someone is uncertain about recovery that the suggestion of meditation might be counterproductive. The reality is this: meditation can mean the difference between recovery and relapse. When someone has made a commitment, set their intention, and become willing to go to any lengths, the idea of meditation should not be too overwhelming. As soon as someone is willing to attempt meditating, they should.

Step Eleven presents prayer and meditation as the principle means of conscious contact with a higher power. Meditation is much more than that. It is the best method for changing ourselves. Certain aspects of our personalities, certain behaviors and feelings that are part of the old addicted way of being are hardwired—literally—into our brains. Meditation is the best way to unwire those mental circuits. Meditation is the instrument of transformation.

Literally hardwired? Yes, "wired" right into the brain. Neurons, the primary functional cells of the nervous system, serve the basic function of transmitting signals called impulses. Like wires, they are long with ends that have little arm-like structures called dendrites, the purpose of which is to connect to the next neuron, ultimately forming long circuits.

Now, suppose I'm learning a new skill, like playing a tricky drumbeat. It's new to my brain, which has to form neural connections to facilitate my playing. The act of playing the drums involves my thinking about how it should sound, and making all four limbs do exactly what they're supposed to. This mental/physical activity will use available neurons, but must route the signals through the brain and out to my arms and legs.

Now, the brain wants to work smart instead of working hard. When I come back day after day, playing that same complicated rhythm, the connections will start to become routinely used. Those little dendrite/arms on the neurons will start to reach out to one another, forming a more permanent connection. As the connections become "wired" circuits, the nervous system is now able to transmit the signals of that drumbeat more efficiently. That is how all types of skills become easier with practice. This quality of our nervous systems is known as neuroplasticity, the ability of our brains to change and adapt.

The same is true for thoughts, feelings, and behaviors. The more we think certain thoughts, experience certain feelings, and behave certain ways, the more "hardwired" they become. This is how our addictive behaviors became so strong, almost to the level of instinct, as though we were born with them. Just like driving a car, the tendency for thoughts, feelings, and behaviors is to move from being an effort toward being effortless, and finally becoming automatic. The vast majority of what we do in life has become a preprogrammed, conditioned response that runs deep. Much of our lives, good or bad, are spent in a state of "autopilot".

So I think to myself, "Wouldn't it be great if all those thoughts, feelings, and behaviors that are running on autopilot were the thoughts, feelings, and behaviors that I want to think, feel, and do as part of my highest recovery? How could I reset or re-program that autopilot?" The answer of course, is meditation.

So what is meditation? Simply defined, it is the entering of a relaxed and focused mental state. As previously mentioned, there are many reasons to meditate; there are many ways to meditate; there are many benefits to meditation. There is a proverb in which Buddha was asked "What have you gained from meditation?" He replied, "Nothing! However, let me tell you what I have lost: anger, anxiety, depression, insecurity, fear of old age and death."

This is where we are much like computers. Along the lines of automatic thoughts, feelings, and behaviors and the idea of being on autopilot, we could think of anger, anxiety, depression, and fear on the downside, with security, compassion, and love on the upside as programs that the system of our mind is running. Our physical brains are the hardware. Our minds are the operating systems. We have, like them or not, a whole bunch of installed programs. Just like software on the computer, we have been programmed with our emotions, our way of thinking, and our way of doing things. In short, our way of being is like information on our personal hard drive.

If I wanted to change a software program on my home computer, I would click on a few tabs and settings and open up access to the operating system. That is where programs are accessed or added, modified and changed, or even deleted! How then do I access my own operating system to access, add, change or... delete programs? Meditation? Well, yeah!

To better understand meditation, and at the risk of sounding like a nurse again, it's helpful to understand a few things about the brain. The average adult brain weighs about three pounds, which is a small percentage of the total body weight, maybe about 2 percent. In a disproportionate fashion, the brain uses 20 percent of available blood sugar, or fuel. That means the brain is an energy hog. As explained earlier, the function of brain cells is to transmit impulses, which are measurable as electrical vibration. All this electrical energy generated by the brain is measured in official metric system units called hertz (Hz). The energy is measured with a standard type of test called an electroencephalogram (EEG). The EEG is to the brain what the electrocardiogram (often called EKG, but properly ECG) is to the heart. It represents the energy as a waveform of amplitude (power) over time. Brainwaves run from 0.5 Hz all the way up to 80 Hz per second.

The amount of energy or number of hertz that the brain generates depends on what we're doing at the moment. If I'm in a deep sleep, my brain might generate 0.5 up to 3 Hz on an EEG, which is known as delta activity. If I'm reading a book, my brain is functioning at between 14 and 30 Hz, commonly referred to as low beta activity. If I'm at work handling some serious situation, I might be between 30 and 40 Hz, known as high beta. Depending on how much information I'm processing, the measurable energy of my brain corresponds on the output measured by the EEG. When we meditate, the ideal brain energy output is at a point between being awake and being asleep. It is referred to as the alpha brainwave pattern and is measured as 9 to 14 Hz. There is also a level of "deep" meditation in the range of 4 to 8 Hz, which is known as theta brainwaves.

The objective of a basic meditation is to quiet the mind chatter, which characterizes a "busy" brain as it functions in the beta state. By bringing the brain into the alpha state, a number of positive effects occur. The brain will become more coherent. This means that the different regions of the brain will communicate more effectively. Because the subconscious part of the brain actually processes a million times faster than the conscious brain, this is like tapping into a huge reserve of mind power. This enhanced communication also has the benefit of allowing the intentional changing of subconscious beliefs. We can literally rewrite our minds' programs.

All this takes is practice. Anyone can do this.

After acquiring the skills of basic meditation, we can begin to apply those skills in other ways. Using our minds, we can begin to rewire our brains. We can focus on a behavior or character defect and actually change or begin to eliminate it. After meditating becomes part of our regular spiritual practice, the phrase "change my mind" will never be the same.

Though there are many techniques for meditating, for the sake of developing basic skills, I am going to outline two simple methods. Later, after you have made a beginning, feel free to explore other methods including prerecorded guided meditations. Initially however, it's best to develop the ability to quiet your own mind. In consideration that it's best to form a habit of meditating, here are some helpful guidelines:

1. **Find a place that will become your meditating place.** It should be a comfortable place where you can sit. You should have privacy and be able to spend time there undisturbed for as long as you meditate. This includes being away from pets, phones, children, and any predictable interruptions. Removing glasses, watches, and even shoes might be helpful. Sitting with your hands resting in your lap or on your legs works best for most people.

2. **Background music or no background music?** This is an individual preference, and it should depend on what works for you. Familiar, calming music that does not distract is the best. Instrumental music is probably the best choice, as lyrics are a potential distraction. There's a wide variety of available commercial music intended for the purpose of meditation.

3. **Set aside a specific time to meditate.** Develop a routine. The amazing neuroscientist, Dr. Joe Dispenza, says, "The hardest part of meditating is making the time to do it." Some people prefer meditating before bed. I prefer soon after waking in the morning. Planning and making the time is important because the excuses not to meditate will start to come along. "I'm too tired; it'll take too long; it's too hard; it won't help; *Seinfeld* reruns are on..." Do it daily for three weeks, make a commitment.

4. **Sit when meditating.** A comfortable chair that enables you to sit with your back straight and erect, feet on the floor, is best. The problem with lying down is that we are accustomed

to sleeping when in this position. If you experience sleepiness during meditation, try sitting forward in the chair so you're not reclined the next time. If you have trouble relaxing, sit back in the chair more the next time. Find a comfortable position before you begin, as one of the objectives is to stop thinking about how your body feels.

5. **Remember to "be" light.** This is not an uptight, rigid experience. Relax, be yourself at your random, happy-go-lucky best. This is not a job interview; this is not a tax audit; this is not a dental procedure. There is nothing to screw up, but everything to gain. You CAN'T lose here. The best things happen when we are just taking it as it comes.

6. **Be aware that your body will play tricks on you until your mind teaches it that the mind is in charge.** Use the bathroom first. Anticipate itches, twitches, coughs, congestion, sneezes, wheezes, aches, pains, burps, belches… every imaginable little physical sensation that will distract, irritate, annoy, and tempt you to give in and be sidetracked. At the outset, set your intention and resolve. Sit with it, knowing that you can handle anything your body throws at you. Wait it out, and believe that your body is the servant, your mind the master, and not the other way around. With patience, your mind will prevail.

7. **Your brain will attempt the same.** José Silva, creator of the famous Silva Mind Control Method, said, "The brain is like a drunken monkey." Shopping lists, to-do lists, replays of conversations, events, things you heard, saw, felt, or otherwise experienced will come flooding into your head in an avalanche of unwanted mental chatter. This is natural. The analytical part of the brain is running, and it's just doing its job. Do not be annoyed. Simply become aware that it's happening, and calmly move back to the process of meditating. With practice and perseverance, the brain will transition from beta to alpha, and your ability to settle yourself down will improve quite rapidly.

These guidelines are merely suggestions. Meditation is a unique and individual experience. By trial and error, you will find what works for you. Remember that the objective is to quiet the mind, which eases the brain into the alpha state between wakefulness and sleep, the specifics of how this is accomplished are secondary. There are no rules, only freedom. If something isn't working, simply learn from it and move on to something that does. The settling-down phase is referred to as the induction. Here are a couple of suggested methods for settling into a relaxed, meditative state:

1. The Countdown Method

Prepare yourself as suggested above. Begin by closing your eyes. As though looking toward the ceiling across the room, point your eyes upward 15 to 20 degrees underneath your closed eyelids. For many, this little trick with the eyes has the physiological response of moving the brain toward the alpha state. Take several long, slow, deep breaths, holding each breath in momentarily. Then exhale and relax. Then, while breathing slowly and steadily, start to count backwards from 100 with each respiration. Establish a slow, comfortable rhythm. As you are progressing down from 100, you should begin to feel more relaxed. Focus on the count to the exclusion of all everyday thoughts that try to enter your mind. As you get to the end of your countdown, you should feel physically and mentally relaxed with your mind quiet, free from the usual internal dialogue or conversation that typically plays in your head. At the end of the countdown, if you do not feel relaxed enough for your liking, simply go back to 20, or even 50, and resume the counting-down process. Do this every day for a week. It should only take 10 to 15 minutes. At the end of each countdown, simply enjoy the peaceful sensation of being relaxed. After you have gained the ability to do this portion of meditating, the induction, or basic meditation, other skills will be added. The first priority is learning to quiet the mind.

After the first week, begin your countdown at 50. At the beginning of the third week, try beginning your countdown at 30. Remember to go slowly, and focus on the breathing and counting to the exclusion of intrusive thoughts. If counting down from 30 doesn't work the first two days of the third week, go back to counting down from 50. This is fine. The objective however is to gain the ability to move more quickly into the meditative state. This will come with practice. Again, for the first three weeks, practice the skill of calming yourself into the meditative state, and remain there relaxing for a few minutes if you wish. At the end of each session as you decide to conclude, calmly think to yourself, "I'm going to return to beta consciousness now," and slowly come back to alertness and open your eyes. You will feel a sensation as if returning to awareness of your body, which was temporarily suspended. As you gain the skill of mastering the bodily sensations and distractions, you'll be able to detach from your body. This will have tremendous benefits as you take the meditation process to the next level, active meditation, which will be discussed later.

2. Focus on Body Parts

This is another technique for the induction phase of meditation. It entails a methodical focusing on the parts of the body in sequence. When focusing on each body part, it is important to feel, or sense, that body part as opposed to visualizing the body part. This is because visualization engages the analytical part of the brain, which defeats the purpose of attempting to move from a beta state to an alpha state. The part of the brain which senses and feels our bodies usually runs below the level of consciousness, so this type of sensing is consistent with alpha function.

Begin by closing your eyes. Use the same technique of looking toward the ceiling across the room, pointing your eyes upward 15 to 20 degrees underneath your closed eyelids. Take several long, slow, deep breaths, holding each breath in momentarily. Then exhale and relax.

Now start by sensing your toes. As you feel your toes, let them relax. Feel your toes completely relaxing. Feel a warm, comfortable sensation in all your toes. Now sense your entire feet, and slowly feel them relaxing, all tension and discomfort leaving them, being replaced by warmth and comfort. Slowly move to your calves and lower legs. Feel them relaxing, and sense any discomfort or tension leaving them. Feel them bathed in warmth. Next, move your attention to your knees, feel them relaxing, and sense warmth and comfort filling them. Slowly move to your upper legs. Sense your thighs, and feel them relax. Feel them become bathed in comfortable warmth. Remembering to feel and sense rather than picturing the parts of your body with your mind, move your attention to your hips and pelvis. Sense them, and feel them consumed in warmth and comfort, completely relaxed. When you're ready, move to your midsection and lower back. Sense them, and feel them relax. Feel the muscles of your midsection and lower back relaxing, all tension leaving them, and sensing any strain or pressure being replaced with relaxation as they're bathed in comfort and warmth. Now sense your chest and upper back. Take a slow, deep breath, and as you exhale, feel the tension leave your body, being replaced by a sensation of warmth and relaxation. Now feel your fingers and hands. As they rest in your lap, sense them, and feel any tension or strain slowly leave them, being replaced by warmth, comfort, and a relaxed sensation. Next, feel your lower arms and elbows, first sensing them, and then feeling them filled with warmth and a sensation of comfort. Now move to feeling your upper arms and shoulders, then sensing all tension and stress leaving them as you take a slow, deep breath, and exhale slowly. Feel warmth and a relaxed sensation filling your shoulders and upper arms. Now feel your neck and the muscles between your neck and shoulders. Take a slow, deep breath, and feel any tension and stress you're holding leave your body as you exhale slowly. Repeat the slow, deep breath, and as you exhale, feel your neck and the muscles between your neck and shoulders becoming relaxed with a warm, comfortable sensation. Now sense your eyes, and feel any strain or tension leaving them to be replaced with warmth. Next, feel your face, feeling the muscles of your forehead, jaws, and mouth relaxing. Sense any tension leaving your face, and being replaced by a sensation of warmth. Sense your entire head, and feel it become relaxed, warm, and comfortable. Finally, feel and sense your entire body. Remember not to visualize or form pictures of your body, but rather sense and feel it in its entirety. Sense any remaining tension leaving your body, being replaced with a feeling of warmth and comfort.

This meditation induction takes a little learning and a little practice. The basic guidelines are to feel and sense rather than picture and visualize. Do this every day for three weeks, attempting to improve each day, releasing more tension and stress, while becoming more skilled and practiced at moving through the meditation. It should take 15 to 20 minutes. At the end of each session, enjoy the peaceful sensation of relaxation. Bear in mind that this is the first stage, and other skills will be added down the line. The focusing of the attention on sensing the body has the effect of quieting the mind. Again, the objective is to gain the ability to move more quickly into the meditative state. This will come with practice. At the end of each session as you decide to conclude, calmly think to yourself, "I'm going to return to beta consciousness now," and slowly come back to alertness and open your eyes. You will feel a sensation as if returning to the beta consciousness of your body, which was temporarily replaced with alpha consciousness awareness.

~~~~~~~~~~~~~~~~~~~~~~~~~~~~

Now that the stage is set, I want to relate an idea I discussed earlier to this notion of building a foundation. From my nursing experience, I discussed the concepts of preventive medicine, primary, secondary, and tertiary (bet you thought there was no reason for that being there, huh)? My experience of recovery has been that it is a lot like my physical state. Like my body, I want my recovery to be "healthy." Like my physical condition, my recovery goes up and down. In fact, I could think of my recovery as being on a continuum. The high end of that range is a strong, robust recovery. Like the wellness continuum, where the opposite end and downside are death, my recovery would be considered dead with the first drink. My recovery continuum ranges from being in love with life all the way down to being drunk.

By building a strong foundation, complete with the above concepts and their practice, am I not practicing recovery maintenance? As in health maintenance, I am ensuring that my recovery will not move down that scale toward the thoughts, feelings, and behaviors of active alcoholism, or at least I am working to minimize the possibility. In effect, I am practicing primary prevention in my recovery. When my recovery suffers the equivalent of the common cold, the remedy is to strengthen the foundation. It's the same as boosting my immunity. And if my recovery suffered a more serious infection, such as actually thinking about or wanting to drink, the remedy is the same, only the dosage and urgency are both higher.

By working toward the establishment of a foundation in my recovery, I have prepared myself to move forward. The benefits of the foundation are a new sense of stability, both in my life and my thinking. The thoughts no longer race, and the frustration, worry, and anxiety have started to settle down. As my thinking becomes better, I feel better. It is now time to turn my attention toward my vision for my life and my recovery.

CHAPTER 23

The Vision

This is the point at which we are officially departing from the Twelve Step model. We have made a beginning and come to terms with the standard way people have been getting sober for 80 years. We accept the ideas, principles, and actions that have worked the best for the most. We want to use our foundation in Alcoholics Anonymous as a basis for moving toward the goal of transformation. While we were previously people enslaved by alcohol, our objective is to become new people. Free people. We will now establish a vision for that transformation.

Without doubt, people in Alcoholics Anonymous transform daily. With the foundation we are building, that happens naturally. However, we are talking about something different and more profound. Our intention is to literally become different people, from the way we think all the way down to our cells.

I could begin by asking myself what makes me happy. If I'm honest, I might be surprised to find that I want the things in life that most everyone wants. I thought I was unique, a rebel, but when I got down to it, the real and meaningful things in life sounded pretty good.

I had never envisioned life in sobriety. I had never even been able to picture life in my 30s, while I was in the midst of my wild 20s. Superficially, I began to get in touch with the guy hidden inside me, the one who was just like everyone else, and that I never knew was there. That guy was okay with the steady job/health insurance/paid vacation semi-respectable, guy-next-door existence; in fact, he liked it. To the contrarian, nonconformist maverick that was the "previous Keith," the notion of being so normal, so run-of-the-mill... so average... was unthinkable. The old mindset was the result of years of living in opposition to everything, the power struggle of addiction. After surrendering in this undeclared war, the world began to look like a different place, and I began to wonder, "What was I thinking?"

As I flirted with different mental pictures of imaginary futures, some ideas stuck. They remained in the back of my mind in the first months to years of my recovery.

Years ago, I began to tentatively explore ideas that were off the beaten path of mainstream AA. Ultimately, I had to summon my courage and bravely step off the edge and into the void of infinite possibility where a higher potential existed. This was not easy. Earlier, I talked about how others reacted negatively to things I said and did. I had to come to understand how these reactions were rooted in a type of fear. It was never personal. The reaction of others is much more about them than about me. For those entrenched in a limited way of being, I am more a mirror than a candle in the dark. It is unfortunate, but in my limitlessness, some people can only see their own limits. The important thing for me was to divorce myself from the judgments and opinions of those who are not ready to embrace a bigger picture. My obstacle is not the fear, lack, or limitation of others. My obstacle is my reaction to that negativity; in other words, my obstacle is me. What I need to get past is my own fear. I need to transcend my own limitations. Most of all, I need to rise above my judgment of myself. The words "I can't, I shouldn't, or I won't" have no place in my vision process.

I must not base my own happiness on the opinions or approval of others.

We must set our intention that we are now on a new adventure. Are you ready to be courageous? Are you ready to reject limits? Are you ready to give yourself permission to do something that no one else has given you the permission to do? If you know that you are worth it (AND YOU ARE!), the answer is a resounding yes! Yes! YES! A 3-foot tall Jedi Knight named Yoda once said, "There is no try... only do."

The next challenge in establishing my vision is to understand my role in the transformation process. Specifically, it's helpful to understand that there is going to be a clear division of labor. Understanding my role in the bigger picture of this process will help me avoid thoughts and concerns that have no place in my making a vision for my highest recovery. A good analogy might be going on a trip...

When going on a long-distance trip, I need to make a plan. This is like a vision for my trip. I have a specific destination in mind, and perhaps an itinerary when I get there. Arrangements must be made. I need to choose a mode of primary transportation (flying, for example), and incidental transportation (airport to hotel, etc.). I will also need accommodations and must make all the necessary reservations. I need to be clear on details of the trip, so I can anticipate things I will need and pack accordingly. If my situation warrants, I need to ensure that responsibilities and obligations, perhaps the care of pets, will be met in my absence. I make these plans to the best of my ability, and this is the vision for my trip.

The day of this journey arrives, and all my preparations are made. At this point, it becomes my job to simply go on the trip. Perhaps I've specified that a car will come at an appointed time and take me to the airport. I get in the car, and I'm now being transported. I'm at the airport, where I undergo the airport routine, and eventually board my flight. I'm then flown to my destination airport, and as I've specified, I'm eventually taken to my final destination.

While I've made all these plans and arrangements (and paid for them, naturally), and perhaps walked from ticket counter to boarding gate to my seat, then similarly moved around according to my plan, I have been passive in the larger sense during this process. I was driven to the airport. I was assisted with my boarding pass, I was directed onto the plane, and perhaps even shown where my seat was. I certainly did not fly that plane; I had faith in the pilot to do that, especially the landing part! I continued to follow my plan, and eventually was taken where I envisioned going.

I made the plan and then relied on other people and things to get it done. The details were handled, much of them completely behind the scenes. If I checked baggage, it was stored on the plane, which was obviously maintained and fueled, again behind the scenes. The airline also managed and administered all the peripheral areas, such as an online reservation system, staffing, and all the necessary peripheral jobs and services. The airport itself is maintained and run in accordance with aviation standards and regulations. In other words, while I made the plan, the details and execution of that plan were done for me.

The other side of that division of labor is something greater than me: an airline, an airport, a hotel chain, a limousine service... I'm only responsible for the vision, that's it. When establishing my vision, I want to bear that in mind. My job is to create it, and not worry about the logistics of my journey.

My journey in recovery is no different. My job is to create a vision of the life and recovery of my dreams. God will handle the details later.

So, now is the time to create! What is your vision of a tremendous recovery, literally the recovery of your dreams? What kind of life will you have in that recovery?

Remember those beer-soaked, barstool pipedreams? Did you daydream about a fulfilling career instead of a series of meaningless jobs? Did you think about having a strong, healthy body instead of being plagued with never-ending symptoms, discomforts, and physical problems? Did you think about traveling to beautiful or exotic places? Did you imagine having healthy friendships and relationships based on acceptance and trust? Did you ponder a life of abundance, where all your needs and even some of your wants were met? Or, as an active alcoholic, did all these things seem too fantastic to be real? Did you think they were just things that were portrayed on television and in movies? Did your addiction dictate what you thought was real, possible, or within your grasp? Did you alter your perception of your own potential or what was attainable based on the lowered expectations and standards of an addictive way of life? In other words, if your alcoholic way of being didn't match your dreams, did you downsize your dreams to match your alcoholic way of being?

More primarily, what kind of recovery would bring those things into the realm of possibility? A secure, contented sobriety based on a strong foundation in the fundamental principles of Twelve-Step recovery? A sound, spiritual basis for living, complete with a comfort level in the ideas of each of the first, second, and third worlds, as outlined earlier? A firm grasp of a belief system that accounts for "the larger questions," and also some reckoning with something greater than you? In short, a sustainable recovery?

Don't spare the details. How will you act? How will you speak and laugh? How will you stand, sit, and move? And how will you feel? Remember what Step Eleven says... "No man can build a house until he first envisions a plan for it." And when that vision does come true, think about how grateful you will be. Think about how you'll be living in gratitude and the positive emotions of creation, as opposed to the negative emotions of stress. This is imagination in the most constructive sense of the word.

No one told me what I know today, which is that I can be anything I want to be. And if someone had told me, I would have immediately been fixated on "how" it would come about, thereby imposing limitations on myself before even considering the possibilities. The pictures in my head, though no longer beer-soaked, were nevertheless in a mental file drawer labeled "pipedreams."

The truth is that I can be or do just about anything I choose in recovery. I can have what I want; I can be who I choose to be. I can have the characteristics of my choosing. The condition to having what I want is that I must be worthy; the condition to being whom I choose is that I must be willing to change into that person. For the moment, I need to put the conditions, details, and the "how" aside to focus on the "what."

Let go of mental and emotional restrictions. Be open to all possibility. Ask yourself, what was or is my dream? What did I always want to do or be? Before I lowered my sights to correspond to my alcoholism, before I settled for less, before I gave up, what did I want to experience? How would my life be if that dream came true? Let the descriptions and adjectives come to mind. No limitations, only possibilities. Form mental pictures of yourself experiencing the feelings and way of being that goes with the vision.

Let the experience become as real in your mind, as detailed, as the experience of the field trip that I described earlier. Make it so real that you can memorize the feelings associated with it. Keep it in your mind, and think about it over time. Whenever you have a few free moments, return your mind to your ongoing vision "project." Further define those mental pictures and feelings until they become something you can call up when you want to. Like the sculptor who looks at a block of marble and sees the finished statue within, like the artist who looks at the blank canvas and sees a masterpiece, look at the infinite possibilities that are your future and see your own masterpiece of creation. See the life and recovery of your dreams.

It helps to write it down. Talk about it. Share it with others to make it more real, just like Step Five. As you begin to give the vision life, you will eat, drink, and breathe it. You might surround yourself with reminders. For example, if you have a vision of transforming your body into a healthier version of you, get some pictures of people who look the way you want to. If you have set a lower target weight, write it down in places where you will be constantly reminded of your goal.

When you were a child, was there something, a toy or bicycle perhaps, that you wanted and set your sights on getting? Did you think about it day and night? Using a bicycle as an example, did you think about every aspect of it? You probably thought about how it looked, how it felt to sit on it, to ride it, and you thought about how happy you would be when that happened. You made a complete mental rehearsal of the future experience of the thing you wanted. It's time to do that again. It's time to live your highest vision of the life and recovery of your dreams.

CHAPTER 24

Process of Change

Now that we have a vision of the life and recovery of our dreams, it is time to go to work and start changing. The next phase of deliberate transformation is accomplished during meditation, and also daily in each waking moment of our lives. The important thing is that we set our intention on change and realizing the accomplishment of our vision.

Frequently I hear recovering alcoholics say, "I'm an alcoholic, and I'll never change." While this is mostly said innocently, it has hazards. They might be sharing about feeling jumpy from too many days without a meeting, or reacting to a situation where there is alcohol present. Sharing about this is desirable; seeking identification and validation is part of the process of moving away from this way of being and toward freedom from those types of worries. Reinforcing the behavior or situation in the context of "never changing" is not good, however. Words have power. When we say we will never change, even rhetorically or as a joke, we send a message to our subconscious, where the feeling part of "thoughts and feelings" live. Thinking back a few pages, we decided that it's important to have our thoughts and feelings united, as this tends to be the signal we "broadcast." When we say something negative, even as an expression or to be funny, and especially if it's reinforced by some group approval (or what seems like it), we are telling our brains to wire that in. We are telling ourselves that it felt good, and we want that experience to continue or repeat. We are learning and fortifying a way of being that no longer serves us.

This type of negative thinking is an illustration of what we need to change. It's a prime example of a program that we want to delete. It doesn't fit anywhere in our vision of life or recovery. The subtle emotions, thoughts, and behaviors that do not serve us will be numerous, insidious, and deeply entrenched. Something like undesirable self-talk is much more subtle than a glaring character defect, such as impatience or being judgmental. Still, they are no less detrimental.

Fear not! These harmful, but gray-shaded issues are just as responsive as the obvious ones to the methods we will use to weed them out and remove them from our way of being. Just like combing through a garden for unwanted, opportunistic plants, we will prune out of our minds the unwanted, useless thoughts that are still wired in, sapping our energy, emotional resources, and peace of mind.

As with any project, it is helpful to be organized. When we cook, we gather the recipe, the ingredients, and the necessary pots, pans, and utensils. Before beginning construction, the builder assembles his plan, his tools, and his building materials. Further, in both those examples there is some practical knowledge underlying those tasks. Certain principles of food preparation and construction are understood. The transformation we are undertaking is no different. In addition to the division-of-labor idea, there are some other concepts that we will use. While these were laid out as information previously, we will put them in the context of what we are doing now.

By this time, we've hopefully established a relationship with something greater. Whether our personal conception is a religious-type God; a natural or elemental force; an all-encompassing, unifying field of energy; a universal creative intelligence; some combination of the above; or something else entirely, our relationship with this greater power now becomes paramount. In the division of labor, this higher power will now become our partner in the act of transformation.

My personal perspective, as discussed earlier, is that we are eternal consciousness having transient human experiences. Our physical selves, at the most fundamental level, are in the nature of energy that is: 1. nonlocal, 2. subject to entanglement, and 3. not strictly governed by linear time. We are therefore connected to this greater power, and we can use our intention to enjoy a relationship that is more of a collaborative partnership rather than one-sided. Whatever your personal conception of this greater power is, you will be calling on this power to assist in this transformation.

Reality, the universe in which we exist, is essentially neutral. It functions like a cosmic copy machine in which the reality we receive is based on the reality we project. This copy machine responds not only to our thoughts, but places more emphasis on how we really feel. The subconscious, much more powerful than our conscious-thinking brain, has a more direct connection to the universe.

To effect change in our lives, we make a vision of the desired outcome, the future reality that we want. One of infinite possible futures, this is the one we have selected. By using our conscious minds and connecting to our subconscious, we will connect ourselves to the future we desire. We will use the quantum property of entanglement to energetically attach ourselves to our desired outcomes. We will use the power of our minds to "premember" our vision for the future, just as if it's something we are experiencing physically. We will make it real in every sense, except that it just hasn't occurred historically—yet.

Because our consciousness has the power to influence our physical reality, our physical bodies will begin the transformation ahead of the actual events. By rewiring neural pathways in our brains, our thoughts, feelings, and behaviors will begin to shift and change. These new thoughts and feelings will send new signals to our bodies at the cellular level and below. In keeping with the epigenetic model, the tiny protein sleeves around our genes will respond to the new vibrational and chemical messages we are producing by shifting and reconfiguring, thereby literally changing our DNA. The modified DNA will act as a blueprint for our new physical selves in our new reality. We are literally transforming into different people.

In the quantum model, where the reality we experience collapses into the present moment from infinite possibilities, we have established a direct connection to the possible future of our vision. By mentally, emotionally, behaviorally, and physically becoming the actual version of ourselves that exists in that possible future, we draw that possible future toward and into our present reality. The things that go on around us will begin to reflect this, and come into line with the new reality.

This is where the cosmic copy machine now goes to work for us. The division of labor that I spoke of earlier, where we have done the preparation and must now simply take the trip, comes into play. The future is coming. The who, what, where, when, and, most important, the how is completely out of our hands. Our job is to become the new person. Our job is to change ourselves internally before our external environment changes.

All these creative ideas that were also presented earlier are precisely the underlying principles and concepts that make our transformation possible. Like the cook who knows the effect of heat on the ingredients, and like the builder who knows the correct tool for any phase of construction, we have attained the basic knowledge necessary for a personal transformation. We, who formerly could not go a day without a drink, are now ready to literally become a different person who doesn't drink.

We will now turn our attention to beginning the reprogramming procedure. The first piece of this is about enlisting help from our higher power so that we are in harmony with the universe and the quantum model. The second aspect will represent our efforts to change our thoughts, feelings, and behaviors at the level of our automatic mental programs.

So far, we have practiced a basic form of meditation. We have calmed our minds (and bodies in the process) and worked on moving into the alpha brainwave state. It is in this state that our brains are coherent and unified. It is in this state that we can access our subconscious. It is in this state that we can effectively rewire how we think. And most importantly, it is in this connection to our subconscious that we are best able to access that part of us which is an aspect of the divine. Here is where we are best able to talk to and listen to God. To do this, we will take the next step in our meditation by becoming active during the process. Sometimes referred to as dynamic or active meditation, we will develop the skills necessary to perform life-altering brain surgery of the most positive type. Like going into the operating system of our mind, we will begin the process of upgrading ourselves to the newer, better version.

This new step in the procedure will build directly off the basic meditation. It is essential to practice and develop the ability to settle your brain into the alpha state. I strongly recommend practicing a basic meditation for three full weeks before moving on to the next phase.

Begin by meditating as you have been. After settling into the calm, relaxed (and by now hopefully familiar), meditative state, you are now going to start doing things. Asking for help with a negative emotion, character defect, undesirable habit, or troubling dilemma are examples. You can plan what you want to work on beforehand, or simply go into the meditation and spontaneously "see what happens." The emphasis here is on asking for help. This is where having a solid conception of a higher power and what your relationship with that power is can be amazingly useful.

Some information to bear in mind... remember that the meditative level of consciousness is somewhere between alertness and sleep. The analytical mind, that constant ongoing conversation we have with ourselves that is always playing in our brains, has mostly gone quiet. We are still conscious. We are capable of calmly and deliberately performing certain mental tasks.

Always remember that meditation is a wonderfully free process. It's certainly okay to meditate on anything. You can put any kind of question out there, and simply see what floats up from your subconscious. This will be one source of your response from your higher power. And it's okay to be Apollo astronauts here; you can understand as much or as little about what your higher power is or how it works as your gut tells you. Whatever that is, it's just right for you. You can even ask it what it is! The possibilities are limitless. The one important thing is that you reach out consciously in some way to something greater that is both connected to you and beyond you. Remember that you need to access a greater resource.

Initially, I suggest meditating and working on negative emotions. The basic ones, such as fear or sadness, are fairly common to all of us; emotions such as impatience and being judgmental are a little more gray, but just as common. I do something like this: "Universal creative intelligence (or God, higher power, etc.)," I think to myself, or even say out loud. "You know me, and you know I struggle with fear (or sadness, envy, hate, etc.). I humbly ask for your help to be free of this negative emotion. Please remove it from me as you would, in the way that is just right for me. Thank you for this gift, and all the blessings you've put in my life"

The next step in this meditation is to think about how it would feel to be free of that negative emotion. We're going to use that vision process, and it's like we're going to go on that field trip in our minds. How great I will feel without fear! The things I will do and the way I will do them, absolutely fear free. And I will be so grateful for my life without fear. Ah, to be fearless...

Place emphasis on imagining and capturing in your mind the feeling of gratitude. Notice that I already said "thank you." Just as if you have already attained that state of fearlessness, think about how happy you'll be and actually allow and direct yourself to feel that. You can make it absolutely real in your mind, and truly experience the thoughts, emotions, and even the way of being ahead of experiencing it with your five senses in the real world. These thoughts, these pictures of how you will think, feel, and behave come from your subconscious. They have formed somewhere in the back of your mind where your consciousness connects to a greater consciousness. This is God showing you your possible future.

By connecting to that possible future, and enhancing your thoughts with gratitude and joy, you begin to broadcast a signal that tells your body to be the body of the person having that experience. Though you are working in the operating system of the mind, the program changes you are making are changing you physically. You are materially doing two things simultaneously. While wiring new circuitry, actual new brain cell connections that will support your fearless way of being, you are disassembling the old circuits of fear. The next step will continue that process and begin to prepare you to take your fearless way of being from inside your head to the world outside.

The next step in the active meditation process is to think about a situation, circumstance, event, or even person who brings up or causes the same negative emotion or character defect that you just asked for help with. You're going to think of something that is part of your everyday, real-world that will interfere with the transformation to a new way of being. If you've been working on fear, think of something you fear. If you're working on sadness, think of something that makes you sad. As you do this, your feeling of being beyond fear or sadness, along with the elevated emotions and freedom will start to fade. Fear or sadness will begin to return. At the precise moment when you feel the negative emotion return, interrupt this little process by thinking of a big red stop sign, and say to yourself the word "STOP!" As though you are cutting off the return of the negative emotion by ordering it to stop, you are using the power of your mind to control what that "drunken monkey" of a brain will do to you if you let it.

Next, THINK about how engaging that negative emotion does not serve you. You're absolutely worthy of making this transformation and you need to care about yourself enough to do it.

Now CHANGE! Order that automatic program to stop switching itself on and running. Consciously bring back that real feeling of fearlessness and gratitude that you meditated on previously.

Stop, think, and change. Repeat.

This will take some practice. You will need to read and review this section a few times to acquaint yourself with the directions and the basic concept. Once you understand what to do and how to do it, you are on your way to accomplishing some significant change in your way of being. Once you begin this process, you will be amazed. Things will start to happen. When you ask your higher power for help, assuming that your words, thoughts, and actual feelings are consistent, you better be ready. No, not because you're going to be instantaneously transformed. Although that is possible in the quantum reality, something else is more likely to happen. For example, as you move toward that fearless future, you will be presented with opportunities to face and overcome fear.

I hope you didn't think this was going to be too easy, did you?

Information, ideas, and thoughts that come from your subconscious are one source of response from your higher power. The other source will come indirectly, seemingly from the universe itself. What we are doing, as in the example above with negative emotion, character defects, or the like is working on Steps Six and Seven, but on steroids. The act of reprogramming ourselves will have the effect of drawing experiences to us that will test us. There is no substitute for this kind of legwork. My brain is rewired in meditation, but also through my behaviors. I need to be absolutely willing to do some heavy lifting. This comes in the form of response to the situations that arise; I must face my fear, demonstrate patience, make a conscious decision to move beyond sadness, etc. This is my part of the collaborative effort with that power greater than me. I must have absolute willingness to accept my assignment in this division of labor.

When the universe sends these situations and things to test you, now you can better expect them. When things such as fear, negative emotion, and character defects begin to come up, think of the stop sign and say "Stop," as in your meditation. You will eventually condition yourself that the fear, negative emotion, or character defect will never pass by your awareness. You now have the opportunity to respond mindfully rather than react as you would in the past. And, as you keep making different choices, you will rewrite your old mental programs.

The tremendous potential for meditation as a tool of transformation should be apparent. If we can use meditation to make inroads with character flaws and negative emotions, why would we stop there? Abstracting a little bit, the possibilities that come to mind are only limited by our imagination and... our vision for our life and recovery. In the same way that we created mental pictures of ourselves free from negative emotion or character defects in our meditation, we can create mental pictures of our lives and recoveries.

By using my mind to think about the details, the specific ways that I will think, feel, and act—in other words, my way of being in the life and recovery of my dreams—I am transforming myself into that person. I am rewiring my neural circuitry and signaling my body to modify and change into the mind and body of the person I wish to become. I am entangling myself, energetically connecting to that possible future. I'm not only thinking about the blessings I will experience and the gratitude I will feel. I am actually creating those feelings with the power of my mind and consciousness, thereby strengthening that connection to the future by experiencing my new way of being ahead of that future. I will be willing and ready to experience that future as it begins to come true, doing whatever work is necessary to become that new person. I am worthy, and I will continue to make myself worthy.

CHAPTER 25

Acceptance: Living the Dream

Recovery is challenging. It takes a lot of effort. There are many difficulties, but the greatest obstacle we face turns out to be ourselves. My refusal to be open-minded, my lack of willingness, and my dishonesty are vestiges of my old way of being that I must transcend. Only my thoughts, feelings, and actions can replace limitation with possibility. It is not simply an issue of motivation; no internal drive or external incentive will compensate for lack of willingness on my part. My capacity to view and accept myself, my circumstances, and my life objectively and honestly is what defines my readiness to change.

Acceptance is a means and also an end; it is both a catalyst and a result of my surrendering and believing. As I gain more capacity for acceptance, my ability to withstand emotional pain also increases. I become better able to delay gratification, a mature attribute of recovery (or a recovery attribute of maturity). I'm doing a lot of changing. Change is now a daily priority. What used to be called a psychic shift, I now refer to as transformation. It is an alteration of mind, body, and spirit. They are inseparably linked. My consciousness, including the aspect of me that is my spirit, is the master of my physical domain. It now becomes imperative that my belief in my recovery be absolute. I need to think, feel, and be that new person of my dreams.

The challenge becomes accepting the process and fact of transformation. I must integrate every element of my new way of being. I have to put it all together. My upgraded way of thinking, my healthier emotions, and the healthy behaviors that follow them, and my entire way of being in the world serve to redefine me. I need to step into that. I need to make it solid, concrete, and real. I need to accept this amazing gift of recovery in every way. It only becomes real when I decide it is. The minute I believe it, I will see it.

There are some expectations that I must manage. I must not expect that I am and will remain "an alcoholic who will never change." I must expect to change every day. New things and ideas will come into my life daily, and I must embrace them. I must not expect that I am and will remain "a person who can no longer drink." I am instead a person who will remain sober under any and all circumstances. The acceptance of my recovery, my freedom from the disease of alcoholism or addiction, is evidenced by the change of focus away from a state of limitation, and instead to an affirmative, positive way of being. No more "I can't, I won't, or I never"; from now on, it's "I can, I will, and I always." It's about where I place my energy.

Consider the importance of belief and expectations. The premise of healing in any sense is based on an agreement. I once heard Eric Pearl, a recognized energy healer, explain how this works in the context of alternative healing in his Reconnective Healing seminar. The agreement is based on certain expectations.

In an alternative modality, someone has a problem and seeks treatment from a healer. In alternative healing, especially energy-based, where there is often nothing physically tangible happening, the healer performs his work as he was trained to do. He does what the healing calls for, to the best of his ability, and his part is then done. It now becomes the client's role to accept that healing. The client has sought the service of the healer and has agreed on what will be done. Acceptance might be based on faith in the healer, or belief in the healing technique, or any related element or combination. Implicit for both healer and client are their respective parts in the relationship. The point at which the client will likely begin to feel better is the point in the process when they accept the healing.

We might be inclined to think that's fine for such energy stuff. Of course it would have to work that way, it's only logical. But is it any different in our traditional Western system with its biomechanical/pharmaceutical approach to healthcare? It's really no different. In the more traditional Western model, the same concepts apply, but it looks a little different.

A person has a problem and decides to seek treatment. They call the doctor's office, negotiate the automated phone menu, and schedule an appointment. The time of the appointment arrives, and the person, now assuming the role of patient, arrives at the doctor's office. They check in, perhaps sign the privacy agreement or update their personal information, and sit in the waiting room. This is part of the routine; the call, the appointment, the forms, the waiting room are all exactly as expected based on previous experience. We all know how this works.

The routine continues—the patient's name is called, they are led to a smaller exam room where they again wait, and finally a knock comes on the door and the doctor steps in. He or she reviews some information, asks a couple of questions, performs some examination and in less than two minutes (the time the doctor has allotted for this entire exchange is a total of four or five minutes) says one of two things. The doctor essentially says, "It's going to be okay," or, "We need to do some tests." Assuming we have heard option number one, the doctor is simultaneously reaching for something as he utters those reassuring words. As with every step in this process, this is exactly what the patient has come to expect.

The doctor reaches for his prescription pad and writes an order for a chemical medication. For the sake of example, we'll say the patient has some type of infection, and the prescription is for an antibiotic. The doctor gives the prescription to the patient along with some instructions. A quick progress note is written for an assistant to transcribe and file, and the doctor says goodbye.

Just as expected, the patient has been in the office an hour, and spent four minutes of that time in the presence of the doctor. The patient will now proceed to a pharmacy to wait for the prescription. On receiving the medication, the patient will begin taking the antibiotic as instructed to start combating the infection.

The point at which the patient begins to feel better is not when they begin taking the medicine. It's not eight hours later, when the bacteria count begins to go down. The point which the patient begins to "feel" better is when the doctor says, "It's going to be all right," and, just as importantly, when the doctor reaches for that prescription pad. That is the moment that the Western-model patient accepts the Western-model healing. That turning point, which happens before any actual physical effect has happened, is based on the patient's acceptance of agreed-on expectations that have been met. Faith in the doctor is supreme, but more important is the belief and acceptance that what is being done works.

So the question then is if we can accept a healing prior to receiving any material treatment, why can't we recover from addictions before our physical environment changes? Why do we need something outside of us to change what happens inside of us? We don't! We are just so conditioned to thinking we need a cause-and-effect, biochemical solution to our ills and problems that we have come to expect it. We can absolutely transform. We just need to give ourselves permission.

I am not cured. Almost daily, I suffer from all manner of character defects, negative thoughts and emotions, and generalized issues that constantly remind me that I am a work in progress. We all are. In the big picture, a step small backward following a significant step forward is not a disaster.

My medical-minded colleagues would say I have "alcoholism in remission." Whether medically minded or not, those who have known me over time freely acknowledge that I have become a different person. To remain that different person will never be enough. I will work to continue changing every day I continue breathing. The minute I stop, my transformation becomes subject first to subtle erosion, then obvious decay, and finally reversal. That would be the slow, painful option. The fast, immediate option would be to merely get drunk. If I continue to do what sustains my recovery to the best of my ability on a daily basis, it is reasonable for me to say, as a transformed person, "I will never drink again."

Gratitude is essential. I am grateful every day. The fact of my life that I don't ever think about drinking still amazes me daily, without failure. Though it's never been tested, I have no doubt that a subtle but distinct expression of my actual genetic code has modified over time. I am a different man with different DNA than the man with the bottle of vodka under the seat of his car who could not go a day without a drink. Today, I would not willfully alter my consciousness in any way. Good or bad, joyous or sad, I would not forfeit one more second of full participation in this industrial-strength human experience that my spirit is here on earth to manifest. The challenge is to remain grateful every day, to continue to grow and improve, and to never forget that I would revert back to my old way of being in every way if I got physically drunk. Transformation reversed.

The challenge is also to constantly improve my connection to the creative intelligence, that something greater, higher power, or God that gives me this gift of life. As one leaf on a vast tree, I must be aware of my connection to all the other leaves. We all have the same stake in our collective welfare; we need our tree to thrive. There is no point in being the happiest, healthiest, most robust leaf on the tree, while numerous other leaves are struggling with disease and decay. We are all in this together.

In life in general, we worry about ourselves and "our own." In business we compete, and keep the secrets of our success to ourselves. The Darwinian survival of the fittest mentality seems to be much more prevalent than any type of instinct for cooperation. To sum it up, I wasn't naturally inclined to tell the next guy how I got my smile so white and my lawn so green. The secret of my success tends to remain a secret. That's how it is in life, business, and that's certainly how it is in the bars. If the first and second worlds are any indication, that's how things work. But as mystic philosopher Swami Beyondananda (Steve Bhaerman) once said, "If all someone does is look out for number one, they're treating everyone else like number two."

AA works by cooperation, an entirely different principle. Early on, I realized that the fellowship of Alcoholics Anonymous had a unique and distinguishing property. We freely share our experience and knowledge in ways that distinguish AA from most other areas of life. If someone is remotely interested in knowing, I will tell them exactly how I've succeeded in my quest for recovery. In fact, if I could actually wrap up and package my amazing recovered way of being and give it to the clueless, struggling new people, I absolutely would. If I could just hand it to them with a bow on top so that they can experience what I have, I would. Unfortunately, that can't be done, which is actually a good thing. Just as I have experienced and learned these things for myself, we all must do that. That struggling new person, to whom I would give the gift of recovery if I could, is also eternal consciousness having a transient human experience, just like me.

We can't give it away. We do the next best thing. We share it. That's why there is such tremendous power in our experience.

And that's what drives me. The need to raise our collective consciousness is something we become responsible for once we become aware of it. Before I knew I had a disease, I was responsible, but not to blame. Once I learned I was responsible, I could accept the blame or change, not even a choice really. And so it goes as more information comes to me. Now that I'm aware of the bigger picture, I'm responsible for that. The awareness that I can predict my future by creating it, the awareness that we are all connected, and the awareness that I can use my transient human experience to humbly make a contribution toward something greater makes me responsible for all that. Now I know what I didn't know.

As I move forward, there are some principles that I try to incorporate into my way of being. These are consistent with the spirit of perpetual transformation, and also the type of spiritual evolution we are going to need if we are collectively going to do better with the scourge of alcoholism and addiction at large. These are liberally borrowed from a great thinker named Stephan A. Schwartz.

I need to practice what I preach. Commonly referred to as "walking my talk," I have to be the living embodiment of the ideas, concepts, and practices I've discussed here. They have worked for me. I have really done these things and continue to do them. If the private or real Keith were not actually what I am portraying here publicly, obviously this wouldn't work for me. It couldn't work for anyone else either. My private/personal identity is consistent with my public persona.

I take no particular credit for these ideas. At best, they are my personal adaptation of ideas and concepts that have been around for a long time. Therefore, they are now just information that is out there in the world, free for anyone to use, modify, pass along, but hopefully benefit from. It is my hope that through acknowledgment and bibliography that I have adequately given credit where it is due. There is a saying that nothing in AA is original; that no matter what you hear someone saying, chances are they heard it somewhere before. So it should be with Sustainable Recovery.

As I put this information out there, I must detach from the outcome. While I will do what I can to support and perpetuate Sustainable Recovery, the moment I punctuate the last sentence of this book, it's out of my hands. Perhaps the writing of this will help no one but me, or perhaps there will be some greater benefit. This might come about long after I'm gone, and that's okay. In being true to the larger spiritual objective I'm laying out here, I am fine if I don't ever see it manifest, though I hope it does manifest.

While AA has done the best, for the most people, for the longest time, it is my intention that we do better for more. This is an inevitable byproduct of Sustainable Recovery. I am so grateful for my transformation that I just want to give back, thereby continuing the transformation. As people manifest their own transformations, it would be self-evident that they would feel as I do about giving back. It is not my expectation, but rather my hope that this would take the form of doing better for more. Common purpose and intention would tend to reinforce the likelihood of achieving the desired outcome.

Within the entire scope of the recovery movement, and despite the appearance of hierarchy or rank, everyone is essentially equal. The newest, sickest newcomer to the oldest, most established long timer in recovery are both exactly where they belong at any given moment on their respective journeys. Even active alcoholics or addicts, first becoming aware of their issues, are in the process of recovery. As such, their contributions, to themselves and all who witness them on their journeys, are intrinsically of equal value. Everyone plays his or her part in the big picture, whether that of amazing role model or wretched advertisement of everything that can go wrong. We might not be alike, but we are all equal.

The most basic challenge, and the real key to Sustainable Recovery, lies not in simple maintenance, but in unceasing motion in the general direction of improvement. While it doesn't feel like I grow every day, I still have to try. I need to learn, develop, and change every day, hour, and minute. The notion of recovery maintenance (like health maintenance) is a good one, but it's more of a prevention of deterioration than a guide for growth. The only time anything in the universe is absolutely still is that tiny instant of time when it is in between the two basic states of being, the positive or negative state. Growth or decay. Gratitude or insecurity. Survival or creation. For a split second, I can have the appearance of being still. My preference is to be in motion toward gratitude, growth, and creation.

Finally, if acceptance is both a means and an end to a sustainable recovery, when does it occur in that recovery process? In the example of an energetic healing, acceptance of healing came when there was a belief in the process and, to a much lesser degree, when expectations were met. In the traditional setting, acceptance of the healing came when the expectations were met, belief being implicit. If the healing, that is, the recovery, is contingent on acceptance, which is in turn contingent on belief supported by met expectations, when and how will this acceptance arrive?

In the old, traditional twelve-step recovery, acceptance was a by-product of belief in the process. As the results of that process started to become apparent in the external world, they affirmed first belief, then ultimately acceptance. A gradual process, seeing came before believing; the change inside came as the external environment changed. Acceptance was a matter of degree.

In the process of Sustainable Recovery, acceptance comes when we understand that the disease of addiction is, in reality, a gift. It is part of that industrial-strength human experience that is the true purpose of our spirits. Embracing the growth opportunity, both in purely human and also spiritual terms, allows us to step into the greatness that is part of our potential. Understanding and accepting this gift is the means to achieving transformation, which is the end and also the ultimate state of acceptance. In that ultimate acceptance, we know we are always connected, and that everything about us and everything in our entire reality is exactly as it should be.

Bibliography

AA World Services, Inc. *Alcoholics Anonymous, 4th Edition.* New York: Alcoholics Anonymous. 2002.

AA World Services, Inc. *'Pass It On'—The Story of Bill Wilson and How the A.A. Message Reached the World.* New York: Alcoholics Anonymous. 1984.

AA World Services, Inc. *Twelve Steps and Twelve Traditions.* New York: Alcoholics Anonymous. 1953.

Armstrong, Karen. *A History of God: The 4,000-Year Quest of Judaism, Christianity, and Islam.* New York: Ballantine Books. 1993.

Beauregard, Mario. *Brain Wars: The Scientific Battle over the Existence of the Mind and the Proof That Will Change the Way We Live.* New York: HarperCollins Publishers. 2012.

Choquette, Sonia. *The Psychic Pathway: Reawakening the Voice of Your Soul.* New York: Crown Trade Paperbacks. 1995.

Choquette, Sonia. *Your Heart's Desire: Instructions for Creating the Life You Really Want.* New York: Three Rivers Press. 1997.

Dispenza, Joe. *Breaking the Habit of Being Yourself: How to Lose Your Mind and Create a New One.* New York: Hay House. 2012.

Dispenza, Joe. *Evolve Your Brain: The Science of Changing Your Mind.* Deerfield Beach, Florida: Health Communications, Inc. 2007

Lipton, Bruce H. *The Biology of Belief: Unleashing the Power of Consciousness, Matter and Miracles.* New York: Hay House. 2008.

Lipton, Bruce H., and Steve Bhaerman. *Spontaneous Evolution: Our Positive Future (and a Way to Get There from Here)*. New York: Hay House. 2009.

McTaggart, Lynne. *The Field: The Quest for the Secret Force of the Universe*. New York: HarperCollins Publishers. 2002.

McTaggart, Lynne. *The Intention Experiment: Using Your Thoughts to Change Your Life and the World*. New York: Free Press. 2007.

McWhorter, John. *Doing Our Own Thing: The Degradation of Language and Music and Why We Should, Like, Care*. New York: Gotham Books. 2003.

Myss, Carolyn. *Anatomy of the Spirit: The Seven Stages of Power and Healing*. New York: Three Rivers Press. 1996.

Myss, Carolyn. *Sacred Contracts: Awakening Your Divine Potential*. New York: Three Rivers Press. 2002.

Pearl, Eric. *The Reconnection: Heal Others, Heal Yourself*. Carlsbad, California: Hay House. 2001.

Radin, Dean. *The Conscious Universe: The Scientific Truth of Psychic Phenomena*. New York: HarperCollins Publishers. 1997.

Radin, Dean. *Entangled Minds: Extrasensory Experiences in a Quantum Reality*. New York: Paraview Pocket Books. 2006.

Schwartz, Stephan A. *Opening to the Infinite*. Langley, Washington: Nemoseen Media, 2007.

Sheldrake, Rupert. *Morphic Resonance: The Nature of Formative Causation*. Rochester, Vermont: Park Street Press. 1981.

Siegel, Daniel J. *Mindsight: The New Science of Personal Transformation*. New York: Bantam Books. 2010.

Silva, José, and Philip Miele. *The Silva Mind Control Method*. New York: Pocket Books, a Division of Simon and Schuster, Inc. 1977.

Talbot, Michael. *The Holographic Universe: The Revolutionary Theory of Reality.* New York: HarperCollins Publishers. 1991.

Targ, Russell. *Limitless Mind: A Guide to Remote Viewing and Transformation of Consciousness.* Novato, California: New World Library. 2004.

Tompkins, Peter, and Christopher Bird. *The Secret Life of Plants: A Fascinating Account of the Physical, Emotional, and Spiritual Relations between Plants and Man.* New York: HarperCollins Publishers. 1973.

Vaillant, George E. *Spiritual Evolution: A Scientific Defense of Faith.* New York: Broadway Books. 2008.

Weiss, Brian L. *Many Lives, Many Masters.* New York: Fireside Books. 1988.

Wilcock, David. *The Source Field Investigations: The Hidden Science and Lost Civilizations behind the 2012 Prophecies.* New York: Dutton. 2011.

Zukov, Gary. *The Dancing Wu Li Masters.* New York: HarperCollins Publishers. 1979.

Zukov, Gary. *The Seat of the Soul.* New York: Fireside Books. 1989.

Suggested Reading

For a new perspective on the world, and how to effect significant and positive change, I suggest reading or listening to these three books, in this order:

The Field: The Quest for the Secret Force of the Universe by Lynne McTaggart. This work documents and explains things we always thought were true. Everything is connected.
http://www.lynnemctaggart.com/

The Biology of Belief: Unleashing the Power of Consciousness, Matter and Miracles by Bruce Lipton, PhD. The quantum approach to biology tells us that environment determines our genetics; our consciousness affects our environment.
https://www.brucelipton.com/

Breaking the Habit of Being Yourself: How to Lose Your Mind and Create a New One by Dr. Joe Dispenza. This book, in addition to the body of Dr. Dispenza's work, is my template for personal transformation. This is the original source for rewiring the brain through active meditation. Many excellent resources and wonderful guided meditations are available through his website, http://www.drjoedispenza.com/

Please follow and like *Sustainable Recovery* on Facebook at Sustainable Recovery book.

About the Author

Keith Kay is a fake name of a real man who has worked in the mainstream of healthcare for three decades, and focused on the specialty of substance abuse. Additionally, he has studied a variety of alternative healing modalities, as well as the latest techniques in personal transformation. These attributes, in combination with more than 20 years of personal recovery, give him a unique and fresh perspective on addictions and rehabilitation. He continues to work as a registered nurse in the substance-abuse field, where his passion remains helping others and pursuing greater insight into the process of recovery. He has chosen to publish under a pseudonym in keeping with the Twelve-Step tradition of anonymity at the level of media.

Made in the USA
Lexington, KY
21 January 2015